White Fire

White Fire

THE INFLUENCE OF EMERSON ON MELVILLE

John B. Williams

California State University, Long Beach
Long Beach, California

PS
2388
.P5
W5
1991
Feb. 1996

Distributed by arrangement with
University Publishing Associates, Inc.

4720 Boston Way
Lanham, MD 20706

3 Henrietta Street
London WC2E 8LU England

Library of Congress Cataloging-in-Publication Data

Williams, John B., 1941-
White fire : the influence of Emerson on Melville
/ John B. Williams.
p.   cm.
Includes bibliographical references and index.
1. Melville, Herman, 1819-1891—Philosophy.
2. Emerson, Ralph Waldo, 1803-1882—Influence—Melville.
3. Influence (Literary, artistic, etc.)   4. Transcendentalism (New
England)   5. Philosophy in literature.   I. Title.
PS2388.P5W5   1991
813'.3—dc20   90–28923 CIP

ISBN 1–878981–02–1 (cloth : alk. paper)

"Yet it is quite out of character to say Mr. Emerson lectures—he does no such thing . . . HE CHIPS OUT SPARKS. . . . he lets off mental skyrockets and fireworks—he spouts fire, and conjurer-like, draws ribbons out of his mouth. He smokes, he sparkles, he improvises, he shouts, he sings—HE EXPLODES LIKE A BUNDLE OF CRACK-ERS—he goes off in fiery eruptions like a volcano, but he does not *lecture*."

—Review in *The Boston Daily Evening Transcript*, February 8, 1849

CONTENTS

PREFACE

The title phrase, "White Fire," appears twice in *Moby-Dick* in descriptions of turbulent seas. In "First Lowering" (Chapter 48), Melville pictures waves forking and crackling during a squall "like a white fire upon the prairie," in which the men in whaleboats are unconsumed though burning: "immortal in these jaws of death!" Again, in "The *Pequod* Meets *The Virgin*" (Chapter 81), he refers to "blinding vapors of foam and white fire" at the climax of a whaling scene. The term also is used by Henry Seidel Canby to describe Emerson's powerful appeal to listeners and readers of his own time. As part of my title, the phrase suggests the vitality of Emerson's thought, which was like a spark to the tinder of Melville's art.

Though contemporary critics have linked Melville to traditional intellectual sources extending as far back as Plato, they have underestimated the influence of Emerson, who eloquently articulated the ideals of his era. This book puts forth new evidence of that connection and demonstrates the keenness and pervasiveness of Melville's response. The argument assumes that Melville indeed read with a "lynx-eyed mind," not only in books that opened to him the literature and philosophies of the world, but also in current newspapers and magazines that offered incisive critical interpretations of Emerson and New England Transcendentalism. It assumes further that Melville retained much of what he heard directly from Emerson, the lecturer, on one or more memorable evenings early in 1849, and from others who were familiar with Emerson's thought.

The case this book makes turns largely on an examination of ideas in

Emerson's unpublished lectures of 1848–1850, which provide new insight into what Emerson was saying at the time of Melville's greatest literary productivity and receptivity to influence. It also considers public reaction to Emerson in the Boston and New York press. Evidence from these sources, which is crucial to an understanding of ideas available to Melville, has so far remained largely outside the discussion of Melville's creative progress, with the effect that Melville is often portrayed as being far more the independent critic of Emerson than he actually was at that time.

When we think of Melville's mature art, which dates from about 1849, the notions that come to mind are likely to include thought diving, cracked human nature, life as an angle of vision, the quest for commanding insight, and the shipwreck of the soul. All of these find dramatic expression in Emerson's lectures of 1848–1850. In addition, Emerson was reasserting ideas from his earlier writings, including the principle of identity, polarity as an underlying tension in experience, evil as a consequence of too much consistency and conformity in human relationships, moral compensation as an underlying ordering principle in nature, natural aristocracy as transcending social hierarchy, and art as an abstract or epitome of the world in miniature. These, too, are significant ingredients in Melville's art. Though we can recognize in them elements of Platonism, European Transcendentalism, and American Puritan thought, the point too often overlooked in critical discussions is that Emerson was Melville's most immediate and probably his most evocative source.

This book proposes that the influence of a living writer differs from, and may transcend, that of writers of tradition whose messages, even though timeless, are not responses to events and pressures of the current moment. Influence therefore has a social dimension, since it is part of the environment in which an artist works. Such a power to affect in Melville's day could spread like heat from a central source, with ideas and images passed from person to person as well as through magazine and newspaper commentaries. Though Melville's extensive but random reading gave him a broad background in traditional learning, the words of an established writer-mentor like Emerson helped to bring his knowledge into focus and thereby enhanced his art. It is probable that what Melville gained from Emerson's richly allusive sayings was a selective reinforcement of ideas already stored in his memory from reading, but not fully assimilated. In fact, the stages of Melville's artistic development coincide with his growing awareness of, and reaction to, ideas and images from traditional sources that Emerson had made popular.

The evidence indicates that Melville's first direct access to Emerson's words probably was through the lengthy reviews of Emerson's writings in *The New York Literary World* at the time Melville was working on *Mardi*. Though Melville later learned from Hawthorne, whose well-known influence on craft is discriminated from Emerson's aesthetic and ethical notions in the discussion of *Moby-Dick*, Melville began responding in *Mardi* to Emerson's complex challenge, especially the advice for the artist to compress the world into a work of art. So primarily as a result of Emerson's immediate influence, Melville became the first American novelist to offer his readers a comprehensive view of the human condition—the world reduced to an island archipelago, the deck of a ship, or a seven-storied office and apartment building. In this sense, works like *Mardi* (1849) and *Moby-Dick* (1851) compare with others like Thoreau's *Walden* (1854) and Whitman's "Song of Myself" (1855), which are acknowledged inheritors of Emerson's aesthetic ideals.

The design of this book is in two parts:

Part I: From Emerson to Melville consists of three chapters that discuss the theory of transactional relationships among creative people, identify Emerson's leading ideas in the late 1840's, and show how Melville reacts to them and to the ambivalent reviews in the New York and Boston press. To establish a connection between the two writers, I have reconstructed the contents of Emerson's lectures of that era and noted resemblances to particular passages in letters and novels that Melville was writing at that time.

Part II: The Path of the Creator includes six chapters that follow Melville's career as a novelist and short-story writer. They indicate how he encountered Emerson's ideas, responded to them in his early novels, then partly rejected them after *Moby-Dick* in rebelling against the literary establishment, only to reassert them in his last novel, *Billy Budd*.

In developing this subject, I have been sensitive to the difficulty of singling out a major influence on Melville from many others that have contributed to the rich texture of his fiction. My focus on Emerson's impact, therefore, does not seek to imply that there were not other significant shaping pressures. Still, a consideration of how Melville responded to a great contemporary over the years is useful not only for a fuller understanding of Melville's mind and art, but also for insight into the more general issue of how talent develops. Melville's reaction to Emerson has to be inferred, for there is no record that the two ever met. Even so, Melville was sensitive enough to absorb the best of Emerson's well-publicized line, as one newspaper described his ideas, since Emerson was far more self-revealing on the lecture stand than in informal gatherings. Melville's responsiveness to Emerson is here viewed as the natural reaction of a developing writer to an older and more mature spokesman on literary matters, who inspired him to assimilate ideas and find direction to his art. As Emerson himself said, "Genius borrows nobly." So art stimulates art, and even an original talent will find and depend not a little on what James Russell Lowell described as "partners in the labor of thought."

I wish to thank the Ralph Waldo Emerson Memorial Association and the Houghton Library of Harvard University for permission to quote from Emerson's lecture manuscripts for 1848–1850. These are crucial years in Melville's development as a writer. In addition, I wish to express appreciation to the Boston Athenaeum and the Henry E. Huntington Library of San Marino, California for their assistance in my research of reviews of Emerson's lectures and published writings in newspapers and magazines at the time Melville was writing. These materials, though not abundant, are significant not only for the information on Emerson which they made available to Melville, but also for their reflection of public attitudes on Emerson. I am grateful to the C.S.U.L.B. Foundation for grants in support of my research at these libraries.

Among individuals who offered valuable assistance and advice, I should like to mention in particular Professors Neal Tolchin and Albie Burke, whose careful readings of the manuscript helped me to sharpen insights and to trim the language. Also, I am indebted to the late Donald A. Drury for his perceptive criticism of the manuscript in its early stages. For her astute help in computer-assisted research, I wish to thank Leslie Swigart, Associate Librarian at California State University, Long Beach. Lastly, I dedicate this book to my wife, Jean Elizabeth Williams, whose unwavering support encouraged me to dig beneath the obvious surfaces into "the little lower layer."

Long Beach, California
August 1990

ABBREVIATIONS USED IN THE TEXT

Manuscripts of Emerson's "Natural History of Intellect" lecture series, 1848–1850. (See Chapter 3, first part, for descriptions of selected documents.)

    I. "Powers and Laws of Thought" (three drafts)

I, A	1848 draft
I, B	1849 draft
I, C	1850 draft

    II. "Relation of Intellect to Natural Science" (two drafts)

II, A	1848–49 draft
II, B	1849–50 draft

    III. "Tendencies and Duties of Men of Thought" (two drafts)

III, A	1848–49 draft
III, B	1849–50 draft
M	Treatise entitled "Mind and Manners in the Nineteenth Century"
N	Lecture: "Natural Aristocracy"
W	*The Complete Works of Ralph Waldo Emerson*. Ed. Edward Waldo Emerson. 12 vols. New York: Houghton Mifflin, 1903.
L	*The Letters of Herman Melville*. Eds. Merrell R. Davis and William H. Gilman. New Haven: Yale UP, 1960.
Log	*The Melville Log*. Ed. Jay Leyda. 2 vols. New York: Harcourt, Brace, 1951.

64 Conceal the want of knowledge.

One would say, that, whoever had tasted this beatitude, would think all other goods cheap. _Quantum scimus sumus._ How much we know, so much we are. What is life, but the angle of vision? A man is measured by the angle at which he looks at objects. What is life — but what a man is thinking of all day? This is his fate & his employer. The brain is the man. The eyes outrun the feet, & go where feet & hands will never come; yet it is very certain that the rest of the man will follow his head. The history of intellect will be the best of all chronicles & will quite supersede them.

"What is life, but the angle of vision?" Page 64 of Emerson's lecture, "Power and Laws of Thought," 1850 manuscript, reproduced by permission of the Ralph Waldo Emerson Memorial Association and of Houghton Library of Harvard University.

PART I

FROM EMERSON TO MELVILLE

CHAPTER 1

CREATIVITY AS A SOCIAL PHENOMENON

1. The Problem of Influence

Few modern readers are wholly prepared to accept the notion that creative genius is partially a dependent attribute, that a writer with a distinctive style and integrity is not the sole originator of his images and meaning. Dependency suggests such hallmarks of mediocrity as imitativeness, conventionality, lack of imagination. And yet almost any sample of powerful writing yields evidence of its creator's dependence on the stimuli of other intellects, particularly those of his own time. Their communication to him is a sharing of consciousness providing him with ideas that he modifies in original ways to suit his artistic purposes. Creativity has a social dimension that is as vital to a writer's development as are his native gifts of expression.

This tendency of creative individuals to respond to one another's work is a well understood characteristic of scientists and scholars, who frequently collaborate as members of investigative teams, organize into professional associations, and share the results of their research. The popular view of the poet or novelist, however, is of a person alone in a room with his writing instruments, trying to match words to feelings. Thoreau's advice in *Walden* would seem to apply especially to the writer: "Nay, be a Columbus to whole new continents and worlds within you, opening new channels, not of trade, but of thought" (321). Writing in this traditional view is an act of self-discovery.

3

The truth is more complex. As historians and biographers tell us, the self exists in a context of external events and influences that help to define it. In the broadest sense, self-discovery as it occurs in the production of art results from an orientation of the artist's inner world to the outer world of the senses. Though critics often seek to connect individual works and their writers to external forces, such as the prevailing climate of opinion of an era, the history of ideas, and traditions of a genre or literary structure evolving in time, the difficulty of obtaining objective evidence often prevents them from adequately accounting for the pressures of temperament by which one writer can sway another. Such pressures actually may dominate the work of a responsive artist, as Morris I. Stein has observed: "Creativity, like all other behavior, is a function of the transactional relationships between a person and his environment. The creative individual affects and is affected by the social context in which he lives."[1]

This book seeks to examine the social context in which Ralph Waldo Emerson and Herman Melville wrote, to analyze and assess the relations between these two great individualistic writers of the American literary renaissance. The task would be easier if the two had been acquainted with one another as, say, Melville was with Hawthorne. Still, evidence to be presented in the following pages indicates that creative relationships do not necessarily require personal friendships. Nor do they entail reciprocity. As Merton M. Sealts, Jr. and others have indicated, Emerson as the older, established writer influenced Melville, though there is no evidence that Melville had any impact on Emerson.[2] Underlying this study are three basic questions that so far have received unsatisfactory answers in twentieth century criticism: What was Emerson saying at the time Melville was developing as a writer of prose fiction, that is, from 1845 to 1856 (between the ages of twenty-six and thirty-seven)? How much of Emerson's timely message and manner did Melville know? What creative use did Melville make of these ideas and images that Emerson, more than any other contemporary of Melville, espoused?

The importance of these questions becomes apparent when we consider the thrust of critical studies of the Melville-Emerson relationship. F. O. Matthiessen in *American Renaissance*, published in 1941 and still the most influential treatment of the pre-Civil War literary revival in America, has established the tone of most later investigations with his comment, "How an age in which Emerson's was the most articulate voice could also have given birth to *Moby-Dick* can be accounted for only through reaction" (184). Matthiessen argues that both Hawthorne and Melville were indebted to Emerson by being forced to react against his assumptions of a benevolent nature. Emerson's vision, he asserts, is defective because it lacks a viable understanding of evil. To support his argument, he cites Melville's largely negative comments written in the margins of two volumes of Emerson's essays which Melville had acquired in 1862, six years after he had bitterly ended his career as a professional writer because of a lack of an audience (185). When we consider that the essays were first published in 1841 and 1844, before Melville had begun writing, the impression that Matthiessen creates is that Melville's attitude toward Emerson was consistent through the years. The obvious weakness in this argument is that it stereotypes both Emerson and Melville. It does not consider the Emerson that Melville knew of, listened to, read and also wrote about when he was serving his literary apprenticeship. This Emerson of the late 1840's and early 1850's was a mature, still vigorous commentator on the times, and not a replication of the Emerson of the essays. The evidence shows that Emerson changed through the years. And so did Melville.

One important consequence of Matthiessen's study is that most critical histories of our literature in the period preceding the Civil War have followed his lead in grouping the major authors on the issue of whether or not they project a vision of evil. In one category, we find the optimists, with Thoreau and Whitman joining Emerson, who is the acknowledged chief spokesman for self-confidence in his day; in the other, the pessimists and doubters, with Poe and Hawthorne linked to Melville, who offered the most inclusive tragic view of man. Such a classification is useful in understanding contrasts in tone, but it imposes restrictions on inferences that may be drawn as to the individual writer's complex interrelationships with other writers. To be sure, within each of these antithetical groups, critics have identified a number of dependencies, such as the indebtedness of Thoreau to the older Emerson and of Melville to the older Hawthorne. But when critics have viewed Melville in relation to Emerson, logical consistency has led to an emphasis on the contrasts. As a result, those elements in Melville pointing to an aesthetic interest in Emersonian thought and the use of Emersonian images, despite Melville's occasional criticisms of Emerson, receive consideration only to the extent that they agree with the critical model.

Among the more notable critical studies influenced by Matthiessen, Charles Feidelson's *Symbolism and American Literature* (1952) places Emerson and Melville at the opposite poles of the mid-nineteenth century symbolistic movement, though he recognizes their interdependence in this comprehensive statement:

> Emerson represented the upsurge of a new capacity, Melville the relapse into doubt. Emerson was the theorist and advocate, Melville the practicing poet. Emerson embodied the monistic phase of symbolism, the sweeping sense of poetic fusion; Melville lived in a universe of paradox and knew the struggle to implement the claims of the symbolic imagination. Yet neither was really an independent agent; their methods were reciprocal, and each entailed the other. Though Melville speaks to us today as Emerson does not, they stand on common ground with our own sensibility. Melville assumed the ambient idea that Emerson made explicitly, and if we feel Melville as one of ours, we must take Emerson into the bargain, whether we like it or not. (120)

Here the power of doubt overmatches Emerson's assurance, as it does also in Harry Levin's *The Power of Blackness* (1958), in which Poe, Hawthorne, and Melville are described as rejecting the "one-sided platitudes" which form our "national credo." Levin asserts:

> Our most perceptive minds have distinguished themselves from our popular spokesmen by concentrating upon the dark other half of the situation, and their distinctive attitude has been introspection, dissent, or irony. Where the voice of the majority is by definition affirmative, the spirit of independence is likeliest to manifest itself by employing the negative: by saying *no* in thunder—as Melville wrote to Hawthorne—though bidden by the devil to say *yes*. (7)

By implication, whatever genius Emerson had is deficient because of its affirmation, even though Emerson's essay "Self-Reliance," as well as many of his other writings, taught the generation in which Melville came of age to apply the spirit of the "Declaration of Independence" to their own lives and work.

Many other texts can be cited that stress the contrasts between Emerson and Melville, despite acknowledgements that they "stand on common ground." At times, Emerson has been treated as an uninvited guest in the movable feast of twentieth century criticism. No more is he viewed as "the wisest American," poetic father, and golden moralist. A. L. Yoder, for one, sees Emerson merely as a "representative of his time," whose work "stands as a remarkable transition from Romantic to Victorian." Yoder reflects an important contemporary view in asserting, "Emerson is an American classic, which is to say at the least that like the nation he has survived. Just why is not certain."[3]

Among the few critics who perceive the essential connection of Melville to Emerson's thought, Perry Miller says in his essay, "Melville and Transcendentalism," that "What links Melville with Emerson is not that they necessarily acquired anything from the 'high German metaphysics,' but that they were both aware of a configuration of ideas which, popularly identified with Germany, challenged the regnant ethic and esthetic of nature." Emerson, he observes, is the incubus of Melville's thought, and Melville's works are "to the end, implacably, defiantly, unrepentantly, Transcendental."[4] Similarly, Nina Baym argues in "Melville's Quarrel with Fiction" that the contact with Emerson's thought "was the single most significant influence on the shape of *Moby-Dick*." Her reference is not merely to the idea of "transcendental self-reliance as embodied in Ahab's story" or to the "attack on transcendental optimism in occasional reflective passages," but to "the more pervasive and definitive influence evident in the concepts of truth and of the divine authorship of nature and language, concepts that Emerson expressed most concisely in the 'Language' section of *Nature*."[5]

More recently, Merton M. Sealts, Jr. has reviewed Melville's responses to Emerson in *Pursuing Melville: 1940–1980* (1982), concluding that Melville "not only read Emerson with understanding over a period of more than twenty years, but knew very well exactly where he agreed and disagreed with Emerson's provocative thinking" (276). Sealts speculates on which particular lecture Melville attended in early 1849 and which essays of Emerson that Melville read in the years he was writing, since there is no record. In Sealts' view, however, Plato is an earlier and possibly more important influence on Melville than Emerson.[6]

What is still needed to determine what Melville knew is a consideration of the ideas and images that Emerson was disseminating as a lecturer at the time Melville was writing. They have an immediacy which qualifies significantly, if it does not override, Emerson's earlier opinions in print. The evidence is in Emerson's lectures, particularly the series he delivered during the years 1849–1850 that we know Melville attended at least in part; in the articles on Emerson and Transcendentalism in newspapers reflecting public attitudes, and in periodicals like *The New York Literary World* to which Melville had access. When we consider that the contents of Emerson's lectures were passed about by word of mouth and that review articles extensively quoted from his writings, we can assume Emerson's thought was available to anyone who sought it, particularly a new writer seeking to establish his own reputation.

2. *'Partners in the Labor of Thought'*

Transactional relationships, or the give and take of influence among living writers, have four general characteristics that transcend the special conditions of a given time and place. These are the features of a creative community: a prevailing interest in expression and sensitivity to language; a shared spirit of rebellion or common cause; the stimulus of a mentor to articulate the aesthetic standards and controlling ideas of the time, and a cultural milieu hospitable to expression with open lines of communication. In addition, as in all dynamic associations, there is the mixture of praise and criticism, of individual acceptance and rejection—the flux of temperaments reacting to one another. Since some writers are public figures whose ideas may be widely disseminated, the reactions are not restricted to those of friends or personal acquaintances. Further, though artists of small talent are likely to be subdued by the thinking of a high-powered group, individual genius is enhanced by it, like the single coal which burns brightest in the center of the fire.

Melville's responses to Emerson evolved against this background. The dominant cultural center of the 1840's and 1850's, when our literature was in its first bloom, was Boston and nearby Concord, where Emerson was the leading spokesman for writers and intellectuals. Emerson saw his native city as a source of creative power:

> The climate [of Boston] is electric, good for wit and good for character. What public souls have lived here, what social benefactors, what eloquent preachers, skilful workmen, stout captains, wise merchants; what fine artists, what gifted conversers, what mathematicians, what lawyers, what wits; and where is the middle class so able, virtuous and instructed? (W, XII, 208–209)

To be fully appreciated, Emerson's references to Boston's "electric" climate must take into account the long winters with sub-freezing weather, the summer humidity and heat, storms and other vicissitudes. He was ennobling the weather as being a tonic for the character. Then as now, Bostonians have thought of their city as the hub of the universe.

In this environment, Emerson's influence touched such talents as Henry David Thoreau and Nathaniel Hawthorne, who were considered by their contemporaries as members of his small circle of Transcendentalists, and outsiders, Walt Whitman and Herman Melville, both of rival New York, who nonetheless had personal contacts with members of the group— Whitman with Emerson and Melville with Hawthorne. To all who would read or listen, Emerson demonstrated the possibilities of metaphor, asserting in essays, poems, and lectures in crowded auditoriums even in winter that nature in all its diversity is an emblem of the mind. In *Nature*, first published in 1836, then republished in 1849 when Melville was writing, Emerson wrote that the word is the link between the mind and the sensory world, so that "every appearance in nature corresponds to some state of the mind, and that state of the mind can only be described by presenting that natural appearance."[7] This view, often repeated in his lectures, provided a rationale for writers to dramatize the self in terms of its attitude towards the external world. So Melville speaks through his character Ahab in *Moby-Dick* (1851): "O Nature, and O soul of man! how far beyond all utterance are your linked analogies! not the smallest atom stirs or lives on matter, but has its cunning duplicate in mind."[8] The idea, of course, has many European antecedents, including the writings of Coleridge and Carlyle; but the point is that Emerson was the leading American spokesman for it at the time Melville was maturing as a novelist.

Emerson also was the most articulate advocate for rebellion against an increasing materialism in society and the pressure on American writers to conform to literary conventions imported from abroad. He spoke and wrote with a sense of high mission, pointing out the regenerative power of nature and advocating literary independence and artistic integrity. He had taken this position early in his career with evocative appeals for the artist to rely on his instinct, assuring him in "Self-Reliance" (1841) that "Whoso would be a man must be a nonconformist." He taught that "envy is ignorance" and "imitation is suicide," and he gave encouragement, asserting that the power which resides in each individual is "new in nature, and none but he knows what that is which he can do, nor does not know until he has tried" (W, II, 46). As David S. Reynolds has shown, part of Emerson's power is due to his assimilation of popular attitudes (16–17). In effect, he spiritualized ideas of freedom and equity underlying our democratic system of checks and balances and applied them to the individual life and art.

Writers stimulated by Emerson's buoyant appeal produced works characterized by organic form, rich symbolic structures, and criticism of the encroachments of civilization on the individual. In dramatic terms, the struggle of the self for moral and spiritual growth as opposed to forces leading to its decay provides the underlying subject of all the diverse masterpieces produced in the years 1850–1855, which Matthiessen has justly identified as the time American literature reached full maturity.[9] Whether the views offered in the major works are optimistic, as in Thoreau's *Walden*, or pessimistic, as in Melville's *Pierre*, Emerson's expansive vision affected them all. To many hearers, an address by Emerson was an awakening experience that they remembered for years. As James Russell Lowell put it, Emerson made his audience feel as though they were "partners in the labor of thought."[10]

Such partnership among writers stimulates individual genius as ideas spread from a central source. An important social characteristic of the creative community of the New England area writers, however, is the relative formality of Emerson and the people he influenced. By today's standards, they were studiously genteel. Emerson, for example, exchanged letters with Margaret Fuller on aesthetic matters while she was a guest in his home. Even Melville, who was well-acquainted with colloquial language as an able-bodied seaman, signed only one of his many letters to his friend Hawthorne with his first name (L, 143).

Even so, formality and social distance are no less effective than the informality of writers of our time as a means of transmitting ideas and attitudes. Both traditions have deep roots in the history of the English language and culture. With the New Englanders, formality can be explained on two social grounds. In the first place, Emerson and his associates were inheritors of Puritan idealism, which set forth the view that all things have equal significance before God. Even though people with this perspective may be committed to speak plainly, they are likely to take all matters, including trivial ones, seriously. Yankee humor, rooted in earthy realism, was more the province of the working classes—farmers and traders—than of intellectuals like Emerson, who were concerned with educating the conscience.

More importantly, the New Englanders, and Melville as well, felt they were participating in establishing an independent national literature for the young republic. They took their mission seriously. As Henry Seidel Canby has observed, "Emerson, so cold and shy in his personal relations, was in faith, hope, and creative thinking a white fire burning through convention and all hindering obscurantism."[11]

As a lecturer, Emerson represented no organization, but spoke out as an individual conscience. He expressed always a minority opinion on intellectual, moral, or literary matters—his own. Such sayings of his as "To be great is to be misunderstood" represent his answer to being regarded as an "uncommon man" in the public view. But Emerson inspired his listeners with such qualities as eloquence, confidence, a disarming simplicity of manner, gentleness—he seldom raised his voice—pith, a talent for seeming to create dazzling figures of speech at the moment of delivery. Margaret Fuller and others have remarked on the musical qualities of his voice. Lowell reminisced that hearing him was like listening to Beethoven. "We know perfectly well what we are to expect from Mr. Emerson," he observed, "and yet what he says always penetrates and stirs us, as is apt to be with the case of genius, in a very unlooked fashion."[12] The creative impact that Emerson sought to make in his virtuoso performance was calculated to be fundamental and lasting. "The end of eloquence," he wrote, probably in 1847, "is—is it not?—to alter in a pair of hours, perhaps in a half hour's discourse, the convictions and habits of years?"[13]

When Emerson delivered a lecture series in Boston in January and February of 1849, *The Boston Daily Republican* carried an editorial comment which suggests the attitude of his audience and also the public at large:

> Mr. Emerson's reputation is now so well established, that praise would be out of place. Yet we have felt, when inspired by his original eloquence and concentrated thought, that he did little else than shake the chains by which in this earth man is bound, without pointing out how we might break the chains and become the lords instead of the subjects of life. He carries our mind away to a paradise of intellectual and spiritual beauties; but that paradise is beyond the limits of this world; and when his voice comes in our ears, we are recalled to the necessities of life, our bodies which must be fed,

our families which must be provided for, and we find it difficult to reconcile his ideal scheme with the state in which we find ourselves. It seems like the plan of a better world, or a far off future in this, and not now practicable. We are far from imputing this as a fault to Mr. Emerson; such a mind is needed to counteract the practical and material tendencies of the time, and, as he says, "man is an eclecticism of excellent men," and nowhere found more complete in one person. It is natural, perhaps necessary, that as the rest of the world are too practical, so Mr. Emerson should be too ideal. (January 17, 1849: 2)

When we consider that Melville attended one lecture in this series, and read or heard about the others, it becomes clear that his own mixed feelings about Emerson were not unique. In this context, Emerson's "natural, perhaps necessary" function was precisely to arouse these feelings in thoughtful people through voicing his idealistic rebellion against materialism by reminding them of beauties "beyond the limits of this world." In his lectures and essays, Emerson's constant strategy was to place his ideals well outside mortal reach. For example, in an 1842 lecture on Transcendentalism, he asserted there was no "pure Transcendentalist." Of God, he said in "The Over-Soul": "Our being is descending into us from we know not whence." In short, Emerson's contribution as a partner with the public in the labor of thought was to stimulate people to think about their entrapment in the routines and conventions of society by taking a stand that was deliberately "too ideal." "If you would lift me," he said of eloquence, "you must be on higher ground" (W, VII, 94).

Melville's response was to catch this feeling of rebellion in his own writing, in which the Transcendentalist ideal and the real are in continuous conflict. Actually, Melville's ambivalence toward Emersonian optimism mirrors the editorial opinions of the press. The picture of Melville that emerges against the background of public reaction shows him to be much less the independent intellectual critic of Emerson, as Matthiessen and others have asserted, and much more the self-conscious artist absorbing popular attitudes and images from the most readily available sources and imaginatively transforming them into art.

We can see this dynamic creative process at work in Melville if we examine in detail the evidence of his only known direct encounter with Emerson in 1849. The discussion which follows suggests that Melville began thinking of the central images in *Moby-Dick* upon hearing Emerson lecture.

3. *Emerson and Melville: Spark and Tinder*

Emerson did most of his writing in the study of his home in Concord, where he was often alone but never in solitude. The furnishings were uniquely appropriate to the man. He sat in a rocking chair beside a large, highly-polished drum table that could turn on its axis. Around the rim, it had many drawers hand-made by Thoreau, who was adept in woodworking, for storing note pads, pen and ink. Emerson did not have to look far for a reminder that all nature is round and that a circle is the "Flying Perfect." When he would finish writing in a pad which he held on his lap, he would deposit the pages in one of the drawers and turn the table to another drawer when one was filled. We can presume that when he revised, he pulled pages out of the drawers and matched them up to suit his purpose. The manuscripts of his lectures, written in ink on unlined paper, show signs of constant revision, with entire lectures rewritten, pages added or removed, and passages of one version sometimes attached to another. But all revolve on the same axis of thought, the centrality of the self. One reason his lectures have received little critical attention until recent years has been the difficulty of establishing reliable texts. Gaps suggest that he sometimes ad libbed in the lecture hall. And yet the aphorisms and metaphors about the life of the mind and art on page after page, like spokes of a wheel, suggest a vitality and spontaneity of statement that must have been contagious.

The senior Oliver Wendell Holmes has noted that Emerson spoke in cities "to such cultivated audiences as no other man could gather about him" and also in villages to plain people "whose classics were the Bible and the 'Farmer's Almanac.'" Wherever he lectured, his words would be remembered and passed on to others, as Margaret Fuller said, like winged seed. His inspiration filtered down through innumerable channels into every level of society. As the reviewer of the *Boston Daily Republican* said of the lecture series Melville attended in 1849:

> Mr. Emerson's audience was, as it always is, of the most select and intellectual character; and we saw many among the crowd, with whom the public are more familiar as the oracles, than the recipients of thought. These persons, whose own audiences might regard Mr. Emerson as visionary, or, in their incapacity to follow the eagle flights of his intellect, might comfort their weakness by bestowing upon the comprehensible some harder epithet, know very well what inspiration and light their more commonplace and better

appreciated talents derive from the subtle muse of Emerson. (January 17, 1849: 2)

Boston newspapers advertised this lecture series under the general title of "Mind and Manners in the Nineteenth Century" for delivery on successive Monday evenings from January 15 to February 12 at the Freeman Place Chapel on Beacon Street. Since Melville was in New York during the last part of January and attended a reading of Shakespeare by Fanny Kemble Butler in Boston on February 12, it is evident that he attended the lecture given on February 5. He expressed his reactions to hearing Emerson in two letters to his New York publisher friend Evert Duyckinck, dated the following February 24 and March 3 (L, 76-80).

Contemporary critics have often quoted from these letters, but they have misinterpreted the significance of Melville's perceptive remarks since they have viewed the letters almost wholly apart from Emerson's lecture manuscripts and the reviews in the Boston and New York newspapers. William Braswell, for example, observes in his article "Melville as a Critic of Emerson" that "Melville wrote capriciously of 'this Plato who talks thro' his nose' " and advises that his remarks should not be taken seriously because at that time he was "hardly qualified to pass judgment upon the merits of his famous contemporary."[14] Matthiessen notes Melville's praise of Emerson in the comment, "I love all men who *dive*," but sees Melville as quickly feeling suffocated as he followed Emerson in his plunge into ideas. Matthiessen adds, "Melville knew that there was 'a gaping flaw' in all the transcendental yea-sayers to life, that these continual affirmers of perfection were 'all cracked right across the brow.' "[15] The images that Matthiessen cites of thought-diving and the cracked condition of man, however, are both present in Emerson's lecture manuscripts. Sealts offers a detailed analysis of Melville's March 3 letter along with quotations from one of the lectures in the series which in the manuscripts is entitled "Natural Aristocracy," but he is silent on images from other lectures in the series that Melville must have heard because he used them in his letter.[16] When the letters are considered in the whole context of what Emerson and the reviewers were saying, Melville's comments show an extraordinary sensitivity to Emersonian images and to public opinion. Far from indicating capriciousness, outright rejection, or a reserved interest in Emerson, the letters demonstrate Melville's capacity for creative response to Emerson's subtle appeal. Melville paid Emerson the highest kind of compliment by borrowing from him.

The first letter is best known for its record of Melville's discovery of Shakespeare ("Dolt & ass that I am I have lived more than 29 years, & until a few days ago, never made close acquaintance with the divine William"). In passing are these two short sentences on Emerson: "I have heard Emerson since I have been here. Say what they will, he's a great man" (L, 77). No other mention of Emerson might have been forthcoming from Melville if Duyckinck had not written an answer, probably chiding Melville for favoring Emerson, for Melville begins his second letter with the protestation, "Nay, I do not oscillate in Emerson's rainbow, but prefer rather to hang myself in mine own halter than swing in another man's swing" (L, 78).

What had Duyckinck said? Melville's phrasing suggests that the New Yorker had called his attention to a satiric article in the February 6 edition of Horace Greeley's *New York Daily Tribune*, which characterizes Emerson as turning a rainbow upside down and using it as a swing. There is even a cartoon showing Emerson swinging on the inverted rainbow, his hat and one shoe falling off. From Melville's denial, we can infer that Duyckinck had him sharing the swing with Emerson. The article indicates the rivalry between New York and Boston papers, since it is an embellishment of a review published a few days earlier on January 25 in the *Boston Post*. By adding an introduction and four cartoons to the original text, the *Tribune* ridiculed both Emerson and the rival newspaper. But not to be outdone, the *Boston Daily Evening Transcript*, a competitor of the *Post*, picked up the *Tribune's* version with drawings and published it on February 8 with its own introduction. On the following page is the *Transcript's* article, which Melville could have seen, since he was in Boston at the time.

Although the review makes a joke of Emerson's impractical views, it praises his ability with metaphor. Emerson is both a playful sprite swinging as a child, one shoe off, "now sweeping the earth and now clapping his hands among the stars," and a power that "moves in the regions of similitudes" and "chips out sparks." Such a backhanded compliment would be likely to put an Emerson admirer on the defensive, forcing him to say, as Melville does, "Say what they will, he's a great man." Melville garnishes the image in the review, substituting his own formal word "oscillate" for the critic's "swing" and then forswears imitation by declaring he would prefer to hang from his own halter. Emerson would have approved this self-reliant stance.

Melville continues with a compliment of his own that reflects the sense

AN ILLUSTRATED CRITICISM. The Boston Post contained the other day a very fanciful critique upon Mr Ralph Waldo Emerson as a lecturer; and the New York Tribune of Monday happily hits off the article in a parody, followed by some clever wood cut illustrations of the original critique, showing how the writer's ideas would stand the test of the pencil's embodiment. We copy the article and the accompanying engravings, as there has been considerable inquiry for the latter among the curious. "The critic of the Post," says the Tribune, "writes most dazzlingly of one of Emerson's delightful lectures. We can hardly call it criticism, for he does not properly *criticize;* he plays around the subject like a humming-bird round a honeysuckle—he darts at it like a fish-hawk after a pike. He looms up like a thunder-cloud, comes down in a shower of tinkling sleet and rolls away like a fire on the prairies. He plays with figures of speech like a juggler, balancing the sentences on his chin, and keeping up six with each hand. His fancy goes up like the jet of a fire engine, and comes down in a spiral ecstasy, like a Peruvian condor. He is a detonating mixture—a percussion cap—a meteoric shower—a spiritual shuttle, vibrating between the Unheard-of and the Unutterable. Like a child he shakes his rattle over the edge of Chaos and swings on the gates of the Past—and he sits like a nightingale in a golden ring, suspended by a silver cord from a nail driven into the zenith.

"We cannot resist trying our hand at illustrating his description of the lecture—giving form to the writer's phosphorescent fancies. Our attempts in this line accompany the text. Mr Emerson, whose splendid profusion of thought and imagery, combined with the magnetism of his voice and presence, must produce the deepest impression wherever he is heard, has probably never imagined himself, even spiritually, in positions so remarkable. He will be equally amused with ourself at the result. Thus *ecstacises* the writer:"

"Yet it is quite out of character to say Mr Emerson lectures—he does no such thing. He drops nectar—HE CHIPS OUT SPARKS—he ex holes odors—he lets off mental skyrockets and fireworks—he spouts fire, and, conjurer-like, draws rib bons out of his mouth. He smokes,

he sparkles, he improvises, he shouts, he sings—HE EXPLODES LIKE A BUNDLE OF CRACKERS—he goes off in fiery eruptions like a volcano, but he does not *lecture.*
* * * * He went swiftly over the ground of knowledge with a Damascus blade, severing everything from its bottom, leaving one in doubt whether anything would ever grow again. Yet he seems as innocent as a little child who goes into a garden and pulls up a whole bed of violets, laughs over their beauty, and throws them down again. So that, after all, we are inclined to think no great harm has been done. He comes and goes like a spirit of whom one just hears the rustle of his wings. He is a vitalized speculation—a talking essence—

A SORT OF CELESTIAL EMANATION

["*Celestial Emanations*" may properly be allowed to take an airing on Comets. - Illustrator]
—a bit of transparency broken from the spheres—a spiritual prism through which we see all beautiful rays of immaterial existence. His leaping fancy mounts upward like an India-rubber ball, and drifts and falls like a snow-flake or a feather. He moves in the regions of similitudes. He comes through the air like a cherubim with a golden trumpet in his mouth, out of which he blows tropes and figures and gossamer transparencies of suggestive fancies. He takes high flights, and sustains himself without ruffling a feather. He inverts the rainbow and uses it for a swing—now sweeping the earth and now clapping his hands among the stars."

(Electroprint of single-column article in *The Boston Daily Evening Transcript,* February 8, 1849, p. 2.)

of the review: "Yet I think Emerson is more than a brilliant fellow. Be his stuff begged, borrowed, or stolen, or of his own domestic manufacture he is an uncommon man. Swear he is a humbug—then he is no common humbug." (We can appreciate Melville's admiration of an uncommon humbug when we consider that he came back to this idea seven years later and expanded it into a novel, *The Confidence-Man: His Masquerade*, which includes the art of fiction among the deceptions of the confidence man.) Melville's defense of Emerson's brilliance leads to an admission of his own sense of interdependence with other intellects. "The truth is," he says, "that we are all sons, grandsons, or nephews or great-nephews of those who go before us. No one is his own sire" (L, 78).

Melville's general reaction to the February 5 lecture is that of surprise and pleasure:

> I was very agreeably disappointed in Mr. Emerson. I had heard of him as full of transcendentalisms, myths & oracular gibberish; I had only glanced at a book of his once in Putnam's store—that was all I knew of him, till I heard him lecture.—To my surprise, I found him quite intelligible, tho' to say truth, they told me that that night he was unusually plain. (L, 78–79)

What had Emerson said that so attracted Melville? We cannot reconstruct the lecture that Emerson actually delivered on February 5, or any other night in the series, because of his methods of improvisation; but Melville's two most significant images referring to Emerson as a thought-diver and as being cracked across the brow provide clues to passages that particularly impressed him. We can infer that he heard them either from Emerson directly or from people who reported on other lectures which they attended.

The series "Mind and Manners in the Nineteenth Century" is not preserved with that title among Emerson's manuscripts for the years 1848–1850 at the Houghton Library of Harvard University. Instead, the title applies to a single discourse of one hundred and thirty-six pages included among drafts of a series later called "Natural History of Intellect." Evidence in these manuscripts and newspaper advertisements and reviews indicates that they are raw materials of the Boston course. (See Chapter 3 for analysis of these manuscripts.) The first draft of the second lecture in the series, entitled "Relation of Intellect to Natural Science," has this passage describing the man who dives within himself to find the truth that gives him perspective on all men:

The eyes of the man who saw through the earth the ingots of gold that were lying a rod or two under the surface or of the diver who came suddenly down full on a bed of plant oysters that were all pearl were not to be compared to his which put him in perspective of men. *He was the man-diver.* [Italics added.] He was the thought-vampire. He became at once ten, twenty, a thousand men as he stood gorged with knowledge and turning his fierce eyes on the multitude of masters in all departments of human skill, and hesitating on which map of action and adventure to turn his all-commanding introspection. (II,A, 36–37)

The passage illustrates Emerson's tendency to play daringly with images at the risk of ridicule, much as the critics and Melville had noted. Its reference to gold suggests a timely allusion to the Gold Rush to California that was getting under way in early 1849. The succession of exaggerated images is the kind that would draw laughter from an audience assembled for a commonplace discussion of everyday problems. But Emerson's select audience came to be surprised and entertained, as Melville was, with verbal magic. Emerson's deliberate mixing of metaphors amounts to an expression of confidence in himself and in his listeners' ability to follow him beyond the limits of logical consistency. Melville sensed that Emerson was audaciously different, and sided with him in these lines from his letter:

Now, there is a something about every man elevated above mediocrity, which is, for the most part, instinctuly [sic] perceptible. This I see in Mr. Emerson. And frankly, for the sake of the argument, let us call him a fool;—then had I rather be a fool than a wise man.—*I love all men who dive.* [Italics added.] Any fish can swim near the surface, but it takes a great whale to go down stairs five miles or more; & and if he dont [sic] attain the bottom, why, all the lead in Galena can't fashion the plumet [sic] that will. I'm not talking of Mr. Emerson now—but of the whole corps of thought-divers, that have been diving & and coming up again with bloodshot eyes since the world began. (L, 79)

Melville's references not merely to diving but to the diver's eyes indicate how closely he identified with Emerson's imagery and the precarious enterprise of probing for truth. The passage illustrates his ability to select the appropriate image from the many Emerson offered and to develop its potential within the limits of the natural world. But even in this, he may have had help from another Emersonian image. The *Boston Daily Republican* reported that the third lecture in the series, scheduled for January 29, would concern inspiration. A manuscript fragment entitled "Inspiration" consisting of many pages and rough notes that Emerson used in lectures delivered from 1848 to 1850, contains this comparison of poets to whales: "Poets are mammalia of a higher element, and, as the whale must come to the top of the water for air, so they might go to the top of the air for thought."

We can sense in Melville's use of Emerson's diving image his individual perspective on questing for truth. Where Emerson's man-diver, having found the hidden knowledge he sought, turns his "fierce eyes" toward new adventures, Melville's thought-diver comes up from his unsuccessful probes in deep waters with "bloodshot eyes." Significantly, a search through Emerson's lecture manuscripts and published writing indicates that he later discarded his diving metaphor, perhaps because of its lack of focus, though he repeated the underlying idea of self-awareness in many other forms. Melville, however, retained the image, developing the association of thought-diving to whales into the grand tragic quest for truth in *Moby-Dick*.

The second image by which Melville characterizes Emerson also has its antecedent in the lecture series. The single manuscript preserved under the series title, "Mind and Manners in the Nineteenth Century," contains an extended comment on the crack in all nature, including human nature. "We have been accustomed," Emerson says,

> to distinguish two parties, to one of which all men belong, the party of the past, and the party of the future:—the movement or the establishment.— This schism runs under the world, and appears in literature, philosophy, church, state, social customs; a war, it seems, betwixt intellect and affection. *It is a crack in nature* [italics added], which has split every church; Christendom into Papal and Protestant; Calvinism, into old and new schools; Quakerism, into old and new; Methodism, into old and new; England, into conserver and reformer; America, into Whig and Democrat; it has reached into the immoveable East, and is renovating Constantinople and Alexandria and threatens China. It has reached into the Indian tribes of North America, and carries bitter politics of Democracy among the Red Men. (M, 3)

The world Emerson describes is frequently reduced to the individual. "For what is the age?" he says in his introduction, "It is what he is who beholds it. It is transparent in proportion to the powers of the eye" (1). Later, he observes, "In the eye of the philosopher, the individual is the world" (6).

Unlike the image of the man-diver, the figure of a crack in nature was a continuing preoccupation with Emerson. In his essay "Compensation" (1841), for example, he uses it to account for the imperfections of epic heroes:

> Achilles is not quite invulnerable; the sacred waters did not wash the heel by which Thetis held him. Siegfried, in the Nibelungen, is not quite immortal, for a leaf fell on his back whilst he was bathing in the dragon's blood, and that spot which it covered is mortal. And so it must be. *There is a crack in every thing God has made.* [Italics added.] (W, II, 107)

Against this background, Melville's application of the image to Emerson, the immediate source, is more than a criticism of Emerson's "gaping flaw." It amounts also to an imaginative endorsement of the Emersonian thesis that no mortal, not even Emerson, is whole. Melville writes:

> I could readily see in Emerson, not withstanding his merit, a gaping flaw. It was, the insinuation, that had he lived in those days when the world was made, he might have offered some valuable suggestions. *These men are all cracked right across the brow.* [Italics added.] And never will the pullers-down be able to cope with the builders-up. And this pulling down is easy enough— a keg of powder blew up Block's Monument—but the man who applied the match, could not, alone, build such a pile to save his soul from the shark-maw of the Devil. But enough of this Plato who talks thro' his nose. (L, 79)

In Melville's view, Emerson's flaw is egotism, an error Melville saw in most men, including himself. Emerson projects himself in his descriptions of cracked nature. In effect, he has the crack which he sees in others. Even so, Melville is quick to add that Emerson's task of building up is far more difficult than that of pulling down or blowing up.

The image of cracked human nature made a deep impression on Melville, though in his novels from *Typee* (1846) on he presents characters with physical injuries that are outward signs of psychic wounds. Also, in *Mardi* (1849) he mentions in passing "cracked skulls" as the allotments of many combatants in "this cracked sphere we live in," but the idea is undeveloped (441). It is not until *Moby-Dick* (1851), after he had heard Emerson, that the notion of a schism in the nature of man is fully represented in the character of Captain Ahab, his most memorable tragic hero. Besides having lost a leg in an encounter with the white whale, Ahab also has a single scar extending rod-like from his temple down the side of the body. A superstitious crewman proposes that the scar is a birth-mark "from crown to sole." The crack in Ahab's body is symbolic of a profound spiritual schism suggesting all the separations characterizing modern man—divisions of head and heart, intuition and logic, will and fate, knowledge and ignorance, self and nature, and ultimately man and God. In no other character has Melville dramatized so completely what Emerson called "the divided state" of man when out of harmony with the forces that created him.

In these particular ways, then, Emerson's lecture stimulated Melville to think creatively, not only in writing a letter to Duyckinck, but also in developing fundamental images in his major work. If as the reviews of the lecture assert, Emerson's mind cast out sparks, Melville's was the tinder that easily ignited and burned without losing its identity.

4. *The Receptive Imagination*

The line of influence extending from Emerson's image of cracked human nature in 1849 to Ahab's physical and spiritual cracks should illustrate the power of Emerson's suggestiveness and also Melville's receptivity. Even though it has been argued through the years that Melville could have derived the image from various sources, for example, the cryptic "mark of Cain" in Genesis, Milton's scarred Satan, and even the Pittsfield elm, Emerson's reference serves at the very least as a vigorous prompter to a young author casting about for ideas.[17]

Among studies of literary influence, there has been little effort to distinguish between the pressure of a living writer on one of his contemporaries and the influence of writers in the tradition. Peter Conrad offers the broadest view of traditional influence in observing that the literature of a people is "one continuous, unending book" with writers of each generation revising the work of their predecessors.[18] Carlos Baker similarly observes, "No poet can afford to ignore the past, that essential substructure upon which he rears his own superstructures."[19]

Gören Hermerén in *Influence in Art and Literature* differentiates influences from parallels, which are similarities between two works that have no causal relation; copies and paraphrases, which are merely degrees of duplication. Hermerén also distinguishes between general influence, like that of literary borrowings and modeling, and genuine influence, which involves substantial changes in an artist's direction. He offers a comprehensive list of requirements that all types of influence have in common. Those which apply especially to literary relationships may be paraphrased as follows:

1) Two literary works, an earlier and a later, share at least one feature, such as a particular image or idea.

2) Traces of this influence from the earlier work are recognizable in the later.

3) The creator of the later work has had contact with the earlier one, which serves as a contributing cause of the later.

4) The creator of the later work, however, may not be aware of his use of materials from the earlier work.

5) The similarities between the two works are more subtle than those of a copy or paraphrase.

For genuine influence, he offers these further requirements:

6) The influence of the earlier work on the later must be a pervasive feature, affecting the later work as a whole.

7) For the later work to have this pervasive influence, the artist must have assimilated the earlier work; that is, his contact with it is not casual.

8) There is a continuity between the later work and the artist's other works of that or a later time.[20]

If we consider the impact on Melville's art of the images articulated by Emerson in his 1849 lecture, we can argue that by the above standards, the influence is genuine. Not only is cracked Ahab the dominant character in Melville's novel, which offers, as Emerson did, a world view, but as this study also will show, Melville's other fiction from 1849 through the remainder of his career was responsive to the changes dating from his hearing Emerson lecture.

What is especially important in Emerson's statements, besides their evocativeness, is their timeliness to Melville. This is an ingredient lacking in the varied influences on him from writers of the past. They were not, like Emerson, living spokesmen on contemporary literary matters or conditions of life that Melville was facing as an apprentice writer. This element, in fact, may relieve some of the anxiety of indebtedness that Harold Bloom perceives as accompanying influence, since a writer seeking to make his mark may, like a sailor, endeavor to change course with the prevailing winds rather than oppose them.[21]

The case this book makes for a strong Emersonian impact turns on the idea that literary influence has two dimensions, the pressures of the past and those of the present, which affect writers in different ways. Ideas and images originating in traditional sources are much like light from fixed stars, which a writer might study, like a navigator, in his effort to get his bearings. But ideas and images emanating from another living writer, a mentor such as Emerson, are more like the weather, which stimulates immediate attention and reaction and may distort or even blot out the firmament. Though some writers are more familiar with traditions than others, every writer is swayed by the pressure of events and personalities of his own time. Melville's reading in periodicals, to be discussed later, leads to the conclusion that he was at least as responsive to contemporary influences as to those of tradition.

Melville's reaction to Emerson's lecture suggests that Emerson reinforced what Melville already knew from his reading. For example, the image of cracked nature, which Melville had previously used, actually is deeply embedded in American thought, extending back to the fall of man idea of colonial sermons. (We shall consider this tradition in the next chapter.) But its presence in Emerson, especially in the Boston lecture series of 1849, served as a reminder to Melville of its currency and vitality. That he responded so directly to it in his letter to Duyckinck and then made it into the central image in his characterization of Ahab suggests that this and other Emersonian images focused Melville's attention on notions already stored in memory. In effect, they stimulated him to select and thereby helped shape and direct his art. If his reading in traditional literature extending back to Plato gave him experiences of discovery, hearing Emerson lecture or reading him was for Melville and others an experience of rediscovery in the Greek sense of anagnorisis, or knowing again. Emerson himself was aware of this notion, which underlies his observation in "Self-Reliance": "In every work of genius we recognize our own rejected thoughts." In listening to Emerson, Melville sensed the possibilities of what he knew.

Also from the evidence of Emerson's impact on Melville dating from the lecture, we are entitled to infer that the lines of influence, like some marriages, are for convenience. We can describe these lines emanating from Emerson as resembling direct currents of electricity, and not alternating currents, for there is no evidence of a payback. Emerson, who turned elsewhere for his inspiration, was not swerved from his orbit by Melville's writing, though his occasional perceptive comments on novelists and his references to the sea suggest that he was not unmindful of Melville. Melville, for his part, did not seek out Emerson, as he did Hawthorne in 1850. Melville did not have to: Emerson's opinions were available everywhere—in printed matter of all kinds and in conversations among people who had heard him speak. Mentors like Emerson, who themselves learned from older writers, functioned as providers of intellectual stimuli but took very little in return from the younger writers they influenced.

Emerson's formal aloofness was no hindrance to his role as spokesman for the more innovative writers of his time. Though he has been described as shy, modest, and deficient in animal spirits, sharing with Hawthorne a sense of romantic isolation from society, it is probable that no member of his inner circle of intellectuals had greater access to his private opinions than the lecture audiences he addressed. Emerson came to life when he stood alone on the lecture platform, detached from his listeners but responsive to the emotions of the occasion. It was then he set forth his innermost thought, which he believed was the thought of all men, as he said in "Self-Reliance": "Speak your latent conviction, and it shall be the universal sense." He was unequivocal in his intent, not just to communicate but to generate thought: "The eloquence of one," he wrote of lecturing, "stimulates all the rest, some up to the speaking point, and all others to a degree that makes them good receivers and conductors, and they avenge themselves for their enforced silence by increased loquacity on their return to the fireplace" (W, VII, 61).

As we have seen, Melville acknowledged that he was such a receiver and conductor of other men's ideas in his comment, "No one is his own sire." But his reaction was not superficial. Nor does it fit neatly into contemporary theories of influence, such as the one proposed by Bloom, who perceives that "self-appropriation involves the immense anxieties of indebtedness," and asks, "for what strong maker desires the realization that he has failed to create himself" (5)? Melville's response was less that of a writer agonizing over his own creativity and more that of a conscious artist and manipulator, an opportunist, open to suggestions and advice that he sought from a variety of sources, as his frequent allusions to his wide reading clearly indicate. In an apparent autobiographical aside in *Mardi*, he has his narrator, Taji, comment, "In me, many worthies recline, and converse" (367). Melville perceived himself as the host to ideas gathered from far and near, assimilated in his imagination, and bodied forth in his fiction. The anxiety expressed in his letters—such as his ironic desire to write the sort of books "which are said to 'fail' " and his complaint, "All my books are botches"—had more to do with his relations with publishers and the reading public than with other writers of his time (L, 92, 128). For a common sense explanation of a writer's options for responding to influence, we turn to Ezra Pound, a twentieth century writer-mentor, whose comments in "A Retrospect" suggest his role as advisor in the creative community of writers of post World War I Paris:

> Be influenced by as many artists as you can, but have the decency either to acknowledge the debt outright, or to try to conceal it.
> Don't allow "influence" to mean merely that you mop up the particular decorative vocabulary of some one or two poets whom you happen to admire. A Turkish war correspondent was recently caught red-handed babbling in his despatches [sic] of "dove-gray" hills, or else it was "pearl-pale," I cannot remember.[22]

Melville's response, of course, was far more sophisticated than that of the Turkish correspondent. We can infer that Melville's appreciation of disguise, which is apparent everywhere in his fiction and is the main subject of *The Confidence-Man: His Masquerade* (1857), would lead naturally to an effort to conceal influence from the public. For Melville, the most plausible method of hiding an indebtedness to a contemporary would be by counterbalancing one stimulus, such as Emerson's idea of the infinitude of the self, against its opposite, such as the sense of human limitation he came to admire in Hawthorne. It is precisely this tension that characterizes Melville's mature view of art. In the essay, "Hawthorne and His Mosses," written while he was working on *Moby-Dick*, Melville says:

> Certain it is, however that his great power of blackness in him [Hawthorne] derives its force from its appeals to that Calvinistic sense of Innate Depravity and Original Sin, from whose visitations, in some shape or other, no deeply thinking mind is always and wholly free. For, in certain moods, no man can

weigh this world, without throwing in something, somehow like Original Sin, to strike the uneven balance.[23]

The first sentence has appealed to many critics as an expression of Melville's rejection of Emersonian optimism, but it is the second that justifies the inclusion of blackness in his art as a way of achieving equilibrium. Late in life, Melville expressed a similar aim of reconciling opposites in his little poem "Art," which we can describe as his summing up. The artist dreams "in placid hours" of "brave" but "unbodied" schemes. He would lend form and also pulsed life, which tends to break out of conventional molds. Melville continues with a list of polarities culminating with the image of the artist wrestling like Jacob with the angel:

> What unlike things must meet and mate:
> A flame to melt—a wind to freeze;
> Sad patience—joyous energies;
> Humility—yet pride and scorn;
> Instinct and study; love and hate;
> Audacity—reverence. These must mate,
> And fuse with Jacob's mystic heart,
> To wrestle with the angel—Art.[24]

This matching and mating, like the sailor's skilled splicing of rope ends, describes Melville's creative response to the raw materials of art derived from his experience, from his reading, and from his reaction to other creative intellects of his own era.

This chapter has attempted to dramatize the positive influence of Emerson on Melville by focusing on a single example of the creative flow of images and their associations from one writer to the other. The discussion that follows in the balance of Part One includes in Chapter 2 a brief, general consideration of the intellectual background of New England Transcendentalism, the context in which Emerson spoke and wrote, and in Chapter 3 a reconstruction and interpretation of the contents of Emerson's 1849 lecture series, with further illustrations of how Melville imaginatively exploited Emersonian imagery and ideas. Part Two offers an Emersonian perspective on Melville's prose fiction from *Typee*, written in 1845 when his knowledge of Emerson was general and superficial, through *Billy Budd*, composed in his last years, from 1888 to 1891, when he had fully assimilated Emerson's thought.

The governing idea of this book is that creativity is a blend of dependent and independent attributes. It is something like Robert Frost's silken tent, which seems to stand alone in the field but actually is bound to earth by many guys and ropes of love and thought.

CHAPTER 2

TRANSCENDENTAL FIRES
IN NEW ENGLAND

1. Emerson's 'Thought Too Bold'

On August 31, 1837, when Melville was an unsettled youth of eighteen about to begin a brief, unsuccessful engagement as a teacher in Pittsfield, Massachusetts, Emerson addressed the students and faculty of Harvard. It was a time of national depression and panic marked by a collapse in real estate, a precipitate fall in stock and commodity prices, an acute banking crisis, and in New York City demonstrations of the unemployed against inflated costs of food, rent, and fuel. But at Harvard, the routines of academic life were unaffected, even though the University enrolled only forty-four new students that month. As *The Boston Daily Evening Transcript* commented, "The smallness of the number is to be attributed to the difficulties of the times" (September 2, 1837: 2).

The occasion of Emerson's address was the annual Phi Beta Kappa oration to celebrate the beginning of the new academic year. What could he say to his select audience against this background of national malaise? If we put ourselves in Emerson's place, we can sense the appropriateness of his aim—to lift his audience by reminding them of moral and spiritual resources transcending the material. For many, Emerson's oration, "The American Scholar," was a profoundly moving experience, evoking images of the indomitable self. "The man has never lived that can feed us ever," Emerson said, defying the depressed temper of his era:

29

The human mind cannot be enshrined in a person who shall set a barrier on any one side to this unbounded, unboundable empire. It is one central fire, which, flaming now out of the lips of Etna, lightens the capes of Sicily, and now out of the throat of Vesuvius, illuminates the towers and vineyards of Naples. It is one light which beams out of a thousand stars. It is one soul which animates all men. (W, I, 108)

Emerson's address contains the nucleus of his ideas on individual integrity and the life of the mind that he repeated in various ways through the years to generations of Americans. In describing the speech as "our Intellectual Declaration of Independence," Holmes applauded its spirit of rebellion. It reminded him of a fiery oration of Samuel Adams (115). Emerson attacked the complacency of the era in lines that recall Thomas Paine's exhortations about "the times that try men's souls":

If there is any period one would desire to be born in, is it not the age of Revolution; when the old and the new stand side by side and admit of being compared; when the energies of all men are searched by fear and by hope; when the historic glories of the old can be compensated by the rich possibilities of the new era? This time, like all times, is a very good one, if we but know what to do with it. (W, I, 110)

Though Melville did not hear Emerson's words at first hand, his future father-in-law Lemuel Shaw was in the audience.[1] Shaw was then Chief Justice of Massachusetts and fellow of the Harvard Corporation; he had been a friend and legal advisor of Melville's father, Allen, who died in 1832. Also, as a young lawyer, Shaw had been a boarder in the Emerson family home when Ralph was a boy of eleven.[2] Shaw had remained a steady friend of the Melville family, and in the late 1840's and 1850's Herman was a frequent visitor to the Shaw home in Boston, where he had access to Emerson's ideas and to Shaw's informed opinions based in part on the latter's long acquaintance with the Emerson family.

Emerson's topic was traditional. As early as 1809, Dr. J. S. Buckminster of Boston had delivered the Phi Beta Kappa oration on "Dangers and Duties of Men of Letters"; in 1818, Edward Tyrrel Channing, a teacher of rhetoric at Harvard, spoke on "Independence in Literary Pursuits." In 1824, with Lafayette in the audience, Edward Everett spoke on "The Peculiar Motives to Intellectual Exertion."[3] But Emerson's plea, not merely for self-reliance, but also for an independent national literature based on the integrity of the writer must have stirred the young people in the audience—Henry David Thoreau, class of '37, might have been present— and surely jolted the more conservative faculty with the assertion that the growing mind is influenced primarily by nature, not educational systems, and that "books are for the scholar's idle times." Of all American writers who developed in the twenty years following this address, Melville best fits Emerson's description of the great achiever whose vitality is derived essentially from primitive instinct. Emerson's words are prophetic:

> Not out of those on whom systems of education have exhausted their culture comes the helpful giant to destroy the old or to build the new, but out of unhandselled savage nature; out of the terrible Druids and Berserkers come at last Alfred and Shakespeare. (W, I, 99–100)

Emerson's reference to the creative power of "savage unhandselled nature" applies to the entire American experience of settling a wilderness continent, struggling with the Indians, and enduring the hardships of the climate, particularly in the North. But among the acknowledged inheritors of Emerson's ideas, Thoreau and Whitman were relatively limited in their personal encounters with savage nature. Thoreau, two years older than Melville, was a Harvard-educated rebel whose brute neighbors at Walden Pond were such familiar small creatures as the ants which warred among the chips in his woodpile, hoot owls, loons, and the pickerel that he charmed in the summer evenings with his flute music. Whitman, who was the same age as Melville—both were born in 1819—grew up in Brooklyn and abandoned a newspaper career there in 1855 to exalt in poetry the commonplaces of life, the miracle of leaves of grass, the dignity of the simple, separate person whose individuality merges with the whole of creation.

Melville's encounters were far more elemental. The three whalers and U.S. Navy frigate on which he sailed from 1841 through 1844 provided a rigorous education in seamanship. He later wrote that a whale-ship was his Yale College and his Harvard.[4] His experiences harpooning whales, jumping ship, and living for approximately three weeks among reputed cannibals in the Marquesas Islands provided raw materials for his seafaring novels, the best of which illustrate Emerson's intuition with their savage vitality.

Further, Emerson's central representation of the American scholar as "man thinking" set forth a larger-than-life model which artists of that era could react to in their own work. Again, Melville comes closer than any confirmed Transcendentalist poet to dramatizing such a spiritually evolving man in his fiction. His sailor narrators who tell their adventures facing savage nature in *Typee* (1846) through *Moby-Dick* (1851) are images of "man thinking," though they suffer from physical and psychic wounds. They meditate on life's problems while responding to the influences of primal nature, book learning, and action. Like Emerson's American scholar, they stand on instinct, resist convention by going to sea or jumping ship, and strive for moral equilibrium between the inner and outer worlds, which to them are linked analogies. Nowhere else in American fiction of this era do we find characters with such an affinity to the Emersonian model. That Melville's narrators typically fail to make "the huge world come round" to them, as Emerson promised, marked the difference between Emerson's accent on the ideal and Melville's sense of the real. Such a difference, as we have noted, is in harmony with the public's admiring but skeptical view of Emerson's thought. Still the fires of New England Transcendentalism that Emerson set in this address leaped across this gap and burned in the memories of his listeners, and also in others like Melville who later encountered his ideas as "a thought too bold," an exalted dream of perfection and creativity in a troubled era.

2. *Spirits of the New Age*

Emerson's conception of "man thinking" as the ideal quester for truth is at the center of an evolving body of Transcendentalist thought that he began articulating in the 1830's. Though in retrospect we can agree with critics like Joel Porte who label this thought simply "*organicism* in an American setting," it is important for us to understand whence it came and how it developed in America, since the ideas Emerson transmitted were not new to him.[5] What was original was the stimulus of his intellect, with its power to compress concepts of the most general scope into sentences of unusual beauty and intensity. Also, we need to estimate from the record of Melville's reading how much he knew of these ideas from sources other than those emanating from Emerson and the Transcendentalists. In this way, we can gain a timely perspective on Melville's response in the late 1840's and early 1850's to the stimulus of Emerson's genius.

To begin, Emerson offered neither a systematic philosophy nor a theology with hierarchies of definitions and abstractions. (If he had, Melville could not have praised him as a thought-diver striving to touch bottom but coming up unsuccessfully with bloodshot eyes.) Emerson's aim, as "The American Scholar" demonstrates, was to inspire changes in the attitudes of his listeners, not to analyze and classify concepts. He and his followers united initially in rebelling against the dominance of logic and conventionalism in Boston Unitarianism. As protestants against the "pale negations" of Unitarian sermons, they affirmed their faith in God as the "spiritual principle" underlying creation, asserting that divine Truth, Goodness, and Beauty were to be perceived primarily through intuition and imagination. Though they could agree on little else, this was the energizing motive of the cultural movement that developed from their protest and that the public and the press quickly labeled *Transcendentalism*.

The center of the revolt, Emerson's circle, was an informal organization of young clergymen and intellectuals of Boston and Concord, who reluctantly allowed themselves to be called "The Transcendental Club." Of the twenty-six persons who became most active in the inner group, seventeen were Unitarian ministers; the oldest was Convers Francis, who was forty-one at the time of the first meeting on September 19, 1836 in the home of George Ripley, a Boston clergyman. Emerson was then thirty-three.[6]

From the start, the protest Emerson led was not limited merely to church reform. Such a concentration of purpose would have entailed fighting logic with more logic. Instead, Emerson and others who shared his spirit of rebellion drew their ideas from at least two major cultural traditions that served to broaden the appeal of their writings. One was the enthusiasm and intuitionism of German romantic philosophy, which they received largely at second hand through the works of Samuel Taylor Coleridge and Thomas Carlyle. (Emerson had visited both on his European tour in 1832 and 1833 after the death of his first wife, Ellen, and his resignation from the Unitarian ministry at the age of twenty-nine.) The second was the native religious habit of inward communication of New England Puritanism and continuing in Quakerism with the conception of the inner light.[7] Also, they drew upon such varied sources as Plato, Neoplatonism, Swedenborg, and Oriental philosophy. For these reasons, even members of the Transcendental Club were as much aware of their inconsistencies as of their underlying agreement in principle. James Freeman Clarke remarked that the group should have been called "the Club of the Like-Minded" because "no two of us thought alike."[8]

The intellectual vigor of Emerson's immediate circle has led the historian O. B. Frothingham to describe the Transcendental ideas of the group as generating a current in American thought "so strong, that like the Orinoco rushing down between the South American continent and the island of Trinidad, it made a bright green trail upon the dark sea into which it poured but the vehemence of the flood forbade its diffusion" (380–381). Porte, however, explains the vitality in terms of the creative interactions of its members: "We find arranged around Emerson, not a neat circle of little Emersons but rather an odd collocation of resolutely-defined figures who shaped their careers as much in reaction to Emerson as in emulation of him" (vii). Though Melville was not a member of the inner group, this description suggests his creative response to Emerson's appeal, which ranged between reaction and admiration.

One obvious difficulty with an abstract label like *Transcendentalism* applied to a group of individualists is that it implies an unchanging set of ideas, as though the Transcendentalist of 1836 were incapable of modifying his views through the years. But as we can demonstrate in Chapter 3 by examining Emerson's lecture manuscripts of the late 1840's, his interest shifted noticeably from religious protest of the late 1830's to ethical reform and aesthetics when Melville was writing.

Actually, the term *Transcendental*, as used during this period, had at least two distinct classes of meanings. Popularly, the word has suggested, as Dagobert D. Runes notes, "any view that is 'enthusiastic,' 'mystical,' extravagant, impractical, ethereal, supernatural, vague, abstruse, lacking in common sense" (320). The Transcendentalists themselves occasionally used the term in this pejorative sense, which still persists. For example, Theodore Parker, the most radical of the transcendental ministers, wrote in a letter to George Ripley: "You remember the stuff which Margaret Fuller used to twaddle forth on that theme ('absence of art' in America), and what transcendental nonsense got delivered from gawky girls and long-haired men."[9] Similarly, Melville, who was not a member of the nucleus organization, wrote to Evert Duyckinck in the aforementioned letter of March 3, 1849 that he had heard of Emerson "as full of transcendentalisms, myths and oracular gibberish," but was "agreeably disappointed" to find him "quite intelligible" (L, 78–79).

In contrast to this uncomplimentary use of the term, which Melville did not apply to Emerson, is a cluster of more or less technical definitions formulated by German philosophers and asserting the primacy of intuition over logic as an interpreter of experience. These definitions, which derive essentially from Immanuel Kant, refer to knowledge which is not based on experience but is inherent in the mind and essential for an understanding of experience. "I call all knowledge *transcendental*," he wrote in *Critique of Pure Reason* (1781), "which is occupied not so much with objects, as with our a priori concepts of objects" (16). We should recall that Kant's philosophy was in part a reaction to the extreme empiricism of John Locke, whose *Essay Concerning Human Understanding* (1690) denied the existence of innate qualities of the mind. Locke took the position that all knowledge derives from particular sensory experience or combinations of experiences, which are formed into concepts through reflection. In addition, the agnostic David Hume had drawn the further conclusion that if knowledge depends entirely on sensory perception and reflection, then notions of God, the soul, and total nature are beyond human reason because they cannot be demonstrated through the senses. It was for this reason many Transcendental ministers rejected the theology of Unitarianism, which was based on Locke's sensationalist philosophy. Such logic, Emerson felt, led ultimately to skepticism.

Though Kant agreed with Locke on the importance of sensory experience in the acquiring of knowledge, he proposed that the mind itself has inherent concepts and forms of pure intuition, such as causality, time and space, which serve as a patterned screen to give structure to experience. Kant further distinguished between these *transcendental* forms of Pure Reason and *transcendent* ideas that derive from Practical Reason or the moral consciousness. Such concepts as God, freedom, and immortality, he reasoned, were extensions of a posteriori knowledge abstracted from experience, since they have the practical function of guiding moral action (5). These transcendent ideas differ from transcendental patterns already in the mind because they refer to a level of reality that goes beyond both sensory experience and the limits of human comprehension. In other words, the transcendent cannot be scientifically described through the application of the forms of Pure Reason on the faculties of sense perception. Immortality, for example, is an implication of experience which cannot be reduced to the measurement of time.

Kant's careful discrimination between the properties of Pure Reason and Practical Reason served to restrict the scope of comprehension. As a

result, his successors in Germany attempted to unify his conception of
Reason and extend the limits of knowledge. Their searches for an absolute
principle by which all things would be knowable led to the creation of
expansive systems of knowledge in which ultimate reality lay in supersensual, or *transcendental*, processes of thought. In effect, these philosophers
made elaborate maps of the mind with the aim of finding God, as though
He were located there.

Among the earliest revisers of Kant's philosophy, the poet J. G. Herder
proposed the unity of soul-life, with the faculties of thought, will,
understanding, and sensation dependent on one another and springing
from a common source. God is revealed in the soul and in nature,
particularly in religion, art, and history, which are evolving toward
humanitarian ideals of harmony and fullness of growth. H. F. Jacobi
asserted that faith and feeling are intuitive sources of knowledge of God
and freedom. The student of Emerson can sense the affinity of his religious
thought to the ideas of these early followers of Kant, particularly the
poetic vision of Herder.

But other successors to Kant provided even greater stimulation to
Emerson and his inner circle, though much of it came at second hand
through the works of Coleridge and Carlyle. The most important of
these—Gottlieb Fichte, Freidrick Wilhelm Schelling, and G. W. F. Hegel—
devised complementary philosophies, whose logic Emerson ignored while
accepting their conclusions. In brief, Fichte proposed that basic reality is
will, or ego, which intuits its own activity as Universal Reason and rises
above space and time. This transcendental ego produces nature and
expresses itself in moral law. Further, the individual's inward sense of duty
or moral consciousness is an expression of this absolute purpose. Here is
an important philosophical underpinning for Emerson's well-known assertion of identity of the self with spiritual nature: "Standing on the bare
ground,—my head bathed by the blithe air, and uplifted into infinite
space,—all mean egotism vanishes. I become a transparent eyeball. I am
nothing. I see all. The currents of the Universal Being circulate through
me; I am part or particle of God" (W, I, 10).

Schelling agreed with Fichte's conception of Reason as will but broadened it to include the unconscious. In other words, reality is creative
energy; and all nature is an expression of this purposeful spiritual force
trying to realize itself with the aid of time in matter. Schelling reasoned
further that this energy is organic and evolutionary in expression and is

moving toward the goal of perfect self-expression and consciousness. Accordingly, men are capable of imagining better than they know, and art is the highest stage of self-realization, since it serves to reveal nature's own art. The unity in Schelling's philosophy is derived in part from his theory of correspondences between matter and spirit, a notion that is deeply embedded in the history of ideas and that permeates Emerson's writing.

Hegel, the most prominent successor to Kant, rejected Schelling's concept of undifferentiated absolute energy, ridiculing it in his celebrated reference to "the night in which all cows are black." His vision of the universe as evolving through space and time in a triadic pattern of thesis, antithesis, and synthesis represents God as the Idea, the ultimate synthesis or timeless totality of all evolutionary processes. As the culmination of creation, He reveals Himself through religion, philosophy, and art. Hegel's expanded conception of nature, with its underlying pattern of growth, placed greater emphasis on change and contradiction than did Schelling, though both proposed that unity is the result of the reconciliation of opposite qualities in art and nature. We can recognize in Hegel's triads a nearly contemporary source of Emerson's notion of "cracked nature," a thesis and antithesis evolving through space and time toward synthesis, or spiritual wholeness.[10]

These core ideas of German romantic philosophy reached the New England Transcendentalists through three main avenues. Firstly, Emerson and his immediate circle read the German philosophers, either in the original or in translations. Records of Emerson's withdrawals from libraries, for example, confirm his interest as a young man in Herder: in 1829 he checked out of the Harvard library a translation of Herder's *Outlines of a Philosophy of Man* (London, 1800); three years later, he borrowed this work on two occasions from the Boston Anthenaeum. In addition, he withdrew from the Boston Athenaeum in 1837 two volumes of Jacobi's *Werke* (Leipzig, 1812–1815). His extensive personal library contained Kant's *Critic of Pure Reason* (London, 1838), Fichte's *The Nature of the Scholar and Its Manifestations* (London, 1845), and several volumes by Hegel, including *Vorlesungen uber die Aesthetic* (Berlin, 1842).[11]

Of greater significance, however, was the broad avenue to German thought through German romantic literature, which was steeped in what is sometimes called post-Kantian idealism. By 1836, Emerson had read most of his fifty-five volume set of Goethe's works in German. In addition, the interest of the New Englanders in German men of letters is readily demonstrated in the nearly twenty articles and poems about German literature published in *The Dial*, the Transcendentalist journal printed in sixteen issues between 1840 and 1844. The literary historian Stanley M. Vogel rightly concludes: "These New Englanders preferred Herder, Wieland, Schiller and Goethe to Kant, Fichte and Schelling. When the iron regulations of Calvinism began to hem them in, the Transcendentalists turned to these German literary men and not to the philosophers for inspiration" (xiv).

The third and most important route by which German idealism reached Emerson's circle was through the writings of Coleridge and Carlyle. Though neither author redefined the term *Transcendentalism*, both accented special aspects of the German philosophical systems, oversimplifying the ideas in ways that appealed to the Americans, who were not trained in technical philosophy.

Drawing largely on Schelling's philosophy, Coleridge stressed the distinction between intuitive Reason and cognitive Understanding and an evolutionary theory of natural-spiritual correspondences. His conception of the creative imagination as the shaping power of the mind is a variant of his idea of Reason. An important source of Emerson's ideas on polarity, and also Melville's on paradox, is Coleridge's assertion in *Biographia Literaria* that the poetic imagination is activated by will and "reveals itself in the balance or reconciliation of opposite or discordant qualities: of sameness, with difference; of the general, with the concrete; the idea, with the image: the individual, with the representative."[12] Here is the prose forerunner of Emerson's lines on Merlin, the kingly bard who reconciles the extremes in nature to bring forth "poetic peace." Here also is the germ of Melville's image of the writer who strives to match and mate unlike things as he wrestles with the angel Art.[13]

Carlyle, on the other hand, made pronounced use of Fichte's assertive transcendental ego, the individual soul merged with the spirit that encompasses and transcends external nature. Such an idea underlies the various images of the self as representative of spiritual nature in the writings of Transcendentalists, especially Emerson and Thoreau. We find it also in Whitman and with qualifications in Melville.

Emerson's meetings abroad in 1833 with Coleridge and Carlyle, who are credited with stimulating his interest in German philosophy and literature, were supplemented with extensive reading of their major works and by the well-known friendship with Carlyle. Between 1825 and 1836, Emerson's journals indicate a continuing interest in Coleridge's philosophical and critical writings, with references to *Biographia Literaria*, *Aids to Reflection*, and *The Friend*, among other works. Also in 1836 Emerson wrote an appreciative preface to the American edition of Carlyle's *Sartor Resartus*. Its conception of nature as "the Living Garment of God" corresponds to the theme of Emerson's own work, *Nature*, published the same year and accepted with enthusiasm by the Transcendental Club as its manifesto.

When we consider Melville's access to German romantic philosophy, we must conclude from a survey of his extensive reading through 1851, when he completed *Moby-Dick*, that he received none of it directly. The record of books Melville is known to have borrowed or owned, compiled by Merton M. Sealts, Jr., contains no listing of works by Kant, Herder, Jacobi, Fichte, Schelling, and Hegel, most of whom Emerson had read either in the original German or in translation. Nor do we find as much interest of Melville in German romantic literature as Emerson had. From late 1849 through 1851, Melville's period of greatest literary productivity, he did some reading of Goethe, having purchased *Truth and Poetry*, borrowed *Wilhelm Meister's Apprenticeship and Travels*, and received as a gift *Iphigenia in Tauris*. In addition, he obtained a volume of Schiller's poems and one of John Paul Fredrichter's poems. All five works were translations.[14]

Melville's reading of Coleridge and Carlyle also is much less extensive than that of Emerson. Sealts' record indicates that Melville purchased *Biographia Literaria* in 1848, borrowed *On Heroes and Hero Worship*, *Sartor Resartus*, and *German Romances* in 1850. Melville, of course, had available books and journals that offered summaries of the ideas of philosophers and excerpts from works of European writers; but the available evidence indicates that his reading access to the European sources of New England Transcendentalism was limited.

Even so, Melville did have access of another kind. In October 1849, he was introduced to George J. Adler, an honorary Professor of German Literature at the University of the City of New York (the present New York University), who journeyed to Europe with him, and the two spent evenings on shipboard talking about German philosophy. The trip lasted approximately seventeen weeks. In the journal which he kept of this voyage, Melville wrote of one convivial occasion: "We talked metaphysics continually, & Hegel, Schlegel, Kant &c [sic] were discussed under the influence of the whiskey."[15] Though Melville learned from this association, as Sanford E. Marovitz has indicated, the play of his imagination would inevitably direct his interest, like that of Emerson, to the conclusions of the philosophers rather than to the technical details of their arguments.[16] Also, Melville by then had heard Emerson lecture and that same year had written two novels with vigorous dramatic representations of self-reliance: *Redburn* and *White-Jacket*. These, along with Melville's earlier writings, look ahead to the themes in *Moby-Dick*. On balance, despite the personal influence of Adler, Melville's expanded portraits of the self in his novels of this era have their most important source, not in German romantic philosophy, but as the following chapters will show, in the pervasive, contemporary example of Emerson.

The impact of post-Kantian idealism on Emerson and his circle is perhaps most clearly illustrated in Emerson's reference to the term *Transcendental* in this passage from his lecture "The Transcendentalist" (1842):

> It is well known to most of my audience that the Idealism of the present day acquired the name Transcendental from the use of that term by Immanuel Kant, of Königsberg, who replied to the skeptical philosophy of Locke, which insisted that there was nothing in the intellect which was not previously in the experience of the senses, by showing that there was a very important class of ideas or imperative forms, which did not come by experience, but through which experience was acquired; that these were intuitions of the mind itself; and he denominated them *Transcendental*. The extraordinary profoundness and precision of that man's thinking have given vogue to his nomenclature, in Europe and America, to the extent that whatever belongs to the class of intuitive thought is popularly called at the present day Transcendental. (W, I, 339–340)

Instead of limiting the term to Kant's a priori forms and intuitions in Pure Reason of causality, space, and time, Emerson broadened its denotation in the manner of Fichte and Schelling to include supersensual ideas which Kant had declared were beyond human comprehension. Intuitive thought was for Emerson and the New Englanders, but not for Kant, the basis for transcendental knowledge of God, total nature, and immortality. "Nature is Transcendental," Emerson said, "exists primarily, necessarily, ever works and advances, yet takes no thought for the morrow" (339).

Emerson also described the aspirations of the Transcendentalist, who

> adopts the whole connection of spiritual doctrine. He believes in miracle, in the perpetual openness of the human mind to new influx of light and power; he believes in inspiration and in ecstasy. He wishes that the spiritual principle should be suffered to demonstrate itself to the end, in all possible applications to the state of man, without the admission of anything unspiritual. (335–336)

But after presenting this image of human perfection, Emerson adds that he had not yet found a pure Transcendentalist. "I mean," he explained, "we have yet no man who has leaned entirely on his character, and eaten angel's food; who, working for universal aims, found himself fed, he knew not how; clothed, sheltered and weaponed, he know not how, and yet it was done by his own hands" (338). Even though a realist might reject such an ideal as absurd, the image does look ahead to Melville's last novel, *Billy Budd*, which dramatizes the plight of a handsome sailor embodying these characteristics aboard a British warship.

Other members of Emerson's circle offered similar definitions stressing the reality of spirit over sensory experience. For example, George Ripley made this comment in his letter of resignation as pastor of the Unitarian Church on Purchase Street, Boston:

> There is a class of persons who desire a reform in the prevailing philosophy of the day. These are called Transcendentalists, because they believe in an order of truths which transcends the sphere of external sense. Their leading idea is the supremacy of mind over matter. Hence they maintain that the truth of religion does not depend on tradition, nor on historical facts, but has an unerring witness in the soul.[17]

From the comments of Emerson and Ripley, which are expressions of intuition and imagination rather than logical argument, we can infer that the value of post-Kantian idealism to Emerson and other Transcendentalists was not in offering a ready-made philosophical system that would suit their initial purpose of church reform, but in confirming their faith in the divinity of conscience and the spiritual principle underlying nature. The stimulation Emerson received from abroad actually was overmatched by influences from home. "How impossible to find Germany," he reminisced in his journals. "Our young men went to the Rhine to find the genius which had charmed them, and it was not there." Nor was it in Heidelberg, in Gottingen, in Halle, in Berlin: "No one knew where it was; from Vienna to the frontier, it was not found, and they very slowly and mournfully learned, that in the speaking it had escaped, and as it had charmed them in Boston, they must return and look for it there."[18]

Transcendentalism in New England, then, was essentially a native movement, reinforced though not initiated by ideas from abroad. The views Emerson and others espoused were implicit also in the Puritan beliefs of the colonial period, especially those interpreting acts of nature and history as Providences of God and the soul as having a being that transcends the body. These implied the spiritual significance of man and nature. Even the doctrine of Original Sin, which the Puritans' Calvinist theology explained as the separation of man's will from God's purpose, provides an antecedent for Emerson's image of "cracked nature." The seventeenth century Puritan divine Thomas Hooker asserted, "Man was the mean betwixt God and the creature, to convey all good with all the constancy of it; and therefore when man breaks, heaven and earth breaks all asunder; the conduit being cracked and displaced, there can be no conveyance from the fountain."[19] Where the Calvinist reasoned that all human experience must begin with the fall of man and the resultant separation from God, Emerson intuited the closing of the gap through the healing power of imagination and instinct. So we may characterize Emerson in his time as a Puritan released from Calvinistic dogmas, which he called superstitions, and ennobled by the poetic temperament. The historian Perry Miller, who has demonstrated Emerson's relation to the Puritan tradition in America, also has traced the yearning of the Puritans for spiritual purification—a feeling that resonates in Emerson—to the *Confessions* of St. Augustine and beyond to the elemental faith of the Christians of the first century. When Emerson spoke and wrote, he touched deep responsive emotions in his audiences that no doctrines could evoke.

One inevitable result of the stimuli of post-Kantian idealism and the native Puritan tradition of protest on members of the Transcendental Club was the aforementioned early extension of their interests beyond the narrow limits of religious controversy. Although the club met infrequently for a period variously estimated at between four and twelve years, the energies of members found diversified expression in secular activities, such as lecturing, literary criticism, poetry, and reform experiments in communal living. The Transcendental priest soon gave way to the reformer and poet in what Charles R. Metzger has appropriately described as the delayed secularization of New England thought (5–6). It is important for readers of Melville to be sensitive to this change, because it helps to explain how and why he could reject the Transcendental religion at the same time that he was receptive to Emersonian conceptions of right behavior and art that were dominant in the late 1840's and early 1850's. As we shall see in the next chapter, Melville's response to Emerson was timely.

CHAPTER 3

CREATIVE FURNACE: EMERSON'S LECTURES, 1848–1850

1. The Lecture Manuscripts

After nearly four years at sea, Melville returned in October 1844 to his mother's home in Lansingburgh, New York, at a time when Emerson was recognized as the most challenging spokesman for ideas on the meaning of life and art in America. The the time also marked Melville's intellectual awakening, as he later wrote to Nathaniel Hawthorne:

> Until I was twenty-five, I had no development at all. From my twenty-fifth year I date my life. Three weeks have scarcely passed at any time between then and now that I have not unfolded within myself.[1]

By then, Emerson had acquired an international reputation through the publication of his *Essays*, first and second series (1841 and 1844); he had established himself as a lecturer of unusual suasiveness and pith, and his ideas were further disseminated through critical reaction in newspapers and magazines.

To a lesser extent, Thoreau and other Transcendentalists also were attracting public attention through lectures and articles. Although the most significant Transcendental periodical, *The Dial*, suspended publication in that year, a number of its essays on literature and art by Margaret Fuller were reprinted two years later in the *Democratic Review* and made available to Melville, who gravitated, as Sealts puts it, to libraries and bookstores.[2] Also at that time, the Transcendental experiment in communal living at Brook Farm near West Roxbury, Massachusetts, was in its third year, and its participants were preparing to publish in 1845 *The Harbinger*, a weekly newspaper devoted to social reform under the editorship of George Ripley, a founding member of the Transcendental Club.

Though Emerson preferred in his lectures to detach himself from the economic, political, and social upheavals of the 1840's, his rhetorical stance of speaking above the battle was nonetheless aimed at directing the thoughts of people caught up in the daily struggles of living. The general conditions affecting their lives included the depression that continued from the panic of 1837, the unpopular Mexican War of 1845 to 1847, and the deepening crisis over slavery in the South. Emerson's response to these divisive events was to forcefully assert the underlying unity of man and nature.

In Boston, while Emerson was attempting to lift the spirits of his audiences with this theme, Theodore Parker and other Transcendentalists were embroiled in local controversies that pitted Transcendentalists, Unitarians, and Calvinist Trinitarians against one another. Doctrinal differences led to splits in some congregations that in turn led to suits over the division of church properties and much publicity in the press, in what William R. Hutchinson has called "The Great Transcendentalist Controversy" (135). Though these events sustained public interest in Transcendentalism, their details need not concern us; for Emerson's appeal was always to soar above the mundane and project an ideal view of the world that would make "the student independent of the century" (M, 135).

When we attempt to determine the particular Emersonian ideas that Melville absorbed while he was unfolding within himself and writing his seafaring novels, *Typee* through *Moby-Dick*, our problem is analogous to that of the scientist attempting to identify components of the atmosphere at a given time. Nearly all modern research in this area, however, has concentrated on the ideas available to Melville through Emerson's *Nature* (1836), early addresses, and *Essays* (first and second series), initially published while Melville was an adolescent or away at sea. Though Melville left no records of reading anything of Emerson in the late 1840's and early 1850's outside one brief comment to Evert Duyckinck ("I had only glanced at a book of his once in Putnam's store—that is all I knew of him till I heard him lecture"), Sealts for one has speculated on the essays Melville might have read after the lecture, observing that they were available in the public libraries.[3] Others including Matthiessen have turned, as has already been noted, to the marginal comments that Melville wrote in his copy of the *Essays*. Sealts has established, however, that Melville had purchased the work no earlier than 1862, when he was forty-three, some years after he had given up his professional career as a novelist and was bitter over his apparent failure as an author.[4]

Despite the value of these early writings as indicators of Emerson's thought, they do not provide a record of what he was saying in the late 1840's and 50's. Nor can they suggest the public interest in, and response to, Emerson during those years of Melville's greatest literary productivity. The Emerson that Melville heard about and eventually encountered in 1849 was no longer the youthful rebel of "The American Scholar" and "Self-Reliance" but a veteran of the lecture circuit and experienced commentator on the spirit of the times. During 1849 and 1850 alone, he had no less than seventy different speaking engagements, some of them consisting of courses lasting for weeks like the one in Boston. He traveled as far west as Cincinnati and as far south as Philadelphia.[5] What his lecture manuscripts for these years contain is not mere repetitions of ideas and images set forth in the early works on which his reputation rests today, but shifts in focus toward the darker side of human nature, with new perceptions, experiments in phrasing, and applications of his "thought too bold" to the timely interests of his audiences.

In short, Emerson's lectures and public reactions to them in the press are more immediate sources of the ideas and attitudes that Melville reacted to than the early writings. Though Melville may well have browsed through the *Essays* and *Nature* in a library after hearing Emerson lecture, it was the Emerson of 1849 that impressed him most. Everything else that he learned about Emerson would be conditioned by that experience and by what he heard and read of Emerson's ideas of the moment.

Our best source of the ideas Emerson was articulating while Melville was writing is the manuscripts of the lecture series Emerson composed in England in 1848 and delivered with modifications in Boston early in 1849, when Melville heard him speak. We already have noted Melville's employment of images of thought-diving and cracked nature from this series in his letter to Duyckinck dated March 3, 1849. A further examination of the manuscripts will disclose what other Emersonian notions were in the air.

The Boston Daily Republican of Wednesday, January 17, 1849, described the course, which Emerson had advertised under the title, "Mind and Manners in the Nineteenth Century," in these words:

> Ralph Waldo Emerson delivered the first of a course of lectures at the elegant chapel of Mr. Clarke's Society in Freeman Place, on Monday evening. It is to be followed by four more, delivered continuously on Monday evenings. The subject of the course is the Laws of the Intellect. In the first lecture he unfolds the Excellencies of the intellect, the mistakes, which are almost universal in the study of it, and the feasibility of this study. His next lecture will treat of the identity of thought with eternal truth and its correspondences. The third will treat of Inspiration; the fourth will compare the Eastern Mind with the Western; the subject of the last will be Aristocracy. (2)

First mention of a course entitled "Mind and Manners in the Nineteenth Century," however, was in *The Times* of London on the preceding June 6, 1848 for delivery at the Literary and Scientific Institution on Edwards Street, Portman Square (1). Here there were six topics: Powers and Laws of Thought, Relation of Intellect to Natural Science, Tendencies and Duties of Men of Thought, Politics and Socialism, Poetry and Eloquence, and Natural Aristocracy. James Eliot Cabot notes that the first three lectures in the English series were new; the second three were delivered previously.[6]

In describing the contents of the new lectures, which Emerson delivered again in the Boston series and later renamed "Natural History of the Intellect," Cabot observes that "metaphysical notions are treated as if they were poetical images, which it would be useless and impertinent to explain" (560). Since these are precisely the kinds of notions that would have attracted Melville, we need to examine the contents of these lectures in detail, for they contain the fresh materials for the Boston series. To these we add the separate treatise, "Mind and Manners in the Nineteenth Century," which provides the advertised title for the series and probably the contents for one or more lectures, and "Natural Aristocracy," announced in both *The Times* of London and *The Boston Daily Republican* as the closing lecture in the series.

What follows is a brief catalog of the various drafts of these five lectures preserved at Houghton Library of Harvard University among Emerson's lecture manuscripts for the years 1848–1850:

General Title: "Natural History of the Intellect"
First Lecture: "Powers and Laws of Thought"

There are three drafts (hereinafter identified as I, A; I, B; I, C). In the first (67 pages), Emerson writes, "What is the religion of 1848?" In the second (51 pages), he crosses out 1848 and writes 1849; in the third (90 pages), he changes 1849 to 1850. Examination of these drafts discloses repetitions of ideas and phrasing; however, gaps in Emerson's pagination in the second (1849) version suggest that he transferred a substantial number of pages from this short draft to the long third (1850) version.

Second Lecture: "Relation of Intellect to Natural Science"

There are two drafts (identified as II, A and II, B). The first draft is 70 pages and the second 80 pages. Though both are undated by Emerson, they correspond to the second lecture as announced in *The Times* and *The Boston Daily Republican*. Cabot, who was Emerson's literary executor, makes the following initialed comment on the cover page of the shorter draft: "Perhaps it was written in England 1848 or 1847 before he [Emerson] went." Examination of the two drafts indicates that the second is a slightly enlarged version of the first.

Third Lecture: "Tendencies and Duties of Men of Thought"

There are two drafts (III, A and III, B). The first is 68 pages, and the second 77 pages. On the cover of the shorter version, Cabot notes in pencil: "In part at least the third lecture of the London course." On the cover of the longer one, he writes: "Jan. 1849 in Boston, April 2, 1850 at New York." This version is printed in *Complete Works of Ralph Waldo Emerson*, vol. 3, 65–89, under the title "Instinct and Inspiration." Because of its emphasis on inspiration, this lecture corresponds to the third one in the series outlined in *The Boston Daily Republican*.

Treatise: "Mind and Manners in the Nineteenth Century"

There is one draft of 136 pages (identified as M), which seems sufficient to provide materials for more than one lecture. Cabot notes on the cover page: "Probably March 30, 1850 in Spirit of the Age . . . Seems to be a recent variation of Present Age 1839–40. . . . It seems *not* to have been the course in Boston January 1849." Though certainly not the entire course, the manuscript provides the advertised title of the lecture series in London and Boston (for the latter, see the *Boston Post*, January 11, 1849: 2), and the image of cracked nature that Melville applies to Emerson in the letter to Duyckinck, March 3, 1849. Portions of this discourse, which offers a critique of the age, were probably available for inclusion in the London and Boston series. Emerson's announced fourth lecture topic in Boston, a comparison of the Eastern and Western mind, resembles the topic indicated by the title of the treatise and hints at the idea of a schism in thought stressed in the contents of this document.

Closing Lecture: "Natural Aristocracy"

There are two drafts (identified as N, A and N, B). The first draft (74 pages) includes passages in another hand, suggesting that Emerson had a copyist transcribe materials from an earlier lecture. The second draft (192 pages) consists of notes on a variety of allied topics. Though Sealts argues that a version of this lecture was the one Melville heard on February 5, 1849, the listing of the title as the closing lecture of the series in both London and Boston strongly suggests that a version was delivered actually on February 12, the date of the final Boston lecture. Even so, it is possible that Emerson could have used portions of it on other nights in the series.

Houghton Library has several other manuscripts of lectures that Emerson probably delivered in the years 1848–1850, but we need go no further than the above items to obtain the leading ideas and images Emerson was articulating in the late 1840's, including the Boston series of early 1849. Melville was in Boston from January 30 to April 10, during which time he and his wife, Elizabeth, stayed at the home of her parents, where she gave birth to her first child, Malcolm, on February 16. Though Melville is known to have attended only one lecture in the Boston series, Emerson spoke also in nearby Cambridge and Charleston in the same period. It is conceivable that Melville's father-in-law, Lemuel Shaw, Chief Justice of Massachusetts, or other members of the Shaw family were among the "oracles," as *The Boston Daily Republican* puts it, in one or more of Emerson's sophisticated audiences. Shaw was by most estimates one of the most distinguished judges in the United States at that time.

Certainly the intellectual atmosphere in the Shaw home would have encouraged informed conversation on Emerson. Further, the Shaws, if not Melville, could have read a laudatory review of Emerson's lectures in *The Boston Post* on January 25. "No mere description can do Mr. Emerson justice," the anonymous reviewer observes,

> We think he is improving *in his line,* and everybody knows, or ought to know, what that line is, for he is, doubtless, one of the most remarkable men of the day. He is the tallest kind of "corn." He exhibited on Monday evening a wealth of imagination, an opulence of imagery, and of original and peculiar thought which amounted to a surfeit. (2)

If Melville knew little of Emerson before attending one of his lectures, he was in the right place at the right time to become well-informed about Emerson's "line" by the time he returned to New York in April.

2. From 'Man Thinking' to 'Thought Diving'

No statement of Emerson's portrays more vividly the essential nature of the self evolving as "man thinking" than his comment on perspective in "Powers and Laws of Thought," the opening lecture of the Boston series in January and February of 1849. Though the phrasing occurs in the 1848 and 1850 manuscripts (See I,A, 25–26 and I,C, 64), Emerson's penmanship in the latter version resembles that of several pages in the short 1849 draft. The implication is that the page had been part of the 1849 lecture which he later transferred to the 1850 version:

> *What is life, but the angle of vision?* [Italics added.] A man is measured by the angle at which he looks at objects. What is life—but what a man is thinking all day? This is his fate and his employer. The brain is the man. The eyes outrun the feet, and go where feet and hands will never come; yet it is very certain that the rest of the man will follow his head. (I, C, 64)

Though Emerson had expressed this idea as early as *Nature* in referring to a man's developing spiritual perspective, the phrase "angle of vision" was a fresh metaphor in 1849 that has been included in a composite of several versions of this lecture published in Emerson's collected writings (W, XII, 10), where it is available to contemporary readers. Its use by

Sherman Paul in his *Emerson's Angle of Vision* and by A. Carl Bredahl, Jr., in his *Melville's Angles of Vision* suggests the value of the phrase and the idea as an aesthetic frame of reference for critics of our time. But in applying the Emersonian notion to Melville, Bredahl stresses a contrast between the two writers: "Emerson sees the effect of perspective as a liberating influence, freeing man to the possibility of transcending the limitations of his existence. Melville does not draw the same conclusion; to him perspective forces man to realize his limitations" (2).

Bredahl bases his view on statements the two writers made twenty years apart: Emerson commenting in 1836 when he was launching his career as an essayist and lecturer and Melville in 1856 when he realized he could no longer make a living as a writer.[7] The implication once again is that their attitudes were unwavering. As a result, Bredahl's contrast obscures Melville's real indebtedness to the Emerson of 1849 for a principle that gives both shape and texture to the novels Melville produced at least during the next two years. We shall examine some of Melville's problems with angles of vision as we review the pattern of his artistic development in later chapters. Our present purpose is to provide a convincing specific example of how Melville molds the Emersonian idea, even including its image of a man fatefully following his head, into the moment of final suspense in *Moby-Dick*:

During the course of Melville's narrative of whaling, the tragic hero, Captain Ahab, has been thinking all day, every day about the white whale, which looms in his mind as the monomaniac incarnation of all evil. In his ultimate encounter with this object of his hatred, Ahab physically defines his angle of vision by turning his back to the sun. He then curses the whale and hurls his harpoon, crying out, "*Thus*, I give up the spear!" Melville continues with a passage that dramatizes the Emersonian idea in detail:

> The harpoon was darted; the stricken whale flew forward; with igniting velocity the line ran through the groove—ran foul. Ahab stooped to clear it; he did clear it; but the flying turn caught him round the neck, and voicelessly as Turkish mutes bowstring their victim, he was shot out of the boat, ere the crew knew he was gone. Next instant, the heavy *eye-splice in the rope's final end* [italics added] flew out of the stark-empty tub, knocked down an oarsman, and smiting the sea, disappeared in its depths. (565)

Ahab's angle of vision, his eye-splice, is at his end of a line that has run foul. At the other end is his nemesis in nature, the whale of his meditations, which drags him headlong to destruction. The eye-splice smites the sea, since in Ahab's view all nature is evil. The rope end and the man disappear together, for a man's life is identical with his angle of vision. In this manner, Melville's climactic paragraph becomes a metaphor of the entire tragic action of the novel, and of the fallen man that Ahab represents.

If we examine Melville's passage in its immediate context, we can note a further correspondence to an earlier image of Emerson on perspective, set forth in "Compensation" (1841):

> A man cannot speak but he judges himself. With his will or against his will he draws his portrait to the eye of his companions by every word. Every opinion reacts on him who utters it. It is a thread-ball thrown at a mark, but the other end remains in the thrower's bag. *Or rather it is a harpoon hurled at the whale, unwinding, as it flies, a coil of cord in the boat, and, if the harpoon is not good, nor not well thrown, it will be nigh to cut the steersman in twain or to sink the boat.* [Italics added.] (W, II, 110)

In this observation, Emerson connects thought with speech, as though what a man says determines his angle of vision. Ahab's consuming hatred of the whale and all nature leads to his final utterance: "From hell's heart I stab at thee; for hate's sake I spit my last breath at thee." The harpoon of his speech, like that in his hand, is not well put, since the evil Ahab sees in nature is in himself. In reaction, a flying turn of the fouled line bowstrings him around the neck. Thus muted, he is shot from the boat "ere the crew knew he was gone." The whale completes its destruction of Ahab and his world view by ramming and sinking the *Pequod*, the whaleship he commanded in his monomaniac quest.

This evidence of Melville's concentrated use of an idea that Emerson articulated, in addition to the references already cited, strongly suggests the identity in their thinking on perspective extending from 1849 at least through the writing of *Moby-Dick* in 1850 and 1851, despite the contrasts that many critics have emphasized. As will be further demonstrated, the attraction of Melville to Emerson's thought at this time was both intense and inclusive. It is probable that Emerson's concepts filtered into his mind as the heat from a stove until, like Whitman, Melville too was brought to a boil.

However critics of our time judge Emerson's overall angle of vision, the perspective he established in his lecture series of early 1849 develops the limitations as well as the possibilities of human perception. In the quotations cited above, for example, both authors represent individual will as governed by a universal law of compensation, which determines the consequences of every thought, speech, and deed. Emerson, like Melville, also sees physical reality with its restrictions on perception as the starting point for psychological, ethical, and aesthetic questing for the innermost depths of experience and value. In all three versions of the opening lecture, Emerson rejects metaphysical speculation for its own sake, detached from everyday life. "Who has not looked into a metaphysical book?" he asks. "And what sensible man has looked twice" (I, B, 16)? His central effort is to explain the invisible truths of the intellect in terms of the visible, in his words, "to take away from metaphysics its reproach" and "put it into connection with life and nature of recent ages" (I, B, 13).

Emerson begins with a reference to his attending scientific lectures in London and Paris and listening to "Richard Owen's masterly enumeration of the parts and laws of the human body, or Michael Faraday's explanation of magnetic powers, or the botanist's descriptions." He admires the attitude of the naturalist for facts, because they "lend him a certain severe charm."

Emerson continues:

> Then I thought—could not a similar enumeration be made of the laws and powers of the intellect, and possess the same claims on the student? . . . Why not? These powers and laws are also facts in a *natural history*. They also are objects of science and do suffer themselves to be numbered and recorded, like stamens and vertebrae. At the same time they have the advantage of deeper interest, as in the order of nature they lie higher and are nearer to the mysterious seat of power and creation. (I, B, 1–2)

This point of departure for a discussion of the mind and manners of the age would have appealed to Melville, who two years later praised his friend Nathaniel Hawthorne for his respect of the actual:

> We can think that into no recorded mind has the intense feeling of the visible truth ever entered more deeply than in to this man's [Hawthorne's]. By visible truth, we mean the apprehension of the absolute conditions of present things as they strike the eye of the man who fears them not . . . (L, 124)

Melville's strong statement does not preclude an interest in the mind, which was his ultimate topic in *Mardi*, written in 1847 and 1848, reflecting a pattern he described in a letter to the English publisher, John Murray, in these words: "It opens like a true narrative—like Omoo for example, on shipboard—and the romance and poetry of the thing thence grow continually, till it becomes a story wild enough I assure you and with a meaning too" (L, 71).

So also with Emerson's lecture series. After beginning on the solid ground of scientific observation, Emerson launches into the laws of thought as sources of power and creativity, arousing newspaper commentators to depict him swinging on an upturned rainbow and grabbing a comet's tail. But his effort is not to lose touch with the real world. "The wonder of the science of intellect," he observes,

> is that the substance with which we deal is of that fertile and active quality that it intoxicates all who approach it. Gloves in the hands, glass guards over the eyes, wire masks over the face, volatile salts in the nostrils are no defense against this virus, which comes in as secretly as gravitation, into and through all barriers. Everything is mover or moved. And this delicacy of the material does not add to the ease of the analysis. (I, B, 3–4)

In the first lecture, Emerson develops two complementary themes that control everything he has to say in the series. One is the value of a "commanding insight" into the nature of man, a capacity to see life whole, especially in terms of correspondences between the outer world of the senses and the inner world of meaning and value that comprise the organic unity of nature. The second warns of the dangers of "shipwreck" or failure of the inquiring mind in pursuing this lofty goal. Emerson couches these ideas with timely allusions to the interests and needs of his audience.

As to the notion of wholeness of vision, Emerson's insightful man is a descendent of his American scholar of 1837, "man thinking," although the new emphasis is on the quester for knowledge in the real world. Emerson speaks of "the assurance of the unity of nature which always accompanies a powerful mind" by which "Kepler pronounced analogically from music on the laws of astronomy" (I, B, 8). He notes the delight of audiences in "the statement of widest application" (4) and asks, "What but thought deepens life?" (16)

The review of this lecture in *The Boston Daily Republican* suggests the charm of Emerson's appeal:

What! said Mr. Emerson, when our bodies and the world in which they exist are made the subject of perpetual research, should the brain, "that globe of light and flame," be the only province of creation unworthy or uninteresting to be studied! Mr. Emerson said that all men, learned or illiterate, who obtain power and success in the world, did it, not by inductions from outward facts, but from the internal perception and keen study of the nature of man. He said that in his course of lectures he was far from expecting to present a science of the soul; he should be content if he could afford a *memoire pour savoir*, by which the true way of this study might be opened. (2)

Here, then, is Emerson in the role of the pioneer of thought, or "man-diver," as he describes the quester in the second lecture. He does not propose to offer a complete description of the mind, but to motivate his audience to begin such a study themselves. It is, he tells his practical-minded listeners, a means to power:

The search for gold in California or in Canton is for power, possession, and influence. And nobody would go about for indirect means to power who could come at once at the direct means, namely, in knowledge, commanding insight. (I, B, 16)

Though always implicit in Emerson is the belief in the divinity of intuitive thought that leads to this insight, he illustrates his idea with an image at Melville's level of visible reality:

The guide who knows the way will venture on the mountain in night or in storm: The sailor who knows the rig and working of his boat will put out from shore, and fly in the face of dangers, which he knows he can brave. (76)

We should note that in *Redburn*, the novel Melville wrote in 1849 soon after hearing Emerson, the final test of the sailor is whether he can climb the rigging and do his job even in bad weather. Further, in his next novel, *White-Jacket* (1850), it is the nonconformist officer Mad Jack who countermands his captain's orders and saves the warship, *Neversink*, from destruction by skillfully sailing directly into the storm.

Emerson also uses a seafaring image to explain his second important theme, the shipwreck of the inquiring mind "on one of these three vices: egotism, fative [sic], or practicality, insidiously born with him like the weevil in the wheat" (II, A, 1). The word "shipwreck," which calls to mind both the near-disaster of the *Neversink*, a world-frigate commanded by an incompetent, rank conscious captain, and Ahab's fated *Pequod*, occurs in the opening lines of the shorter draft of the second lecture in Emerson's recapitulation of the preceding talk. Although this draft was probably written in England in 1848, or even previously, it could well have been used in the Boston series of 1849. In the slightly longer version that probably was delivered in 1850 and thereafter, Emerson replaces "seeming shipwreck" with "ruin." Even so, the stress on evil, with its sources in the three prevailing attitudes that Emerson found in the world of the senses, is unlike the apparent avoidance of the dark side of the human condition in his early writings, with the exception of occasional passages like the previously cited quotation from "Compensation."

The review in *The Boston Daily Republican* offers this interpretation of Emerson's second theme:

He [Emerson] then proceeded to speak of the causes, which, in our day, have so generally diverted men from the most legitimate of all studies—themselves. The main cause is the universal practicality of the time. Effecting so much as we do with our hands in every department of nature, it is not strange that we should overvalue the hand. This practicality leads the thoughts of men to dwell in the outward world, and tends to make practical effort and power the criterion of merit. Hence our orators and lecturers become imbued with egotism and a desire is induced to signalize their own invention, as if it was not the gift of God. Hence genius becomes talent, and the mind of man a mere wit. Conversation is usually degraded, and society expects for their entertainment that "The stars of heaven shall be plucked down and packed into rockets." (2)

Even though Emerson begins his lecture with praise for men of learning, he sharply attacks intellectual pretension: "Each savant proves in his admirable discourse that he only, knows now, or ever did know anything on the subject. Does the gentleman speak of anatomy? I tell that gentleman and the society, that is my jawbone which the gentleman has stolen and described" (I, B, 17). As Emerson returns to his theme in the later lectures, particularly in the discourse being the advertised title of the series, "Mind and Manners of the Nineteenth Century," he refers to the crack in all of nature, in other words, the potential for a shipwreck of the spirit, or ruin, in every human endeavor. We already have observed Melville's tongue-in-cheek application of this image to Emerson himself and his portrayal of Ahab as having a seam extending from his forehead to his sole. But we also should recognize the correspondence of Emerson's trinity of evils—egotism, fatalism, and practicality—and Ahab's three mates aboard the *Pequod*: Starbuck, who suffers from failure of the will in the final moments before the whaleship sinks; Stubb, who resigns himself to his fate though he is determined to smile back at grinning death; and Flask, who worries at the last how much money his mother will receive after the ship sinks. Ishmael alone is saved from this moral and physical shipwreck because he has acquired the broad vision and self knowledge essential for survival.

In the first lecture of Emerson's series, then, we find the evocative image of perspective and the patterns for survival and ruin that not only establish the tone of the course, but also charge the intellectual atmosphere in which Melville thought and wrote. Emerson's aim to provide a *memoire pour savoir* in order to open up the study of "the science of the soul" is an invitation to his audience, which later included Melville, to respond.

3. *The Mirrored Self in Nature and Art*

If Emerson had chosen to speak at the level of his listeners, instead of from a higher ground in order to lift them, it is conceivable that he could have concluded his opening lecture with some practical advice on increasing mental power. Or he might have offered cosmopolitan platitudes rooted in Benjamin Franklin's adages on achieving material success, with thought reduced to the techniques of salesmanship. But the power Emerson offered was that of personal integrity with its promise of wholeness of vision. It was the kind that he felt would enable one ultimately to see beauty in the commonplace: "The plenty of the poorest place is too great; the harvest cannot be gathered. Every sound ends in music. The edge of every surface is tinged with prismatic rays."

The rhetoric of Emerson's conclusion clearly aimed at inspiring his audience to develop a fresh perspective on the daily struggles of life. Here is *The Boston Daily Republican's* view of the peroration:

> Mr. Emerson closed in his own happy tone of intellectual exaltation. Nothing is so felicitous as genuine knowledge. *Quantum scimus sumus*—our knowledge is the measure of our being. Life is nothing but one tide of thought: happy

is he, who, by a true insight into destiny, can assuage the pangs of our daily trials and afflictions. And this true insight is to be had; "it is accessible and cheap." (2)

This "true insight" that eases the pangs of everyday living is that of the poet.

Even though Melville found beauty in the hardships of the common sailor's life, he surely would have sided with the reviewer in asserting Emerson's vision was "too ideal." Still he was susceptible at this time to the kind of impractical vision of experience that Emerson offered. "So far as I am individually concerned and independent of my pocket," Melville wrote late in 1849, "it is my earnest desire to write those sort of books which are said to 'fail' " (L, 92). He was referring to *Mardi*, his first attempt to encompass the whole of experience in a novel. He had completed the book shortly before he heard Emerson lecture and later ascribed its failure to his immaturity as an artist. Reviewers criticized its lack of cohesiveness, calling it "a hodge podge" and "a shapeless rhapsody."[8] But Emerson's second lecture offered the means for achieving the kind of integrated poetic vision of man's estate that *Mardi* lacked.

Despite its realistic title, "Relation of Intellect to Natural Science," Emerson's second lecture focuses on the unity of nature, including human nature, and art. Emerson calls his topic *identity*, introducing it in these words:

The full fact in the natural history of intellect is its similarity in many remarkable points to the history of material atoms, indicating a profound identity with all parts of nature. All seem to come of one stock. (II, A, 2)

Unlike the treatment of this subject in Emerson's early writings, particularly *Nature*, where the tendency toward pantheism is noticeable, Emerson shifts his focus in this lecture from the divine to the human:

What is the interest of tropes and symbols to men? I think it is that unexpected relationship. Each remote part corresponds to each other, can represent the other, because, all spring from one root. Nature seems like a chamber lined with mirrors, and look where we will, in botany, mechanics, chemistry, numbers, the image of man comes throbbing back to us. *From whatever side we look at nature we seem to be exploring the figure of a disguised man.* [Italics added.] (II, A, 2–3)

This statement is a complement to Emerson's earlier remarks on "angles of vision." It suggests how a poet can represent a perspective by having objects in nature reflect the viewer as well as personify the human condition. Melville approaches the idea in *Mardi* in having the philosopher Babbalanja remark, "The world revolves upon an I; and we upon ourselves; for we are our own worlds" (559). But much of this novel is in the form of an exotic travelogue with events that too often seem detached, as we shall see, from the identities of the participating characters.

After hearing Emerson lecture, however, Melville refines his concept in presenting nature as a disguised man. In the opening paragraphs of *Moby-Dick*, the narrator Ishmael describes the "ocean reveries" that entrance mortal men and then introduces a mirror image that runs through the novel:

> And still deeper the meaning of that story of Narcissus, who because he could not grasp the tormenting, mild image he saw in the fountain, plunged into it and was drowned. But the same image, we ourselves see in all rivers and oceans. It is the image of the ungraspable phantom of life; and this is the key to it all. (3)

"The key to it all" becomes clear in the chapter, "The Doubloon," in which the various characters reveal their angles of vision as they examine the gold coin Ahab has nailed to the mainmast of the *Pequod*. Characteristically, Ahab sees himself in the coin's design, which is an emblem of nature:

> The firm tower, that is Ahab; the volcano, that is Ahab; the courageous, the undaunted, and victorious fowl, that, too, is Ahab; all are Ahab; and this round gold is but the image of the rounder globe, which, like a magician's glass, to each and every man in turn but mirrors back his own mysterious self." (428)

Ahab's image of himself and Ishmael's image of the ungraspable phantom of life blend at the end of the novel, when Ahab looks over the side of the whaleboat and stares, Narcissus-like, into the water for his private vision of the white whale:

> But suddenly as he peered down and down into its depths, he profoundly saw a white living spot no bigger than a white weasel, with wonderful celerity uprising, and magnifying as it rose, till it turned, and then there were plainly

revealed two long crooked rows of white, glistening teeth, floating up from the undiscoverable bottom. (540)

When the white whale rises from the depths with its malice directed toward Ahab, Melville dramatizes the meeting of the mind and its metaphor in nature:

> The glittering mouth yawned beneath the boat like an open-doored marble tomb; and giving one side-long sweep with his steering oar, Ahab whirled the craft aside from this tremendous apparition. (540–541)

The visible reality of the whale perceived by all as it surfaces and the specter in Ahab's mind are one.

In justifying the notion of identity between man and nature, Emerson observes: "Is it not a little startling to see with what genius some people take to hunting, with what genius some men fish, what knowledge they have of the creature they hunt?" His point, which could apply to Ahab and his crew, is that "the fisherman follows the fish because *he* was *fish*" (II, A, 27). The relationship Emerson sees is not merely part to part, but part to whole: "I say that the world may be reeled off from any Idea like a ball of yarn, that the chemist can explain by his analogies all the processes of the Intellect; that the physiologist from his; the geometer and the mechanician respectively from them" (4).

Emerson applied this relationship to art in his published writings as early as *Nature*, in which he comments, "A work of art is an abstract or epitome of the world. It is the result or expression of nature in miniature" (W, I, 23). In the lecture, he represents the mind as encompassing all art and the solar system as well through the synthesizing tendency of instinct:

> If the solar system is art and architecture, the same achievement is in our brain also, if only we can be kept in height of health and hindered from any interference with our great instincts. (The current knows the way.) Something like this is the root of all the great arts, of picture, music, sculpture, architecture, poetry; and the history of the highest genius will warrant the conclusion, that, in proportion as a man's life comes into union with nature, his thoughts run parallel with the creative law. (II, A, 25)

This expansive conception of harmony of self, nature, and art anticipates several refinements in Melville's artistry dating from 1849. For example,

until that year, the digressive passages in his novels were largely unassimilated into the theme and narrative structure. By *Moby-Dick*, however, the
chapters on the whaling industry and cetology serve not only to suggest
the passage of time by separating the dramatic scenes from one another,
but also to provide a perspective on man's total relation to nature. Just as
Emerson's chemist illuminates all processes of intellect, so Melville's
whaler is concerned with religion, art, politics, science, philosophy—the
totality of human endeavor. Since Ishmael tells the story, these interests
amount to his angle of vision.

In addition, until 1849, Melville's ships represent limited aspects of
experience, such as hardship, oppression, and drabness. After *Mardi*,
Melville's ships become miniature worlds. By *Moby-Dick*, though the white
whale represents evil to Ahab, it also reflects qualities of beauty, gentleness, magnificence, power, even divinity; it is a summing up of nature, of
reality and myth in this picture:

> A gentle joyousness—a mighty mildness of repose in swiftness, invested the
> gliding whale. Not the white bull of Jupiter swimming away with ravished
> Europa clinging to his graceful horns; his lovely, leering eyes sideways intent
> upon the maid; with smooth bewitching fleetness, rippling straight for the
> nuptial bower in Crete; not Jove, not that great majesty Supreme! did surpass
> the glorified White Whale as he so divinely swam. (539)

When the whale leaps from the water to form a high arch, "like Virginia's
Natural Bridge," it shows "the wrenched hideousness of its jaw," the focus
of Ahab's preoccupation (540).

The mixing of opposite, discordant qualities in this description is a
tendency Emerson also finds in nature and the mind. In the second
lecture, he stresses in fresh images the idea of polarity as a creative
principle:

> The botanist discovered long ago that Nature loves mixtures, and nothing
> grows well in the crab stock; but the bloods of two trees being mixed, a new
> and excellent fruit is produced. Our flower and fruit gardens are the result of
> that experiment. And not less in human history. Aboriginal races are incapa-
> ble of improvement. The dull melancholy Pelasgi arrive at no civility until
> the Greek comes in. The Briton, the Pict, is nothing until the Roman, the
> Saxon, the Norman arrives. . . . And in the conduct of the mind the blending
> of two tendencies or streams of thought the union of two brains is a happy

result. And usually every mind of a remarkable efficiency owes it to some new combination of traits not observed to have met before. (II, A, 12)

The correspondence of this idea to Melville's view of art as a process of matching and mating unlike things again indicates an agreement of Emerson and Melville on aesthetic principles dating from this period. Although Melville's interest in polarity is evident as early as *Typee*, with Tommo's question "Happar or Typee?" raising the issue of good and evil, the contrasts are not so sharply drawn, nor the mixtures of traits as complex, as we find in Melville's writing following Emerson's lecture series. Tommo's traveling companion, for example, is hardly more than an alter ego; and Taji's successive companions represent individual aspects of mind. Queequeg, however, sums up the noblest qualities of primitive man. The warlike and peaceful tendencies that we recognize in the symbol of his tomahawk peace pipe, his skill with the harpoon and naive worship of a wooden idol, the strangeness of his appearance and his fidelity to Ishmael—these are mixtures that serve to complement the character of Ishmael, a civilized seafaring "man thinking." For Queequeg participates in the weaving of the mat which represents to Ishmael the harmonious interaction of necessity, free will, and chance as determiners of experience. Such complexity of interaction illustrates the extraordinary richness of texture in *Moby-Dick*.

Emerson's idea of identity with its attendant notion that nature consists of mixtures is part of his organic conception of reality. "The idea of vegetation is irresistible in mental activity," he says:

Man seems only a higher kind of corn. What happens here in mankind, is matched by what happens out there in the history of grass and wheat: an identity long ago observed or, I may say, never not observed, suggesting that the planter among his vines is in the presence of his ancestors, or, shall I say, the orchardist is a pear raised to the highest power? (II, A, 4–5)

Emerson proceeds to compare the processes of perception to the growth of a plant in ways that carry over to Thoreau, Whitman, and also Melville:

Under every bud is a new germ, under every leaf the bud of a new leaf and not less under every thought is a newer thought. Every reform is only a mask under cover of which a more terrible reform which dares not yet name itself advances.

The plant absorbs much nourishment from the ground in order to repair its own waste by exhalation and keep itself good, increase its food and it becomes fertile. The mind is first only receptive (passive). Surcharge it with thoughts in which it delights, and it becomes active. The moment a man begins not to be convinced, that moment he begins to convince. (6–7)

Readers familiar with *Walden* can recognize in Emerson's analogy the germ of Thoreau's comment in the opening of the chapter on "Sounds," "I grew in those seasons like corn in the night." The passage also looks ahead to Whitman's description of leaves of grass as "the flag of my disposition, out of hopeful green stuff woven." Melville, too, identifies the erratic course of his inner development with the growth of a plant. In a letter to Hawthorne in June 1851, he writes that "the silent grass-growing mood in which a man *ought* to compose" can seldom be his. Later in the same letter, he confesses:

I am like one of those seeds taken out of the Egyptian Pyramids, which, after being three thousand years a seed and nothing but a seed, being planted in English soil, it developed itself, grew to greenness, and then fell to mold. (L, 30)

Though Melville is referring to a report of an experiment with ancient Egyptian seeds, his organic metaphor is in harmony with Emerson's.[9]

Underlying Emerson's comparison, is an argument on the nature of creativity, in which the mind, nourished with thought, becomes active; that is, it rejects convention and asserts its independence. This view anticipates Melville's well-known praise of Hawthorne in a letter to Hawthorne in April 1851:

There is the grand truth about Nathaniel Hawthorne. He says NO! in thunder; but the Devil himself cannot make him say *yes*. For all men who say *yes*, lie; and all men who say *no*—why, they are in the happy condition of judicious, unencumbered travellers in Europe; they cross the frontiers into Eternity with nothing but a carpet-bag—that is to say, the Ego. Whereas those yes gentry, they travel with heaps of baggage, and, damn them! they will never get through the Custom House. (125)

Though Matthiessen and others have pointed to Melville's strong spirit of denial in this passage in contrasting him with Emerson, Melville's lines are similar to those of Emerson in this lecture. If we allow for differences in rhetorical stance—Melville is writing a compliment to a friend; Emerson is speaking in public—the "heaps of baggage" that Melville objects to are the weight of conventional thought, agreeable platitudes, that Emerson's surcharged mind also says *no* to as it begins to convince. Emerson's image in this lecture for the independent intellect questing for truth is that of the "man-diver" (II, A, 36). It is this idea, and very likely this image, that led Melville to write on hearing Emerson speak, "I love all men who *dive*."

That Melville referred to "thought diving" in his letter to Evert Duyckinck on March 3, 1849 indicates not only that he was aware of Emerson's reference to the "man diver" in the second lecture, but also that he became aware at that time of Emerson's other images, which have, as we have seen, their powerful equivalents in *Moby-Dick*.

4. *The Mind's Shaping Power*

The congruences between aesthetic concepts that Emerson set forth in 1849 and Melville's applications in the novels that he wrote immediately afterwards have their source in shared beliefs in the power of intuitive thought. Even before he heard Emerson lecture, Melville had acknowledged instinct as "better than acquired wisdom" in a letter to the English publisher John Murray in March 1848 (L, 71). In his third novel, *Mardi* (1849), he purports to take the reader on a tour of the world of the mind:

> Oh, reader, list! I've chartless voyaged. With compass and the lead, we had not found these Mardian isles. Those who boldly launch, cast off all cables; and turning from the common breeze, that's fair to all, with their own breath fill their own sails. (556)

Here the author as Taji, the narrator, casts aside the instruments of navigational logic and the cables of tradition and convention to sail with the power of his own spirit. Similarly, in the novel, the Mardian poet Lombardo, representing Melville's ideal of the creative writer, "abandoned all monitors from without" but retained "one autocrat within—his crowned and sceptered instinct" (597).

By comparison, the intuitionism Emerson advocates in the lecture series is not so extreme. Emerson subordinates the Understanding, with its logic and conventional wisdom, to Reason or instinct. He does not reject one set of faculties. Rather, he presents instinct, or the inner voice of conscience, as the guide that enables one to see relationships among parts and to comprehend the shape of the whole. "The poet beholds the central identity and sees an ocean of power" (II, B, 32). In the beginning of both versions of the third lecture, entitled "Tendencies and Duties of Men of Thought," Emerson offers this description of instinct as the mind's shaping power:

> In reckoning the sources of mental power, it were fatal to omit that one which pours all the others into mould, that unknown country in which all the rivers of our knowledge have their fountains, and which by its qualities of structure determines both the nature of the waters and the direction in which they flow. We have a brain of the brain, wisdom, a seminal brain which has not yet organs, rests in outlines and generalities, but which seems to sheathe a certain omniscience; and which, in the despair of language, is commonly called Instinct. (III, A, 1)

This view, with its image of a brain within the brain, suggests split-brain theories of our own age, in which the two cerebral hemispheres represent complementary faculties. Contemporary research has found the left hemisphere to be largely verbal and analytical; the right, imagistic and holistic.[10]

Emerson in effect is asserting the dominance of the right hemisphere's faculties for perceiving and shaping complex wholes and working with metaphors. These comprise his "seminal brain," governed by instinct. Inspiration for Emerson is simply instinct in action (III, A, 11).

We can observe the similarity of Emerson's views to Melville's by noting that Emerson, too, recognizes the need at times to sail without compass or lead:

> We are to know that we are never without a pilot. When we know not how to steer, and dare not hoist a sail, we can drift. The current knows the way, though we do not. When the stars and sun appear, when we have conversed with other navigators who know their craft, we may begin to put out an oar, and trim sail. (III, A, 7)

True wisdom, Emerson adds, is "to make a practical rule of this instinct in every part of life" (8). But in spite of his confidence in drifting with the current, which is essentially spiritual, Emerson does offer considerable advice on steering, that is, directing instinct toward the identity of mind, nature, and art. His navigators are the mentors who, like himself, can show the way.

Melville's commitment to instinct to the exclusion of other "monitors" can account for the lack of cohesiveness in his novels composed before 1849. "When Lombardo set about his work," Melville writes in *Mardi*, "he knew not what it would become. He did not build himself in with plans; he wrote right on, and in so doing, got deeper and deeper into himself, and like a resolute traveler plunging through baffling woods, at last was rewarded for his toils" (595). The evidence of his own early work suggests that the passage is autobiographical.

Emerson had also advocated the exploration of the universe within the self in his published writings from *Nature* onward, but he sought always to match inner awareness with its outer counterpart in the symbols of nature: "The lover of nature is he whose inward and outward senses are still truly adjusted to each other" (W, I, 9). Again, in "The American Scholar," Emerson had asserted that "man thinking," the scholar or poet, is influenced primarily by nature, but also by the mind of the past which is preserved in books and by action. It is probable that Melville did not realize the potential of instinct as this kind of balancing and synthesizing force, uniting all of the faculties of mind and harmonizing experience, until he heard Emerson's elaborations of these ideas in 1849.

Though Melville could confess to Hawthorne in June 1851 that "all my books are botches," he offers a provocative image of the interdependency of "head" and "heart," logic and instinct, that appears to refute the extreme position he takes in *Mardi*. "It is a frightful poetical creed that the cultivation of the brain eats out the heart," he says. "But it's my *prose* opinion that in most cases, in those men who have fine brains and work them well, the heart extends down to hams. And though you smoke them with the fire of tribulation, yet, like veritable hams, the head only gives the richer and better flavor" (L, 129). That is, all of the faculties work together in the creative process. But there is no question about which faculty should dominate: "I stand for the heart. To the dogs with the head! I had rather be a fool with a heart, than Jupiter Olympus with his head" (ibid.). These comments are as close as Melville comes to the Emersonian idea of instinct.

Where Melville and Emerson differ is over the religious significance

Emerson attaches to instinct. Though both writers associate it with artistic integrity, which is enough for Melville, Emerson sees it as divine: "The ship of heaven guides itself, and will not accept a wooden rudder." As a result, the office of the poet is "to justify the moral sentiment and establish its eternal independence of demoniac agencies" (II, A, 50). He must "affirm and affirm," because instinct is "the taper at which all the illumination of human arts and sciences was kindled. And in each man's experience from this spark torrents of light have once and again streamed and revealed the dusty landscape of his life" (III, A, 2).

This spiritual view of instinct is Emerson's higher ground, from which he attempts in the treatise "Mind and Manners in the Nineteenth Century" to view the age. The shape he perceives actually is not much different from the human condition described by his Puritan ancestors with their Calvinistic notion of innate depravity. The divisiveness within the individual and in all of his external relationships, the crack in nature, applies to all men at all times:

> Every man must bear in his own person the badge of his time, grossly or spiritually. The sailor will find it in his boat, the scholar in his college, the statesman in parties. That which may be seen colossally traceable in the movements of masses assumes another shape among the elegant and educated. And we hear more of it, because they know how to celebrate their wars, whilst the others strive and die unsung. (M, 19)

Among the evidences of man in the divided state is "an excess of the reflective habit, tendency to self-dissection, anatomizing of motives and thoughts"—a notion that recalls his criticism of the times in "The American Scholar" twelve years earlier. Then there is the problem of psychological double-vision:

> The hour comes, when, to the mind of the man, the object disjoins itself from the mood of thought it awakens, and he sees that he owes a debt of emotion and thought to a person or thing, which at the same time, he second-sees not fully to deserve the thought and emotion they have awakened, so that he loves, yet shrinks from marriage; he detests slavery, but his servant must not dare to be more than a servant; he burns with a wish to spread knowledge like water, but he will not serve in the school committee; he loves the state, but dislikes all the citizens. . . . He exposes with indignation the hollow charities of the day. He feels the education in vogue to be no education; the religion no religion. But he finds in himself no resources for

the instruction of the people when they shall discover that their present guides are blind. (22-23).

It is important for us to see, as Melville undoubtedly did at that time, that Emerson's insight into human limitation is not superficial, that he is attempting a comprehensive diagnosis of the nation's spiritual malady. In terms of contemporary split-brain theories, Emerson is saying that the over-emphasis on dissection and analysis, mere verbalization—characteristic of the left brain hemisphere, or as Emerson would put it, the Understanding—is preventing the synthesizing power of instinct to heal the individual, and even return him to Eden. "His wit has eaten his heart out," Emerson says, in words that correspond to Melville's later statement favoring the heart over the head. "He excites others by thoughts which do not move his own hand," Emerson adds. "The least effect of the oration is in the orator—a slight recoil, a kick of the gun" (23). Such a flawed individual would be unlikely to speak the truths of the heart.

Though Melville, whose mother was a Dutch reformed Calvinist and father a Unitarian, could reject Emerson's view of the divinity of instinct, he could accept this vision of the age. Melville's novels written in 1849 and later dramatize "the cold charities," hypocrisies, brutalities associated with the life of the common sailor, aboard a merchant ship in *Redburn* and a U.S. Navy frigate in *White-Jacket*. In *Moby-Dick*, the cracked age is summed up in disfigured Ahab, who sails the *Pequod* by dead reckoning, or retrograde instinct, to destruction. But Ishmael's going to sea and his salvation also depend on instinct that leads to a state of harmony between himself and nature. This is the idea that Emerson presents in the conclusion of his treatise in an evocative seafaring image depicting the self in an original relation to the universe:

The age is ours, is our world. As the wandering sea bird which crossing the ocean alights on some rock or islet to rest for a moment its wings, and to look back on the wilderness of waves behind, forward to the wilderness of waters before, so standing perched on this rock or shoal of time, arrived at the immensity of the past, and bound and roadready to plunge into immensity again: What place is here to cavil and repine? What apology, what praise can equal that fact that here it is; therefore, certainly, in the vast optimism, here it ought to be. Wandering we came into this watchtower, this broad horizon, but let us not go hence stupid or ashamed, and doubt never but a good genius brought us in, and will carry us out. (131)

This expansive expression of faith would seem fitting as a conclusion for the entire lecture series, and it is conceivable that Emerson could have saved it for his last words. But the topic publicized for his final lecture, "Natural Aristocracy," develops the idea of hierarchy, which suggests the upward aspiring self. This notion finds its most concise expression, however, in the epigraph Emerson provided for the 1849 edition of *Nature*:

> A subtle chain of countless rings
> The next unto the farthest brings;
> The eye reads omens where it goes,
> And speaks all languages the rose;
> And, striving to be man, the worm
> Mounts through all the spires of form.

In the lecture, Emerson perceives all ranks in nature as having worth, since they are divinely created. "If all mankind were exactly on a par," he says,

> they might perish altogether, say the orientals. We are equally indebted to our superiors and to our inferiors. Our debt to our superiors is, the indispensable one of inspiration. We owe them correction and aim. Our debt to inferiors is not less. (N, A, 18)

He is speaking, of course, of natural hierarchy, not the artificial rankings in society of wealth and birth. We can speculate that Emerson aimed his remarks at his elitist audiences in London and Boston. "The noble ennobles," he told them, as if he would send them forth from the lecture halls with a challenge.

Though Melville's first novels reflect his disdain for social barriers, his writings dating from 1849 often sharply contrast natural aristocracy with social rank. In *Typee*, for example, Tommo's cannibal captors are almost "on a par," except for the divisive influence of the Taboo. Similarly, in *Mardi*, Taji's traveling companions in the voyage around the Mardian islands—a king, a poet, a philosopher, and a historian—represent aspects of the self with no barriers separating them from Taji, who proclaims himself a sun god. But in *White-Jacket*, it is the noble nonconformists like Jack Chase and Mad Jack who save the *Neversink* through excellent seamanship, and not Captain Claret, the antithesis of a natural aristocrat, whom Melville ironically describes as Henry the Eighth afloat. In the "Knights and Squires" chapters of *Moby-Dick*, Melville satirically presents the conventional levels of responsibility and status aboard a whaleship, but demonstrates in the climax that they amount to nothing in an encounter with the white whale. In *Billy Budd*, Melville's natural man, Billy, transcends in his death Captain Vere, who admits to being the prisoner of his uniform and the Articles of War. But perhaps most daringly, Melville presents in *The Confidence-Man* a hierarchy of ignobility in the masquerades of the confidence men who represent all humanity in carrying out their deceptions on the upper and lower decks of the *Fidèle*. Melville's view in these dramatizations of hierarchy in his later novels suggest that over the years he explored the dramatic potential of the Emersonian notion, "Temperament is fortune" (N, A, 19).

From these passages in Emerson's lecture series and their correspondences in Melville's writing, we can deduce the relation of Melville to the genius of Emerson. It should be obvious that it is deeper than the optimist-pessimist classification of the two authors that has appealed to many critics of our time. The images Emerson introduced to his Boston audiences that year of cracked nature, man diving, angles of vision, and the shipwreck of the soul indicate at the least that his optimism was hard won and that he was mindful of everyday reality. Rather, the essential relationship lies in the motives of the artist, the urge to create. It can be phrased as a chiasmus: Where Emerson had developed an art that would meet the test of his faith, Melville was searching for a faith that would meet the test of his art. Even though it is unlikely that Melville attended all of the lectures in Emerson's Boston series, the evidence in Melville's art suggests that he fits well Henry James's concept of the artist as "one on whom nothing is lost."

The significance of Emerson's lectures at mid-century, then, is that they are the means by which he served as spokesman for ethical and aesthetic values in an era dominated by materialism. As mentor for a creative community of artists that included Melville as well as Thoreau and Whitman, Emerson had upgraded the ideas of his essays, making them more timely for his listeners, and introduced vivid fresh imagery aimed at expanding their vision of themselves in relation to total nature. Melville's patterned response to this challenge is the subject of the chapters to follow in Part II.

Great geniuses are parts of the times; they themselves are the times, and possess a correspondent coloring.

—Herman Melville,
  "Hawthorne and His Mosses" (1850)

PART II

THE PATH OF THE CREATOR

CHAPTER 4

QUEST FOR EDEN:
TYPEE AND *OMOO*

Genuine influence, as Göran Hermerén has shown, produces changes in a writer's style that are clearly evident after his contact with the source of that influence. Though the contact itself may be slight, the resulting modifications are substantial over an extended period.[1] These principles apply especially to Melville's fiction, which developed in ways that can be traced to the stimulus of Emerson's thought.

The argument to this point has presented the leading ideas and images that Emerson set forth in his lecture series in January and February of 1849, as well as public reaction to them in the press. To establish their importance to Melville, whose attendance in at least one lecture has been noted, we have considered specific similarities of notions in the lectures to those in Melville's fiction written immediately following the series. In particular, we have examined metaphors of cracked human nature, life as an angle of vision, identity of the self and nature, and the shipwreck of the soul in the lectures and indicated their use in *Moby-Dick*. That Melville incorporated such notions into his art suggests both the power and immediacy of Emerson's appeal and the surprising vigor of Melville's response.

To understand the larger issue of how Melville's art developed in relation to Emersonian influences, we need now to examine the progress of his writing career from its beginning in *Typee*, when he knew little of Emerson but had certain natural affinities for such Emersonian ideas as the good of self-reliance and the evil of custom. Melville's choosing as a young man of

75

twenty-one to go to sea as a deckhand aboard a whaler attests to his independent, adventurous spirit; his jumping ship and living among cannibals in the Marquesas Islands suggests his rebellion against authority. These attitudes, woven into his first novel, indicate that as he sought to establish himself as an author, he was ready for the lessons on artistic individualism and originality that Emerson had been teaching.

In the broadest sense, Melville's career as a writer of prose fiction suggests the image of a tacking ship that at times seeks to take maximum advantage of the prevailing trade winds and at other times sails against them. For Melville wanted to succeed as a serious novelist, but only on his own terms. He found it difficult to compromise with publishers on aesthetic matters. But with Emerson's ideas providing powerful contemporary guidance, Melville absorbed and built on those notions that worked for him, at least through *Moby-Dick*. Afterwards, he turned against them, and also criticized Emerson, partly on the basis of his rebellion against the literary establishment that Emerson represented because *Moby-Dick* had failed to win a large, appreciative readership. By the time Melville wrote *Billy Budd*, however, he had rediscovered the dramatic possibilities of the ethical and aesthetic principles Emerson had advocated.

Though Melville responded to many other influences in the development of his complex art, the focus in Part II on the pattern of his reactions to Emerson offers a useful perspective on his artistic progress. Whatever Melville may have thought of Emerson's view of life, or of Emerson's relative stature in relation to Hawthorne, Melville could not have disregarded what Emerson said about art, imagination, and the life of the mind. The discussion in the following chapters focuses on Melville's prose fiction on the assumption that his considerable achievement in poetry, written largely in his middle years when he was not writing fiction, conveys attitudes that correspond to those expressed in his other work.

1. The Artist's Dilemma: Marnoo or Karky?

In his first two novels, *Typee* (1846) and *Omoo* (1847), Melville saw nature in parts but had yet to see it whole. Though Emerson had long advocated the connectedness of all things, with instinct functioning as a synthesizing power, Melville's tendency at first is to perceive the apparent separateness of events and qualities; there is little of the intricate matching and mating of unlike things that we find in his mature work. Melville's vision at the time of his intellectual awakening is much like that of the young mind Emerson describes in "The American Scholar." Looking at the spectacle of nature, the youthful intellect begins to search for connections:

> To the young mind every thing is individual, stands by itself. By and by, it finds how to join two things and sees in them one nature; then three, then three thousand; and so, tyrannized over by its own unifying instinct, it goes on tying things together, diminishing anomalies, discovering roots running under ground whereby contrary and remote things cohere and flower out of one stem. (W, I, 85)

A compelling example of Melville's initial focus on "contrary and remote things" is his two seemingly disconnected portraits of primitive artists in *Typee*.[2] In them Melville attempts to sort out the essential functions of the artist before he became intimately aware of Emerson's teachings. We can view Melville's career, at least through *Moby-Dick*, as a series of efforts to reconcile these separate roles.

The first artist to appear in the narrative is Marnoo, a roving Polynesian Apollo with free access to all tribes inhabiting the island of Nukuheva. Melville introduces him about midway in the novel (Chapter 18) as a wanderer whose appearance combines "the marble repose of art" with "warmth and liveliness of expression." Like Melville, he is about twenty-five years old and has a flare for the dramatic. That Melville associates this primitive counterpart of himself with an organic concept of art becomes obvious when we consider the tattooing on Marnoo's back: "Traced along the course of the spine was accurately delineated the slender, tapering and diamond-checked shaft of the beautiful 'artu' tree." Tommo, Melville's narrator, comments, "Indeed, this piece of tattooing was the best specimen of the Fine Arts I had yet seen in Typee" (136).

Thus indelibly marked, Marnoo functions as a naturally eloquent social critic, who enthralls the natives with stories of the encroachments of civilization on primitive society. Melville presents him as both a seer and a sayer in the Emerson manner: his vision is comprehensive, extending beyond the enclosed little world of the Typee valley, and his words convey the spirit of defiance:

> The grace of the attitudes into which he threw his flexible figure, the striking gestures of his naked arms, and above all, the fire which shot from his

brilliant eyes, imparted an effect to the continually changing accents of his voice, of which the most accomplished orator might be proud. At one moment, reclining sideways upon the mat, and leaning calmly upon his bended arm, he related circumstantially the aggressions of the French—their hostile visits to the surrounding bays, enumerating each one in succession . . . he exhorted the Typees to resist these encroachments; reminding them, with a fierce glance of exultation, that as yet the terror of their name had preserved them from attack. (137–138)

The character of Marnoo reflects Melville's own gusto in attacking social conventions that dehumanize the individual. Marnoo's eloquent warnings on the evils of French imperialism, correspond also to Emerson's more general criticism of civilized customs and defense of integrity. In short, Melville's first primitive artist is a spokesman for self-reliance. It is Marnoo who arranges Tommo's escape from his cannibal captors, whose secret rituals include eating enemies and violators of tribal taboos.

In contrast to Marnoo, whose art is governed by instinct, is the tattooer Karky, a careful craftsman and traditionalist, an old master of the Typee school, as Melville says, who works on human canvas. Melville introduces him late in the novel (Chapter 30) in a scene that presents him as a tormentor engaged in a pain-producing occupation:

I beheld a man extended flat upon his back on the ground, and, despite the forced composure of his countenance, it was evident that he was suffering agony. His tormentor bent over him, working away for all the world like a stone-cutter with mallet and chisel. (217)

Here is the Typee equivalent of the professional artist, with his array of tools and techniques described as "a great number of curious black-looking little implements of bone and wood, used in the various divisions of his arts" (217).

Karky also is Melville's prototype for the symbolist, since his cryptic designs have religious significance (220). His task is to express in his tattoos the relationship between flesh and spirit, though the connection is obscure to Tommo. Actually, Melville exaggerates fact in establishing Karky's role, for the Typees in real life practiced tattooing largely for ornamentation.[3] Karky's skill working with his pointed instruments is traditional, since it must be learned; and like other kinds of ritualized social activity, its effect is to impose the permanent mark of the tribe on the individual. Every Typee must submit eventually to Karky's trained hand, whose work cannot be undone. We note, however, that Melville's other artist, Marnoo, though tattooed about the body, retains an unmarked face. That is, he has somehow avoided a total surrender to Karky's craft. But when Karky seeks to work on Tommo, presumably to make him one of the tribe—to convert him, as Tommo says—he would start on the face. "I was fairly driven to despair," Tommo comments; "nothing but the utter ruin of my 'face divine,' as the poets call it, would, I perceived, satisfy the inexorable Mehevi and his chiefs, or rather, that infernal Karky, for he was at the bottom of it all" (200).

We can interpret Tommo's fear of being permanently marked on the face as a criticism of craftsmanship that destroys individuality—a stand on art that harmonizes with Emerson's views. Like Marnoo, Tommo would not object to some tattooing, preferring it on his arms between the wrist and shoulder, where it could be hidden by clothes. So Melville at this time would prefer to hide the signs of craft and custom and retain a measure of independence. To be marked on the face would be literally to be placed behind bars and made a prisoner of the Typees for life, as Tommo says: "When his [Karky's] fore-finger swept across my features, in laying out the borders of those parallel bands which were to encircle my countenance, the flesh fairly crawled on my bones" (219).

In these two portraits of primitive artists, Melville evaluates the different claims of instinct and craft, social criticism and symbolism, custom and individuality in the creative process at its most elemental level. That Melville in *Typee* visualizes two artists with separate functions suggests his uncertainty over aesthetic goals. If we can regard the characters of Marnoo and Karky as projections of Melville's unassimilated attitudes, we can infer that he identifies with Marnoo's instinctive approach to art and is repelled by the tedious perfectionism of Karky, though he is fascinated by the mystery of craft.

These portraits indicate Melville's angles of vision on aesthetic matters at the time of his intellectual awakening. Some hints of agreement with Emerson's views on art are immediately apparent. Melville points out, as Emerson did in "The American Scholar," that creativity springs not from systems of education, but out of "unhandselled savage nature." It is not farfetched for us to perceive in Marnoo the primitive equivalent of the nineteenth century New England lecturer and reformer, speaking out for individualism and condemning social conformity. On the other hand, though Karky works with symbols, the emphasis in his art on custom runs against the Emersonian reliance on instinct. Melville's attempt to resolve his dilemma in the first two novels is to follow instinct in the manner of Marnoo. Though occasional incipient symbolism suggests Melville was not entirely indifferent to Karky's sense of craft, his early affinities with Emerson help to account for the spontaneous quality of these narratives of Polynesian adventure. Several hints of Emersonian social criticism that we shall note in the following section suggest not that Melville had read Emerson or heard him speak at this time, but that Melville was aware of Emerson and receptive to the kinds of argument Emerson was making in behalf of individualism and artistic integrity.

2. *Some Early Affinities with Emerson*

Most readers agree that *Typee* and *Omoo* contain signs of Melville's later artistic development. As we have seen, his conflicting perspectives on art, exemplified by the characters of Marnoo and Karky, are the first stage of a struggle between instinct and craft that preoccupied him throughout his career. So also with the hints of his receptivity to Emersonian ideas, which greatly enrich the texture and structure of his later fiction. Melville's path is toward the Emersonian goal of art that offers a symbolic world view and a comprehensive interpretation of the human condition. In the beginning, however, his aim and achievements are modest, even though his vital interest in visible reality is everywhere apparent. We can view these works best as *protonovels*—engaging, spontaneous mixtures of essay and story, lacking in coherent plot and also in character development, but rich in details drawn from personal experience and reading, imaginatively exaggerated in the tradition of the tall tale. They suggest the effort of a young author drifting in the current of his inspiration, frequently changing course from fact to fiction, though agreeing consistently with Emerson's rebellion against customs that debase the individual.[4] Some accounting of these narratives is necessary to show the quality of Melville's vision before he found a mentor whose ideas would help him perceive the aesthetic possibilities of his subject.

An example of how Melville instinctively enlarges on fact is his first description of the sea, which presents a spectacle no sailor is likely to see anywhere in a given moment. It suggests, however, the limited scope of Melville's vision at this time:

> Although I could not avoid yielding in a great measure to the general languor, still at times I contrived to shake off the spell and to appreciate the beauty of the scene around me. The sky presented a clear expanse of the most delicate blue, except along the skirts of the horizon, where you might see a thin drapery of pale clouds which never varied their form or color. The long, measured, dirge-like swell of the Pacific came rolling along, with its surface broken by little tiny waves, sparkling in the sunshine. Every now and then a shoal of flying fish, scared from the water under the bows, would leap into the air, and fall the next moment like a shower of silver into the sea. Then you would see the superb albacore, with its glittering sides, sailing aloft, and often describing an arc in his descent, disappear on the surface of the water. Far off, the lofty jet of the whale might be seen, and nearer at hand the prowling shark, that villainous footpad of the seas, would come skulking along, and, at a wary distance, regard us with his evil eye. At times, some shapeless monster of the deep, floating on the surface, would, as we approach, sink slowly into the blue waters, and fade away from sight. But the most impressive feature of the scene was the almost unbroken silence that reigned over sky and water. Scarcely a sound could be heard but the occasional breathing of the grampus, and the rippling at the cut-water. (10)

Here is a panoramic backdrop for Melville's dramas of men in relation to nature, a composite picture of a watery wilderness teeming with life, conveying a blending of effects of beauty, sadness, splendor, wonder, horror, and final mystery. It is an instinctive synthesis of many different moments, an "ocean reverie" that anticipates the grand scale of Melville's later work; but it is not an example of thought-diving. This narrator is merely a spectator, and the sea he describes is a surface impression, a view from the deck. Though it reflects the narrator's mood, it is not to be compared with a transcendental symbol like Thoreau's Walden Pond, whose waters mirror both the soul's depths and the universe. Such an identity of the "me" with the "not me" Emerson had often articulated, but Melville had yet to perceive.

And yet along with this imaginatively-heightened view of external reality, both *Typee* and *Omoo* have a slight but clearly defined inward progression, as the narrator becomes increasingly preoccupied with the self in relation to the visible world, a prevailing interest of Emerson and other New England Transcendentalists. Melville's aim in representing a return to primal nature corresponds both to Emerson's plea in *Nature* for an original relation to the universe and to Thoreau's purpose in *Walden* "to front only the essential facts of life."[5]

Also like the Transcendentalists, Melville vigorously attacks conforming usages in society that separate men from nature. Because the primitives Melville lived among have fewer arbitrary codes to hamper them than do civilized men, he ironically proclaims the superior virtues of his narrator's cannibal hosts: "They seemed to be governed by that sort of tacit common-sense law which, say what they will of the inborn lawlessness of the human race, has its precepts graven on every human breast." That is, except for their tribal taboos, they are self-reliant: "It is to this indwelling, this universally diffused perception of what is *just* and *noble*, that the integrity of the Marquesans in their intercourse with each other is to be attributed" (201).

This idea, derived from Rousseau, also finds expression in Emerson, who celebrates the "wild virtue" of the savage, unimpeded by the establishments and forms that characterize civilized life. Melville, however, extends Emerson's attack on conformity, popularized in "Self-Reliance," to include primitive traditions like the taboo, which he characterizes as a mysterious web of customs that compose the fabric of primitive society and perpetuate such degradations as tattooing and cannibalism. These he perceives as prototypes of civilized customs. In effect, he applies to tribal life the Emersonian aphorism, "Society everywhere is in conspiracy against the manhood of every one of its members" (W, II, 49). So institutionalized behavior, whether civilized or savage, suppresses instinct, makes indelible marks on character, and ultimately destroys individual identity.

Of the two works, *Typee* is more central to an understanding of Melville's initial attempts to represent in fiction ideas which Emerson also was advocating. Melville's originality lies in his imagery, which sharply contrasts civilized and savage customs, delighting readers with its vigor and novelty. Tommo, his sailor narrator, is not only a keen observer and actor, but also a social critic who asks basic questions about the human condition.

In the opening chapters, Tommo, a restless deckhand aboard the whaler *Dolly*, sorts humanity into two groups, civilized and savage. His experiences lead him to reverse his estimates of the relative merits of the two classes. When the whaler drops anchor in Nukuheva harbor in the Marquesas Islands, he observes how the traditional three estates of civilized men—church, state, and commons—have disrupted the natives' simple, joyous harmony with nature. The Protestant missionaries impose religious conventions but not the Christian spirit on the islanders, with no more than superficial success; the French with their warships subdue the natives and exploit them. Finally, the sailors aboard the *Dolly* engage in unrestrained debauchery with childlike, unresisting Polynesian girls who swim out to meet the ship.

Melville points up the initial contrast between civilized and savage man in his account of a meeting between the French Admiral Du Petit Thouars and the patriarch-sovereign, as the French purportedly take formal possession of Tior, with Tommo an eyewitness. Clothes make all the difference: "Du Petit Thouars exhibited upon his person all the paraphernalia of his naval rank," while "the simple islander, with the exception of a slight cincture about his loins appeared in all the nakedness of nature." The contrast leads Tommo to meditate on the differences between these two representative men. "Yet after all," he observes, "insensible as he is to a thousand wants, and removed from harassing cares, may not the savage be the happier of the two?" (20)

Tommo's question, which suggests the theme of *Typee*, is rooted in the idealism of the "Declaration of Independence," which identifies "the pursuit of happiness" as an inalienable right. It also is in harmony with pleas for simplicity in Emerson and Thoreau. In "Self-Reliance," for example, Emerson objects to the refinements of civilization that have separated men from nature. "The civilized man," he says, "has built a coach, but has lost the use of his feet. He is supported on crutches, but loses so much support of muscle. He has got a fine Geneva watch, but he has lost the skill to tell the hour by the sun" (W, II, 85). Taking his cue from Emerson, and possibly even from Melville in *Typee*, Thoreau exhorts his readers in *Walden* to cut out all excesses in living: "Our life is frittered away by detail. An honest man has hardly need to count more than his ten fingers, or in extreme cases, he may add his ten toes, and lump the rest" (91).

These familiar assertions, which are part of the legacy of New England Transcendentalism, reflect a spirit of rebellion against materialism which finds fresh and vigorous expression in *Typee*. "A gentleman of Typee," Melville writes, "can bring up a numerous family of children and give them all a highly respectable cannibal education, with infinitely less toil and anxiety than he expends in the simple process of striking a light"

(112). Such freedom from worldly cares should release the mind to contemplate higher truths. But in the primitive world that Melville describes, there is a catch.

Unlike the Transcendental ideal of communion of man and God in nature, Melville's cannibal utopia is flawed, as though its inhabitants had picked up some bad habits in spite of their Eden-like environment. Where Emerson proposes that by relying on instinct, men can recover the innocence of Adam before the fall and in effect return to Eden, Melville shows us the joyous but less than perfect state of primitives living in an enclosed earthly paradise that does not, however, render them immune to original sin. His "Happy Valley" of the Typees amounts to a parody of Eden.

The descent of Tommo and Toby into the Typee Valley after wandering for days in the wilderness of Nukuheva provides an image of the fall of man that allows no chance of return. With one leg mysteriously injured, Tommo follows Toby sliding down long roots, which break as they grab for others dangling over rapids. In this action, Melville dramatizes both the impossibility of going back and the hazards of getting down to the roots of things, the absolute conditions of mortal life. When the two travelers arrive on the valley floor, they encounter a naked boy and girl, the Polynesian equivalent of Adam and Eve, whose manner suggests, not so much innocence, as animal fear of the savage living close to nature:

> An arm of the boy, half screened from sight by her wild tresses, was thrown about the neck of the girl, while with the other he held one of her hands in his; and thus they stood, their heads inclined forward, catching the faint noise we made in our progress, and with one foot in advance, as if half inclined to fly from our presence. (p. 68)

This tableau, with its mixture of childlike beauty and fear, represents the dualism of good and evil that pervades the whole of Typee society.

Melville presents his most inclusive praise of the "Happy Valley" in Chapter Seventeen, half-way through the thirty-four chapters of the book. It is here that he notes the "perpetual hilarity reigning through the whole extent of the vale" and comments, "The hours tripped along as gaily as the laughing couples down a country dance" (126). He paints a composite picture of primitive life. First, he observes the young female natives "reclining beneath the shadows of one of the beautiful groves" as they weave blossoms into "chaplets and bracelets," and he comments: "One would have thought that all the train of Flora had gathered together to keep a festival in honor of their mistress." Then he notes the young men, for their part, engaging in such activities as fishing, carving canoes, and polishing ornaments without exhibiting "the least sign of strife or contention"; he sees the warriors, in turn, cultivating a "tranquil dignity of demeanor" as they visit occasionally from house to house, where they are treated with honor and respect. Lastly, he watches the old men reclining for hours on their mats, "smoking and talking to one another with all the garrulity of age" (127). Although the picture Melville gives is incomplete without corresponding details on the pleasures of being middle-aged or elderly women in this society, he says nothing to indicate that they do not share in the general state of well-being.

Despite this view of apparent harmony between man and nature, the narrative portions of the preceding and following chapters trace Tommo's growing conflict with tribal conventions, which tend to promote suspicion of nonconformists and to ritualize fear. Even though the narrative is frequently interrupted by digressions, we can recognize an underlying thematic design reflecting stages of Tommo's struggle against the primitive code which, like the civilized man's conventions that Emerson attacks, is an essential source of evil.

Tommo's initiation into the Typee tribe, which begins with a dramatic life-threatening situation, points up both the power of social pressure and the fallibility of language as a means of knowing. Led into the village by the fearful native boy and girl, the two sailors hope they have encountered supposedly peaceful Happars and not cannibalistic Typees. At once, the wanderers are surrounded by excited, potentially hostile savages, whose chief refuses Tommo's peace offering of tobacco. The chief, "a piece of dusky statuary," asks instead for the tribal password in the fateful question, "Typee or Happar?" Tommo gives the safe answer, "Typee." Partly satisfied, the chief murmurs, "Mortarkee?" which the sailors understand to mean "good." When Tommo replies, "Typee Mortarkee," the natives leap to their feet, clap their hands, and shout "again and again the talismanic syllables, the utterance of which appeared to have settled everything" (71).

Having gained acceptance by saying the right words, Tommo and Toby are subject next to a naming ritual. It is presided over by the chief, a social heavyweight who is appropriately called Mehevi. The point Melville makes is that among primitives, as among civilized people, naming is a communal event over which the individual has no control. Though the narrator offers the one-syllable name, Tom, the chief garnishes it with an extra syllable, according to tribal custom. Then follows an hour-long ritual as the tribesmen introduce themselves individually with names and apparent titles that serve to mystify Tommo, rather than to inform him.

Tommo's struggle against tribal conventions is complicated by his leg injury, which has rendered him helpless in the eyes of his hosts. As a result, he receives treatment accorded to an infant in Typee society. His native attendant, Kory-Kory, carries him everywhere, washes him as a "froward, inexperienced child," and feeds him by rolling food into little balls and putting them one after another into his mouth (88–89). Because Toby is uninjured, he is allowed to take care of himself.

These annoying but seemingly innocuous rituals are part of a tribal pattern for caring for the young and helpless that culminates in a religious ceremony, which suggests a cannibalistic communion service. Melville describes the "cathedral-like gloom" of the forest setting, the sacred building, and then the aged priests—"hideous old wretches, on whose decrepit forms time and tattooing seemed to have obliterated every trace of humanity" (92). Kory-Kory, addressing these keepers of primitive customs and belief, gives "utterance to some unintelligible gibberish," the Typee version of the ritualistic language of religion. At midnight, Tommo and Toby witness a fire ceremony; then Kory-Kory feeds them meat, which the youths suspect is human, though it turns out to be baby pig. Actual cannibalism, Tommo discovers later, is a ritual participated in by tribal leaders, warriors, and priests in great secrecy. Like all tribal activities, it is governed by the taboo.

Melville's satire is uniquely parallel to the Transcendentalists' well-known criticisms of the forms and rituals of orthodox religion, which they said concealed skepticism. Emerson, who had resigned from the ministry in 1832 because he refused to participate in the Ritual of Communion, was still regarded in the 1840's as a religious radical. His advocacy of a faith based on instinct rather than doctrine opposed the conventional theologies of the Unitarian and Calvinistic churches.

In *Typee*, Melville identifies tribal ritual with the ugly and malevolent in primitive society. He sees the savage's denigration of the human body through religious customs as analogous to the civilized man's desecration of the soul through arbitrary ceremonies and creeds that thwart instinct and pressure the individual to conform. Emerson would have agreed. The ultimate target of Melville's criticism is the taboo, an enigmatic institution which regulates Typee society. He presents it as the underlying principle of custom. "I cannot determine with anything approaching to certainty, what power it is that imposes the taboo," Tommo says (224).

As a nonconformist, Tommo rebels against the taboo that prevents the beautiful native girl Fayaway from entering a canoe. He succeeds by appealing directly to Mehevi instead of Kory-Kory, who is fanatically rigid in his attitudes in support of all convention. Although the chief gives in to Tommo's plea, he defends the convention in jargon that suggests the evasive language of civilized men in explaining a custom. Melville describes the chief as "employing a variety of most extraordinary words, which, from their amazing length and sonorousness, I have every reason to believe were of a theological nature" (137). Unimpressed, Tommo counters with an argument in behalf of individual freedom that transcends social barriers: "But all that he said failed to convince me: partly, perhaps, because I could not comprehend a word that he uttered; but chiefly, that for the life of me I could not understand why a woman should not have as much right to enter a canoe as a man" (137).

Melville represents the polarities of good and evil, nature and taboo, which Tommo finds among the Typees in the characters of the narrator's two closest native companions—Fayaway and Kory-Kory. Like the primitive artists, Marnoo and Karky, they represent ideas that appear to have nothing in common. The girl is a youthful romantic conception of beauty in nature. Decorated with flowers and partly clad in a tunic of white tappa—the color which Melville consistently uses in the novels through *Moby-Dick* to suggest varied qualities of nature—she accompanies Tommo everywhere in the valley, except in areas which are taboo to women. Characteristically, her tattoos are so trifling as to be nothing more than beauty marks. Kory-Kory, on the other hand, is Tommo's zealous guide and interpreter of typee customs. He is "alas! a hideous object to look upon," with horizontal bars tattooed across his face representing Karky's best craftsmanship. To Tommo, the girl is an emblem of the free spirit, especially when she stands up in the canoe, disengages her tappa robe, and spreads it out like a sail as the craft glides through the water (134). By contrast, Kory-Kory, a prototype of the modern organizational man, is a complete prisoner of convention and ironically its most outspoken advocate.

Among other native types that Melville introduces, two represent extremes within the Typee Establishment. Mehevi, the chief, is a charming blend of then popular notions of the noble savage of romantic literature, the idealized American Indian of James Fenimore Cooper's *Leatherstocking Tales*, and a prototype of the civilized governor. He rules the Typees with a kindly restraint that suggests Thomas Paine's famous precept, "That government is best which governs least," which Thoreau builds on in his essay, "Civil Disobedience." Though Mehevi respects the taboo, he is independent enough to bend the code for Tommo. This ability to uphold tribal customs and yet respect the individual suggests the natural leader. Unlike the hereditary monarchs of Europe, Mehevi is a man of the people, neither a conformist nor a foolishly consistent hard-liner, but a primitive version of the Emersonian self-reliant man.

In sharp contrast is Mow-Mow, the enforcer of Typee customs, a warrior lacking Mehevi's empathy and flexibility. Melville's description of an encounter between Tommo and this cannibal policeman suggests the diabolic as an active principle in society. Mow-Mow's villainy is suggested by his disfigurement, which recalls James Fenimore Cooper's images of "bad Indians" and looks ahead to the marred features of Ahab:

> I felt a heavy hand laid upon my shoulder, and turning round, encountered the bulky form of Mow-Mow, a one-eyed chief, who had just detached himself from the crowd below, and had mounted the rear of the pi-pi upon which we stood. His cheek had been pierced by the point of a spear, and the wound imparted a still more frightful expression to his hideously tattooed face, already deformed by the loss of an eye. (236)

Mow-Mow's hand on Tommo's shoulder illustrates the pressure on the individual to conform in Typee society and prepares for Tommo's final break with his cannibal hosts in the conclusion of the novel. The farewell scene on the beach with his Typee family—Fayaway, Kory-Kory, and old Marheyo, their father, who also treats him like a son—suggests the ties of love that link the individual and the family of man. But Mow-Mow's pursuit, with a tomahawk between his teeth, as Tommo attempts to leave the "Happy Valley" on a whaleboat, indicates the competing tribal will to destroy those who violate custom. As this fanatic guardian of Typee society closes in, Tommo stabs him with a boat hook and draws blood: "I saw him rise to the surface in the wake of the boat, and never shall I forget the ferocious expression of his countenance" (252). Only through violence is Tommo able to free himself from a society whose code has turned Eden, at least for him, into an open-aired prison.

In *Omoo* Melville turns from depicting the evil inherent in the savage code to representing the degrading influences of civilized conventions, not only on civilized men, but also on the Polynesians, who are compelled to adopt European ways. Again, the Emersonian theme of self-reliance in opposition to social conformity finds dramatic expression in Melville's narrative. He explains in his preface that the title *Omoo*, "is borrowed from the dialect of the Marquesas Islands, where, among other uses the word signifies a rover, like some of the natives known among their countrymen as 'Taboo kanakes.' " Since Marnoo has such a designation in *Typee*, Melville's narrator in the sequel becomes his sailor-equivalent, an observer and commentator who warns of the encroachments of civilization.

Melville gives two objectives for his second novel—to convey some idea of life aboard a whaler by relating his own adventures and "to give a *familiar* account of the present condition of the converted Polynesians, as affected by their promiscuous intercourse with foreigners, and the teachings of the missionaries, combined" (v-vi). Though he asserts that "he has merely described what he has seen," we can perceive an artist's attempt to harmonize his two aims through complementary portraits at sea and ashore of the debasement of the individual by civilized customs. As a sequel, however, *Omoo* is less aesthetically satisfying than *Typee*, largely because the narrator's wanderings have no governing purpose, such as Tommo's desire to return to primitive nature and later to escape from his Typee captors. Despite a lack of suspense in the rambling story, Melville demonstrates a growing skill in the use of symbols to convey his social criticism.

In particular, he develops his theme of the evils of civilized conventions in terms of three contrasting symbols that set off the main divisions of the narrative. The first one is the whaler *Julia*, on which the narrator sails. It is an emblem of the free spirit exploited by a profit-seeking society. Melville portrays this "small barque of a beautiful model" as Yankee-built and heroically "fitted for a privateer out of a New England port during the war of 1812." But captured by a British cruiser, the *Julia* was diverted to ignoble service "as a government packet in the Australian seas." Then condemned and sold at auction, it was purchased "by a house in Sydney, who, after some slight repairs, dispatched her on her present voyage" (6).

The *Julia*, more than the *Dolly*, is a forerunner of the "world ships" that epitomize civilization in such later novels as *White-Jacket* and *Moby-Dick*, though she is not so elaborately described as they. Stocked with condemned foods purchased at auction, the *Julia* is unfit for sailing. Despite her "free, roving commission," the ship is a floating jail for the unhappy crew—"wild, haggard-looking fellows in Scotch caps and faded blue frocks; some of them with cheeks of mottled bronze, to which sickness soon changes the rich berry brown of a seaman's complexion in the tropics" (1). With their sickly, ineffective captain, nicknamed "Paper Jack," the men of the *Julia* form an ironic contrast to the noble cannibal chief and the healthy, high-spirited Typees who sheltered Tommo. Melville's obvious implication is that civilized society is a greater prison than that of primitive culture.

It follows that Melville's second symbol of civilization is the half-completed English jail, or Calabooza Berentanee, on Tahiti, where the narrator and rebellious sailors are confined after refusing to submit to inhuman conditions aboard the *Julia*. The unfinished structure, standing in a beautiful Polynesian setting, suggests the impact of civilization on the island, where the natives find themselves increasingly regimented by the forms of European religion and customs introduced by the missionaries. Melville describes the building as "a mere shell, recently built and still unfinished. It was open all around and tufts of grass were growing here and there under the very roof" Its only furniture, characteristically, is "the 'stocks,' a clumsy machine for keeping people in one place" (131).

Melville's third and most sophisticated symbol is a prison of a different sort. Near the end of the novel, he sums up the encroachment of civilization on primitive culture in his description of the debased court of Tahiti's Queen Pomaree, which the narrator and Long Ghost visit:

> The whole scene was a strange one; but what most excited our surprise, was the incongruous assemblage of the most costly objects from all quarters of the globe. Cheek by jowl, they lay beside the rudest native articles, without the slightest attempt at order. Superb writing-desks of rosewood, inlaid with silver and mother-of-pearl; decanters and goblets of cut glass; embossed volumes of plates; gilded candelabras; sets of globes and mathematical instruments; the finest porcelain; richly mounted sabres and fowling pieces; laced hats and sumptuous garments of all sorts, with numerous other matters

of European manufacture, were strewn about among greasy calabashes half filled with poee, rolls of old tappa and matting, paddles and fish-spears, and the ordinary furniture of a Tahitian dwelling. (356–357)

Queen Pomaree embodies the degradation of her court. Appearing barefooted but wearing "a loose gown of blue silk, with two rich shawls," she impresses the narrator as a plain woman, "rather matronly," with "a careworn expression in her face, probably attributable to her late misfortunes. From her appearance, one would judge her to be about forty; but she is not so old" (357–358). She looks like someone in need of consoling. But unlike the kindly Typees and hospitable Tahitians, the troubled queen is surprised and offended at the intrusion of uninvited guests into her presence and waves them away. "Summary as the dismissal was," the narrator comments, with a pointed reference to meaningless formality, "court etiquette, no doubt, required our compliance. We withdrew, making a profound inclination as we disappeared behind the tappa arras" (358).

Melville's satiric portrait of the half-civilized queen, overwhelmed by an unassimilated foreign culture, is one of a series of memorable vignettes in the novel that have reminded readers of the caricatures of Smollett and Dickens. They also recall Emerson's reference in "The American Scholar" to the divided or degenerate state of the conformist, who lives out of harmony with nature and consequently with himself. Melville's descriptions of the missionaries in particular show them as forms, rather than as whole men and women:

> Of a fine evening in Tahiti—but they are all fine evenings there—you may see a bevy of silk bonnets and parasols passing along the Broom road; perhaps a band of pale, little white urchins—sickly exotics—and, oftener still, sedate, elderly gentlemen with canes; at whose appearance the natives, here and there, slink into their huts. (189)

The image hints at Melville's basic criticism of institutionalized religion, which stresses fear rather than love. One reason the natives avoid the missionaries is that they are whipped into attending church.

Among other images of people is Melville's picture of the half-civilized native jailer of the Calabooza Berentanee, good-natured and indolent "Capin Bob," or Captain Bob, "a corpulent giant, over six feet in height, and literally as big round as a hogshead" (133). In contrast to his grossness, his employer, the English consul Mr. Wilson, "turned out to be an exceedingly minute 'cove,' with a viciously pugged nose, and a decidedly thin pair of legs" (84). Although the Polynesian has the trappings of authority in his title, he is the lackey of the Englishman, an officious caricature of John Bull. The unhealthy native and European master suggest the unnatural dominance of civilized men, supported by physical power, over primitive people. To make his point about the disease of civilization, Melville offers a brief description of some proud, physically well-formed Marquesans, whose culture is less tainted by European influences.

But potentially the most dramatic of Melville's characters is a tattooed renegade white man, Lem Hardy, who suggests the kind of outcast Tommo would have become had he stayed with the Typees and adopted their customs. "Some of us," the narrator comments, "gazed upon this man with a feeling akin to horror, no ways abated when informed that he had voluntarily submitted to this embellishment on his countenance. What an impress! Far worse than Cain's" (28). Though Hardy, like numerous other characters the narrator and Long Ghost encounter, is introduced briefly into the narrative and then dropped, his physical appearance suggests the ultimate degradation—"a white man in South Sea girdle, and tattooed in the face. A broad blue band stretched across his face from ear to ear, and on his forehead was the taper figure of a blue shark, nothing but fins from head to tail" (28).

The assorted exotic images of man, nature, and society that fill *Typee* and *Omoo* charmed most readers and turned Melville overnight into a celebrity, known as "the man who lived among the cannibals." In one sense, the launching of Melville's career as a fiction writer is in the classical tradition of such great epic poets as Virgil, Spenser, and Milton, who began by writing pastoral poetry. Melville, however, was unsure of his direction. The Emersonian parallels indicate primarily his awareness of popular attitudes contained in a few well-known quotations, such as "Whoso would be a man must be a nonconformist" from "Self-Reliance." It had not yet occurred to Melville to attempt to portray anything like the "ideal man" Emerson had visualized. Though there is some experimentation with symbols to reflect criticism of social institutions, both civilized and savage, Melville had not yet discovered Emerson, who had spoken and written on the artist's task of concentrating the radiance of the world to a point.

The significance of *Typee* and *Omoo* to Melville's creative development is that they demonstrate his power to fascinate readers with his vivid travel narratives and his readiness to travel inwardly to new and more exotic territories. The polarities of good and evil, nature and society, instinct and custom, which he explores in these first efforts, continue in his third novel, *Mardi* (1849), with a notable difference. In this experimental work, he attempts to reconcile these opposites in the language of allegory. The Marnoo strain of social criticism and the enigmatic craft of Karky, introduced separately in *Typee* and developed in *Omoo*, partially fuse in *Mardi*, as Melville attempts for the first time to portray nature as a totality. Though this progression in his art would seem inevitable, it does correspond to Melville's discovery of Emerson's ideas and images of wholeness, with their likeliest source in the pages of *The New York Literary World*.

CHAPTER 5

IN PURSUIT OF THE
ABSOLUTE: *MARDI*

1. *The Ideal Man: Emerson in* The Literary World

Melville began *Mardi* in January 1847 as a continuation of *Omoo*, but in June he hinted that his new work of South Sea adventure would occupy "entirely fresh ground" (L, 64). As has been noted, Melville attributed his change in purpose to instinct (L, 71). But there were other forces inducing him to try something new. His courtship of Elizabeth Shaw, culminating in their marriage in August, helps to explain the romantic tone of the novel, especially in those chapters portraying the comic marriage of Annatoo and Samoa and the idyllic interlude of Taji and Yillah up to the moment that she disappears. More importantly, Melville's reading during this period yields evidence of his discovery close at hand of a Transcendental design. *Mardi* evolved as the product of a young artist's urge to create—to hold back chaos for a moment, as Robert Frost said of poetry—swayed by events in his personal life and his reading.

When we consider possible sources of Taji's pursuit of the ideal, which is the central narrative interest in this novel, the romantic quests of Shelley's *Alastor* and Keats' *Endymion* come to mind, but there is no record that Melville had read either writer by the time he was working on *Mardi*. On the other hand, Elizabeth Shaw received from her brother several volumes of Byron's poetry, including *Don Juan*, in July, and we can presume she shared them with her fiance.[1] But by then Melville already had indicated his intent to try fresh ground. We can assume his familiarity with such traditional quest stories as the Golden Fleece and the Holy Grail, as well as others from *The Arabian Nights*, an English translation of which was then in vogue. Even so, a writer like Melville, whose first two works establish him as a rebel against traditions, would be less likely to respond to foreign models in the manner of Irving and Longfellow than to strive to be innovative. With Emerson already well-known for advocating intellectual independence for American writers, it would be natural for Melville to be receptive to Emerson's freshly asserted ideas.[2]

In fact, Emerson's newly published collected poems received praise for their "native strength and beauty" in the April 3, 1847, issue of *The New York Literary World*, a new weekly magazine edited by Melville's friend Evert Duyckinck. Melville had contributed a review as recently as the March 6 issue. Then on April 2, he had sent an excerpt from the forthcoming April 3 issue containing an advertisement for *Omoo* to Edwin Croswell of *The Albany Argus* with a request for an editorial comment in that paper (L, 60). It is therefore unlikely that Melville, who was then casting about for ideas on *Mardi*, could have missed this appraisal of Emerson by Duyckinck:

> His chief capital as a poetical writer consists in the profound belief of a mighty secret in nature, animating, connecting, irradiating, solving all things, which is worth all external things in a mass, which pervades and transcends them all, which it is worth the world and all the best efforts of the world to discover, and to discover all other business, callings, avocations, should be laid aside; and *he has an Ideal Man who is constantly on the search, and whom to delineate so engaged, is the pleasure, and the chief success of our author.* [Italics added.] The Ideal Man, we have a shrewd suspicion, is no other than a first rate man of genius, of the order poetical. (197)

This "Ideal Man" is an updated version of "man thinking" from "The American Scholar." The substance of Duyckinck's review, which fills more than two pages, is to illustrate the quest of Emerson's hero for an unattainable "mighty secret in nature" with quotations from the poems. The notion suggests the central design of *Mardi*.

First among the samples is "The Apology" with reference to the symbolic values of flowers that hint at the floral messages of Hautia's maidens:

> There was never mystery
>   But 'tis figured in the flowers:
> Was never secret history
>   But birds tell it in the bowers.

A quotation from "Hermione" suggests an exotic harmony of man and nature that catches the mood of an oriental romance:

> On a mound an Arab lay,
> And sung his sweet regrets,
> And told his amulets:
> The summer bird
> His sorrow heard,
> And, when he heaved a sigh profound,
> The sympathetic swallow swept the ground.

Beauty personified as a woman hints at the character of Yillah as Taji imagines her:

> 'Tis his study and delight
> To bless that creature day and night
> From all evils to defend her;
> In her lap to pour all splendor;
> To ransack earth for riches rare,
> And fetch her stars to deck her hair.

Lines selected from "Forerunners" embody the notion of the Ideal Man's unending search for nature's secret:

> Long I followed happy guides
> I could never reach their sides;
> Their step is forth, and, ere the day,
> Breaks up their leaguer, and away.
> Keen my sense, my heart was young,
> Right good-will my sinews strung,
> But no speed of mine avails
> To hunt upon their shining trails.
> On and away, their hasting feet
> Make the morning proud and sweet
> Flowers they strew, I catch the scent;
> Of their tone of silver instrument
> Leaves on the wind melodious trace;
> Yet I could never see their face.
>   (197–198)

These touches of Emerson suggest not only the quest motif in *Mardi*, but also Melville's early attempts at poetry through the character of

Yoomy. For example, toward the end of the novel, in a chapter entitled "A Flight of Nightingales from Yoomy's Mouth," Taji's versifying companion is commanded to "regale us with something inspiring." Yoomy's poem, which he describes as "a song-full of songs," begins with the identification of Yillah with morning light:

> Half-veiled above the hills, yet rosy bright,
>> Stands fresh, and fair, the meek and blushing morn!
> So Yillah looks! her pensive eyes the stars,
>> That mildly beam from out her cheek's young dawn!
>
>>> But the still meek Dawn,
>>> Is not aye the form
>>> Of Yillah nor Morn!
>>>> Soon rises the sun,
>>>> Day's race to run:
>>> His rays abroad,
>>> Flash each a sword—
>>>> And merrily forth they flare!
>>>> Sun-music in the air!
>>> So Yillah now rises and flashes!
>>> Rays shooting from out her long lashes—
>>> Sun-music in the air!

The poem concludes with an image of generation:

>> Light wells from her soul's deep sun
>> Causing many toward her to run!
>> Vines to climb, and flowers to spring;
>> And youths their love by the hundreds bring!
>>>> (560–561)

Duyckinck's comment describing Emerson's secret in nature as "animating, connecting, irradiating, solving all things" could apply just as well to Melville's poetic description of Yillah. Further, the rude vigor of this verse with its reference to "sun-music" catches the essence of lines which Duyckinck also quotes from "Merlin." In these, Emerson suggests the kind of poet that Melville through Yoomy sought to be, one who would convey the sun's secret and more:

The kingly bard
Must smite the chords rudely and hard,
As with hammer or with mace;
That they may render back
Artful thunder, which conveys
Secrets of the solar track,
Sparks of the supersolar blaze. (198)

Melville's verse has more in common with these vigorous, irregular lines than it does with the carefully crafted, more traditional meters of Byron, Keats, Shelley, and others among the courtly muses of Europe.

In addition, the point made in the review that Emerson's Ideal Man appears "under the various names of 'Alphonso,' 'Mithridates,' 'Bacchus,' 'Xenophanes' " suggests Melville's use of avatars in the second half of *Mardi*, in which Taji's traveling companions appear to be aspects of himself. (Nearly a decade later, Melville satirizes the Ideal Man concept in *The Confidence-Man: His Masquerade* (1857) by representing a shipload of confidence men as projections of One Confidence Man.) Lastly, the conclusion of the review also would have appealed to Melville, who believed that to write like an American one had to write like a man. Duyckinck said of Emerson, after criticizing his coolness: ". . . we have enough left of manly feeling, of delightful fancy, of pure and lucid expression, of melodious measure, to confer on the author a distinct and conspicuous position as a poet" (199).

The significance of the April 3 review is that it is the first tangible evidence of Melville's access to Emerson's words. The review conveys Emerson's invitation to turn from dull routines to explore the possibilities of romance. It offers not only images of the quest in nature and the mind for a vital principle, but also suggestions on the poet's art and nature of symbolism. Even though Melville denied having much knowledge of Emerson before 1849, the gist of Emerson's current thought and samples of his expression were available to him at the time he was seeking a new direction for his art. In effect, Melville's response was to match and mate his instinct to these ideas so conveniently placed in his path.

Since Melville's exposure to Emerson through the review is at best slight, we may wonder why Melville did not attempt to investigate Emerson thoroughly at this time. A reasonable answer is that Melville acted on impulse and also that Duyckinck printed articles and reviews during 1847 that were critical of Emerson and Transcendentalism. The prudent course for a young writer would be to follow his own presentiment and take what he needed from both sides of the controversy. Certainly the ambivalence Melville exhibits toward Emerson in *Mardi* corresponds to the mixed reaction to Emerson in *The Literary World*.

In the issue of February 20, Duyckinck attacked New England literati with a full-page article entitled "Bad News for the Transcendental Poets." It warns that Transcendentalism has become "a bad card for a young author to play," an idea Melville must have pondered and perhaps even discussed with Duyckinck, whom he frequently visited. The article reflects a popular view of the movement Emerson was associated with, though Emerson is not mentioned by name:

> Poor time-crushed martyrs of the "infinite"; sorrowful knife-grinding "friends of humanity"; souls of destiny tripped up by fortune; very "high natures" laid correspondingly low; sublime lovers turn critic-haters; mockers of " the dead corpse of old king Custom" subdued with laughable retribution by Fashion herself. That it should come to this! (53)

Duyckinck's delight in mocking the New Englanders reflects in part the rivalry existing between New York intellectuals and their counterparts in Boston. He asserts, "The transcendental balloon is rapidly suffering collapse," and makes his point by quoting from both the English paper, *Athenaeum*, and *The Boston Courier* to the effect that the Transcendental poets are "essentially imitative, not original," despite their claims to the contrary (ibid.).

Then on November 6, 1847, when Melville and his bride of three months were living in New York City, *The Literary World* came out with another extensive review of Emerson, this time the fourth edition of his *Essays* (First Series). Though Duyckinck praises Emerson for "a rare beauty and occasional freshness of expression" and quotes extensively from "Self-Reliance," "Spiritual Laws," and "Friendship," his overall judgment is negative:

> Mr. Emerson's opinions are founded too exclusively upon his consciousness to be generally adopted with impunity. He is a man with more intellect than sensibility, more fancy than affection, and more thought than sympathy. His philosophy is based upon egoism. His prevailing doctrine is the sufficiency of the individual. He lacks the human element. (135)

The substance of Melville's later criticism is in this passage. Of Emerson's lack of warmth, Melville wrote to Duyckinck in 1849: "His belly, sir, is in his chest, and his brains descend down into his neck, and offer an obstacle to a draft of ale or a mouthful of cake" (L, 80). In *The Confidence-Man*, he portrays Mark Winsome, a caricature of Emerson in the mid-1850's, as admiring both the beauty and the unscrupulous nature of the rattlesnake. Lastly, sometime after 1862, when Melville purchased a copy of Emerson's *Essays*, he criticizes Emerson for "a self-conceit so intensely intellectual and calm that at first one hesitates to call it by its right name" and for blindness that "proceeds from a defect in the region of the heart."[3] In the conclusion of the November 6 review, Duyckinck offers advice that Melville apparently heeded: Emerson should be read "to excite thought rather than enlist, without reserve, individual convictions" (326).

Exposed in this manner to favorable and unfavorable impressions of Emerson, Melville took some risk in conceiving *Mardi* as a Transcendental quest. In Duyckinck's view he was playing "a bad card." But mindful of popular skepticism of the "time-crushed martyrs of the infinite," Melville satirizes the notion of a sailor-idealist, beginning with Taji's absurd decision to jump ship in the middle of the ocean with a Skyeman as a companion. It is ironical, then, that Duyckinck considered Transcendental elements in *Mardi* to be among the book's strengths. Reviewing the novel in the April 14, 1849, issue of *The Literary World*, he observes: "There is a world of poetical, thoughtful, ingenious moral writing in it which Emerson would not disclaim."[4]

The evidence of Emersonian echoes in *Mardi*, with their most available source in *The Literary World*, suggests both the vitality of Emerson's thought as it filtered through magazines and the responsiveness of Melville's genius even before he heard Emerson speak in 1849. But a little of Transcendentalism, even at second hand, goes a long way. Unfortunately, the little that Melville acquired at this time was not sufficient to give *Mardi* coherence.

2. The Problem of Sailing in Circles

Midway in *Mardi*, in the digressive chapter "Dreams," Melville describes the emotional throes of authorship. "Fire flames on my tongue," he writes. "My cheek blanches white while I write; I start at the scratch of my pen." At the moment he feels embarrassed, but compelled to continue: "Fain would I unsay this audacity; but an iron-mailed hand clenches mine in a vice [sic], and prints down every letter in my spite" (368).

What had he written that would provoke this self-conscious outburst? The short chapter contains a description of the infinity of the self that is as expansive as any in Emerson. His narrator, Taji, aspires to connect himself to the universe:

> But beneath me, at the Equator, the earth pulses and beats like a warrior's heart; till I know not, whether it be not myself. And my soul sinks down to the depths, and soars to the skies; and comet-like reels on through such boundless expanses, that methinks all the worlds are my kin, and I invoke them to stay in their course. (367)

And to thought:

> In me, many worthies recline, and converse. I list to St. Paul who argues the doubts of Montaigne; Julian the Apostate cross-questions Augustine; and Thomas-a-Kempis unrolls his old black letters . . . Zeno murmurs maxims beneath the hoarse shout of Democritus . . . divine Plato, Proclus and Verulam are of my counsel . . . Bacchus my butler, Virgil my minstrel, Philip Sidney my page. My memory is a life beyond birth . . . (367–368)

The passage illustrates Melville's version of "man thinking," who as Taji tours "the world of the mind" in his search for ideal beauty. In this sense, *Mardi* is a Melvillean "Song of Myself" that derives mostly from Emerson, the immediate source, and looks ahead to Whitman. The difficulty with the novel, however, is that Taji's inner world, dominated in the second half by his vision of Yillah, is dissociated from the outer world that Melville randomly describes. Where Emerson's Ideal Man cultivates a delicate adjustment of his inward and outward senses, so that nature becomes a mirror of the self, an "other me," Taji turns inward after Yillah disappears and rejects the world: on his travels around the Mardian isles in search of her, he finds nothing outward to identify with. As a result, the various parts of the world that Melville depicts comprise a succession of separate images, instead of contributing to a unified angle of vision.

Though modern readers see in *Mardi* the signs of Melville's developing genius—Matthiessen has called it a source-book for plenitude—many early reviews stressed its defective form. As an example, the London *Examiner* on March 31, 1849 referred to it as "a transcendental *Gulliver,* or *Robinson Crusoe* run mad." The reviewer offered this description of the contents: "A heap of fanciful speculations, vivid descriptions, satirical insinuations, and allegorical typification, are flung together with little order or connection," so that "the interest is curiously disproportioned to the amount of cleverness and ability employed in it . . ."

Four years later, Melville alluded to the design for *Mardi* as well as to reasons for the book's failure in his semi-autobiographical novel *Pierre.* This evidence offers an insight as to how Melville used his sources. Observing that "Pierre immaturely attempts a mature book," Melville describes an effort like his own to encompass the whole of human experience:

> . . . perceiving, by presentiment, that the most grand productions of the best human intellects ever are built round a circle, as atolls (i.e., the primitive coral islets which, raising themselves in the depths of profoundest seas, rise funnel-like to the surface, and present there a hoop of white rock, which though on the outside everywhere lashed by the ocean, yet excludes all tempests form the quiet lagoon within), digestively including the whole range of all that can be known or dreamed; Pierre was resolved to give the world a book which the world would hail with surprise and delight. (333)

What could go wrong with the story of an idealist sailing around a cluster of islands representing the world in a quest for perfect beauty? Melville hints at an answer in referring to Pierre's mistake:

> He did not see,—or if he did, he could not yet name the true cause for it,— that already, in the incipiency of his work, the heavy unmalleable element of mere book-knowledge would not congenially weld the wide fluidness and ethereal airiness of spontaneous creative thought. He would climb Parnassus with a pile of folios on his back. (334)

In "The American Scholar," Emerson had cautioned against excessive reliance on book learning in well-known aphorisms: "Books are the best of things, well used; abused, among the worst" and "Books are for the scholar's idle times" (W, I, 89). Melville's comments on Pierre's creative efforts are in harmony with the Emersonian line that nature is the primary influence on the scholar. Melville continues by noting that one author dominated Pierre's thinking:

> Though Plato was indeed a transcendently great man in himself, yet Plato must not be transcendently great to him (Pierre), so long as he (Pierre himself) would also do something transcendently great . . . there is no such thing as a standard for the creative spirit. (334)

These allusions to unassimilated reading and a strong attraction to one author as a standard of creativity suggest Melville's own struggle to control his sources. Though he undoubtedly had access to volumes of Plato in libraries, there is no evidence that he owned or borrowed any of Plato's works before the publication of *Mardi*.[5] Since Melville occasionally referred to Platonists in his later writings and in 1849 even described Emerson as a "Plato who talks through his nose," the name may well apply to any strong Transcendentalist influence. Melville's instinct led him to read widely with a "lynx-eyed mind," as he said of Pierre, but he had not learned by the time he was writing *Mardi* that the reading he had absorbed should be "federated in the fancy" without "dictating to his own mind" (*Pierre* 334).

One example of Melville's early dependency on his reading is the use he makes of circle imagery in reference to places, characters, events, and the passage of time. Roundness is everywhere. Though Melville may have perceived this figure by presentiment, as he said, it is probable that his instinct was reinforced by the numerous references to Transcendental circles in Emerson's writings. If Melville had browsed in a book store through the newly published volume of Emerson's poetry, he could have seen lines like these from "Uriel," which set forth the idea of organic unity:

> Line in nature is not found;
> Unit and universe are round;
> In vain produced, all rays return;
> Evil will bless, and ice will burn.
> (W, IX, 14)

Or he could have glanced at the beginning of Emerson's essay on "Circles," republished in 1847 in the fourth edition of *Essays* (First Series). These lines suggest the theme of *Mardi*: "The eye is the first circle," Emerson says, referring to the self as the center of the universe,

> the horizon which it forms is the second; and throughout nature this primary figure is repeated without end. It is the highest emblem in the cipher of the

world. St. Augustine described the nature of God as a circle whose center was everywhere and its circumference nowhere. We are all our lifetime reading the copious sense of the first of forms. (W, II, 301)

Like many writers stimulated by Emerson's genius, Melville experimented with an idea that attracted him and sought to represent it in original ways, as in these specimens of Transcendental geometry:

As Melville suggests in *Pierre*, the underlying unit of structure in *Mardi* is a circle, physically represented by the coral reef surrounding the Mardian isles. Beyond this boundary is the horizon of the sea that undulates for Taji like the coils of a huge serpent. Above this circle of error, the Platonic sun, "a jocund disk" is a "fellow-voyager" traveling westward towards truth in the cycle of the day. Within the coral reef, the various islands represent aspects of mortal mind, with Odo, where Taji settles with Yillah, appearing as "a little round world by itself, full of beauties as a garden" (190). From this Eden-like setting, he looks up at night and meditates on heavenly circles:

Wondrous worlds on worlds! Lo, round and round me, shining, awful spells: all glorious, vivid constellations, God's diadem ye are! (179)

When Taji quests for Yillah, who vanishes unexpectedly from Odo, his route is curved: "Coiling through the thickets, like the track of a serpent, wound along the path we pursued. And ere long we came to a spacious grove, embowering an oval arbor" (205). Landscape features impress Taji with their roundness: "All round, embracing a circuit of three leagues, stood heights inaccessible, here and there, forming buttresses, sheltering deep recesses between" (217). Taji perceives the enervated Donjalolo's impenetrable retreat as an "insphered sphere of spheres" (240). By contrast, the outgoing Epicurean Borabolla is himself a sphere: "Round all over; round of eye and of head; and like the jolly round Earth, roundest and biggest about the Equator" (285). As we might expect, the Mardian word for God is Oro and heaven, Oroolia. Though Babbalanja says the world turns on an "I," its perfect form is an "O."

The two dimensions of Melville's narrative—outside and inside the reef—correspond to the traditional distinction between the comic and tragic half-cycles in the revolution of the wheel of fortune. In the opening chapters, Melville establishes a mood of romantic comedy and adventure, which evolves from incidents that mildly satirize the Transcendental view of self-reliance. Melville's narrator expresses his dissatisfaction with the monotony of his deck hand existence aboard the whaler *Arcturion*, arc-named and sailing "round-about" the equator in an unsuccessful search for the sperm whale. To escape boredom, he elects to jump ship in mid-ocean with confidence in the underlying divinity of nature. "All things form but one whole," he observes with unconscious irony, "the universe a Judea and God Jehovah its head. Then no more let us start with affright. In a theocracy, what is to fear" (12)? From the *Arcturion*, the narrator and his taciturn sailor companion, Jarl, steal away in an open boat into the circle of nature and time, which Melville describes in terms of "grey chaos in conception" (48).

Two contrasting episodes on the high seas emphasize the aesthetic values of the narrator's instinctive journey. In each encounter, Melville employs details that reflect his reading of Coleridge's "The Rime of the Ancient Mariner," in which the natural blends with the supernatural. The voyagers' initial meeting is with an outcast Polynesian Adam and Eve, adrift alone on the brigantine *Parki*. The vessel first appears on the horizon, its spars outlined against the setting sun, in a manner recalling the appearance of Coleridge's specter bark. But instead of finding ghosts aboard the ship, Taji and Jarl discover a quarrelsome primitive couple, one-armed Samoa and his acquisitive wife Annatoo, who portray the incongruities of married life. Their petty bickerings end when she is washed overboard and lost in a storm.

Although some critics discount the *Parki* episode as an inset story with no direct bearing on Taji's quest for a vital principle in nature, the comic realism provides an antithesis to the romantic fantasy of Taji's following encounter with the beautiful maiden Yillah.[6] This relationship, which is essentially spiritual, also ends abruptly with Yillah's disappearance, a romantic counterpart to Annatoo's violent death.

In introducing Yillah, Melville again draws a parallel with the arrival of the specter bark in Coleridge's "Ancient Mariner." Where Coleridge prepares for the introduction of supernatural elements by describing "death fires" which like "a witch's oils," burn "green, and blue and white," Melville offers a vivid description of marine phosphorescence that conveys the impression of first hand experience:

Starting, we beheld the ocean of a pallid white color, coruscating all over with tiny golden sparkles. But the pervading hue of the water cast a cadaverous gleam upon the boat, so that we looked to each other like ghosts. For many rods astern our wake was revealed in a line of rushing illuminated foam; while here and there beneath the surface, the tracks of sharks were denoted by vivid, greenish trails, crossing and recrossing each other in every direction. (121)

Melville follows up, however, with bookish allusions: Taji observes a sea bird with snow-white plumage suggesting Coleridge's albatross. It lights on the sail as a good omen, but Samoa frightens it away in an effort to catch it. Then Taji sees the canoe that bears Yillah. Melville describes its approach as that of a speck intruding into nature. The correspondence to Coleridge's imagery should be noted:

Just tipping the further edge of the sky was a speck, dancing into view every time we rose upon the swells. It looked like one of many birds; for half intercepting our view fell showers of plumage: a flight of milk-white noddies flying downward to the sea.
　　But soon the birds are seen no more. Yet there remains the speck; plainly a sail; but too small for a ship. (126)

Similarly, Coleridge's ghost ship draws into view:

> At first it seemed a little speck,
> And then it seemed a mist;
> It moved and moved, and took at last
> A certain shape, I wist.
>
> A speck, a mist, a shape, I wist!
> And still it neared and neared;
> As if it dodged a water sprite,
> It plunged and tacked and veered.

Melville's allusions to Coleridge suggest the otherworldliness of Yillah, who has a dual function in the narrative, serving initially as romantic heroine in the manner of the title character in Thomas Moore's *Lalla Rookh* and later as a symbol of ideal beauty.[7] In the pivotal action of the novel, Taji rescues the maiden by slaying her captor, the priest Aleema, who is transporting her by canoe to be sacrificed. Symbolically, this action portrays the liberation of beauty from tradition, for Aleema and his sons are following an old custom which the girl has been carefully groomed to fulfill. Though Taji, aided by Jarl and Samoa, wins the battle and takes the prize, the dead Aleema becomes his albatross, since the priest's sons pursue him endlessly as reminders of his guilt.

In contrast to the romantic comedy of the initial voyage, which is a circular journey to unexpected good fortune motivated by instinct, Taji's second voyage, within the coral reed surrounding the Mardian isles, is a monomaniac quest for perfection. Taji's first act upon landing in Mardi is to proclaim himself a sun god and his companions demigods. The natives accept them at face value and respond that many of them are divine, too. The result is a convivial association that gently satirizes the Emersonian ideal of self-reliance which emphasizes the divinity of the individual. "Upon the whole," Taji muses, "so numerous were the living and breathing gods in Mardi, that I held my divinity but cheaply. And seeing such a host of immortals, and hearing of multitudes more, purely spiritual in their nature, haunting woodlands and streams; my view of theology grew strangely confused" (176). Taji worries that he is "overtopped all round" and counsels himself, "Be not a 'snob' " (177). But with Yillah in this earthly paradise, Taji is ideally happy.

What happens thereafter is true to the compensatory nature of a circle, as though Melville had read and taken literally Emerson's notion that it is both "the inspirer and condemner of every success" (W, II, 301). Since Yillah is the last to enter Taji's orbit, she is the first to leave, her sudden unexplained exit from the narrative matching the abruptness of her entrance. As to Taji, his instinctive, outgoing manner that led him from the *Arcturion* to Yillah reverses; and he becomes the prototype of Melville's later tragic heroes, imprisoned by a fixed will. "For a time I raved," Taji says. "Then falling into the outer repose, lived for a space in moods and reveries with eyes that knew no closing, one glance forever fixed" (194). Three years later in *Moby-Dick*, Melville expands this conception of willfulness in the character of Ahab, whose eyes similarly stare with an "infinity of firmest fortitude," as he searches for the white whale. As Taji's monomania grows, he becomes increasingly withdrawn. His main companions in his travels around Mardi—Media, a king; Babbalanja, a philosopher; Yoomy, a poet; and Mohi, a historian— take over the story as commentators on experience.[8] Together they represent faculties of mind, such as self assurance, intuition, imagination, and the understanding, leaving Taji wholly absorbed with his obsession to find Yillah. Though they search with Taji, they are detached from him and talk mainly among themselves. In the end they abandon him as he sails out to sea alone, still pursuing his ideal and pursued by Aleema's avenging sons, under the light of the fixed star Arcturus. The implication of suicide in Taji's final theatrical comment, "Now, I am my own soul's emperor; and my first act is abdication! Hail! realm of shades!" marks the completion of the turn of the circle from self-fulfillment to self-annihilation (654).

In this manner, Melville develops the Emersonian idea of a circle, so that it determines the course of Taji's supposed "chartless voyaging." Where Emerson and Melville differ is in the directions of thrust. For Emerson, circles expand ever outward from the self, so that each turn transcends the old to infinity. "Our life," he says, "is an apprenticeship to the truth that around every circle another can be drawn; that there is no end in nature, but every end is a beginning" (W, II, 301). What is dying is continually being replaced by what is being born. He notes, for example, that "Greek sculpture is all melted away, as if it had been statues of ice" and "the genius that created it creates now somewhat else" (302).

For Melville, however, the circles in *Mardi* turn inward on the self, moving from nature to the mind in pursuit of the elusive secret of life, so that whatever is born is in the process of dying. Taji visits around twenty islands, each of which presents a fanciful image of the human condition, though none reflect Taji's inner ideal of beauty. Appropriately, he sets out at sunrise on a spring morning to stop first at Valapee, an isle that "seems divided by a strait." It is Melville's symbol for the divided state of childhood before the mind, as Emerson said in "The American Scholar," begins to reconcile the polarities of nature. "Little King Peepi," the infant monarch, has within him the assorted souls of his ancestors, who govern him one by one. The other isles reflect variations of this divided state as it is perpetuated in the adult world by social conventions and traditions.

Taji's allegorical voyage makes up in broadness of scope for its lack of verisimilitude. There are random stops at Mondoldo, the island of epicurean living; Maramma, the island of empty religious conventions; Diranda, the island of war; Hooloomooloo, the isolated isle of cripples, whose inhabitants consider Taji and his companions to be monsters. Yillah, of course, is not to be found there. Not is she on any of the islands representing nations of Western Europe and the United States. Melville's criticism of the Americans, portrayed as the boastful inhabitants of Vivenza, and his attack on slavery are in harmony with activities of

Transcendentalist reformers, who in the late 1840's were turning from idealistic experiments in communal living to participation in the abolition-ist movement. But always in these stops, it is Taji's companions who provide the commentary and debate the issues.

Babbalanja's search "to probe the circle's center" in an effort "to evolve the inscrutable" ends for him on the Isle of Serenia, whose peaceful inhabitants practice a faith that resembles the Transcendental religion with its freedom from tradition. Like other Mardians, the Serenians worship Oro, whose name suggests both the Spanish *oro* for gold and the transcen-dental *One*. Their love of Oro and his prophet Alma, suggesting the relation of God to Christ, is intuitive rather than rational. As one islander explains: "We love him because we do" (628).

Even though Babbalanja and the other Mardian companions of Taji accept a faith like that of the Transcendentalists as the closest man can come to truth, Taji's dedication to his idea of absolute beauty leads him onward alone on his tragic course. The last island for him before he heads out to sea beyond the coral reef is Flozella, ruled by Hautia, who entices him to enjoy sensual pleasures in an exotic, watery cave, where the sun does not shine. The circle's center for Taji, however, is nowhere in Mardi, and so he gives up the sensory world with its imperfections to follow a dream.

The irony of Melville's conclusion, that absolute beauty is beyond mortal reach, offers an insight into Melville's own quest for a faith that meets the test of art. He was too independent to portray any convention, institution, or social group as the possessor of the creative spirit. Ulti-mately, the artist must search for it alone at the peril of being destroyed either by primal forces or by those of tradition that relentlessly close in on him.

In the development of Melville's art, *Mardi* is perceived by Matthiessen and others as the midpoint between *Typee* and *Moby-Dick*. It also marks the beginning of a serious attempt to apply Emersonian ideas. It extends the incipient symbolism and specific social criticism of Melville's first novel into a portrait of the world as inclusive as that of *Moby-Dick*, but without the focus of a suspenseful plot, fully-developed characters, and all-inclusive Transcendental symbol, which would, as Emerson said in *Nature*, "concen-trate this radiance of the world on one point" (W, I, 24). Though Melville's circles encompass nature, their center is essentially an abstraction. Yillah, as beauty, is less romantic heroine than phantom. Her brief appearance in the novel, with its supernatural overtones, is hardly sufficient to establish her character as representative of all nature. The other characters and the Mardian isles appear as loosely connected figments of the mind, which together offer a composite picture of the world rather than a synthesis. At this stage in Melville's development, however, he defended the lack of cohesiveness of the novel in a manner that recalls Emerson's notion in "Self-Reliance" that "a foolish consistency is the hobgoblin of little minds" (W, II, 57). In an apparent description of is own work, Melville has Babbalanja comment on the art of Lombardo, the great Mardian poet:

> And what, if he pulled down one gross world and ransacked the ethereal spheres, to build up something of this own—a composite: what then? matter and mind, though matching not, are mates; and sundered oft, in his Koztanza they unite:—the airy waist, embraced by stalwart arms. (597)

Though Melville does indeed ransack the spheres, the failure of *Mardi* to win public approval because of its lack of cohesiveness impelled him to revaluate his conception of the artist's task. His next two novels, *Redburn* and *White-Jacket*, both written in 1849, illustrate his renewed interest in representing visible reality and his continuing search, stimulated by his encounter with Emerson early that year, for a unifying Transcendental symbol. In effect, Melville's realization upon hearing Emerson of the artistic possibilities of the principle of identity spurred him to look for something in matter that would match and mate with the mind of the perceiver.

CHAPTER 6

SELF-RELIANCE ALOFT: *REDBURN* AND *WHITE-JACKET*

1. The Lessons of Failure

In October 1849, after completing *Redburn* and *White-Jacket*, Melville characterized his work to his father-in-law, Lemuel Shaw, as "two *jobs*, which I have done for money—being forced to it, as other men are to sawing wood." He felt that "no reputation that is gratifying to me can possibly be achieved by either of these books" (L, 91). The comments suggest Melville's bitterness over the failure of *Mardi* to win favor with the critics, not to mention disappointment over the loss of readers who had enjoyed *Typee* and *Omoo*. He had invested almost two years in his grandiose experiment in allegory and fantasy, and apparently his heart was set on encompassing the whole of nature in a work of art. That he still yearned to write other books like *Mardi* is implicit in his further comment to Shaw:

> And while I have felt obliged to refrain from writing the kind of book I would wish to; yet, in writing these two books [*Redburn* and *White-Jacket*], I have not repressed myself much—so far as *they* are concerned; but have spoken pretty much as I feel. Being books, then, written in this way, my only desire for their "success" (as it is called) springs from my pocket, and not from my heart. (L, 91–92)

But in spite of his disclaimers, *Redburn* and *White-Jacket* are something more than just two jobs. As responses to the failure of *Mardi*, at least in

113

Melville's view, they mark an important turning point in his art. He realized first of all the value of drawing on his personal knowledge of a sailor's life for his fictions, if he would keep his readers. The dull realities of being a deckhand that led Taji to jump ship might not be dull to readers who have never sailed before the mast. For them, the everyday hazards of climbing the rigging, surviving storms, and enduring the harsh treatment of tyrannical officers would be the stuff of romantic adventure. The continuing popularity of James Fenimore Cooper's *The Pilot* (1823) and *The Red Rover* (1827), whose authentic details derive from the author's experiences in the Navy, and Richard Henry Dana's autobiographical *Two Years Before the Mast* (1840) offered ample evidence of the public taste in seafaring narratives. Though Melville may have felt in 1849 that he was retreating from his artistic goal, he actually was advancing by having to restrict his focus to what he later describes as "visible truth."[1]

A second consequence of the failure of *Mardi* is Melville's heightened sense of craft. His references in that novel to Taji's "chartless voyaging" and to Lombardo's random methods of creation suggest his own awareness of deficiencies in the structure of *Mardi* even before readers began calling it a hodge-podge. His attempt to explain himself in its pages is not unlike that of a raconteur elaborating on the point of a joke. In December 1849, he confessed to his friend Evert Duyckinck: "I admit that I learn by experience and not by divine intuitions. Had I not written and published *Mardi*, in all likelihood, I would not be as wise as I am now, or may be" (L, 96). The comment suggests Melville's awareness of his own growth.

Though Melville says that he became wiser through experience with its trial and error, evidence already presented indicates that he received timely cues on the uses of symbolism from Emerson's 1849 lecture series, "Mind and Manners." He also had time, as Sealts suggests, to follow up his attendance at one or more lectures by reading into Emerson's works available in public libraries.[2]

Redburn and *White-Jacket* demonstrate Melville's increased control over his materials, whether drawn from experience or reading. Elements of character, setting, and action tend to unite in symbolic relationships that reflect some of Emerson's subtler lessons on self-realization. These include the notions of thought as an angle of vision, the identity of the inner and outer worlds of the perceiver, and the debasement of the individual in a compartmentalized, depersonalized society. We can characterize both novels as dramatizing in terms of the routines of a sailor's life the

Emersonian theme of self-reliance. Further, and perhaps most importantly for Melville's future development, both novels apply the Emersonian principle that the whole of experience is implicit in every part, so that the world is likened to the deck of a ship and the fall of man to the fall of a sailor from the main top.

In these ways, Melville transcends the achievements of writers like Cooper and Dana, who do not share his concern with exploring the relation of the mind to the world of the senses. Though *Redburn* and *White-Jacket* were written in haste and lightly regarded by their creator, both succeed, where *Mardi* failed, in appealing to readers with their lively, realistic narratives and in symbolic portrayals of the self evolving through the crucible of experience toward manhood and wholeness of vision.

2. Discovery of Symbolic Form

In *Redburn* and *White-Jacket*, Melville shifts his focus from his unabashedly exotic "world of the mind" to the commonplaces of a sailor's life in a search for what Emerson in 1849 described as "commanding insight" into human nature. Like Emerson's "man diver," he probes into the everyday happening for its secret. *Redburn* recalls Melville's first sea voyage from New York to Liverpool and return in 1839 as a nineteen-year-old crewman aboard the trader, *St. Lawrence* (Log, I, 42). Critics have long been aware of the numerous parallels between the fictional events and Melville's own growing up experiences.[3] The close attention to detail in this novel led Evert Duyckinck to characterize it as "Defoe on the ocean." *White-Jacket*, in turn, is a fictionalized account of Melville's service aboard the frigate *United States*, which he boarded in Honolulu in the summer of 1843 for the homeward journey around Cape Horn to Boston (Log, I, 102). His vigorous attack on flogging and other inhumane military customs in this novel helped to arouse public indignation which led to the mid-century reformation of the Navy, including the abolition of corporeal punishment.[4] Considered together, both novels reveal a new cohesiveness in Melville's art which is due substantially to his application of lessons on symbolic form that he acquired from Emerson.

The term *symbol*, in a literary sense, refers to an object or an image which suggests a meaning beyond itself. Emerson, however, employed the term to denote the concrete language of nature and art by which the complexity of the invisible whole is concentrated in the visible part. He considered nature, and any individual detail in nature, as a metaphor of the mind, a representation through the senses of a supersensual reality. As he wrote in *Nature*, reprinted in London in 1848 and in Boston in September 1849, "A fact is the end or last issue of spirit. The visible creation is the terminus or the circumference of the invisible world" (W, I, 35). No matter how small, "a leaf, a drop, a crystal, a moment of time, is related to the whole and partakes of the whole. Each particle is a microcosm, and faithfully renders the likeness of the whole" (44). Like nature, a work of art also is a metaphor of the mind, since it consists, as Emerson said, of a fact of nature modified by the will of the artist. He therefore could perceive the universe in a drop of water or in a poem.

These ideas, we have noted, also appear in the Boston lectures of early 1849 with a secular emphasis, as Emerson speaks of perceiving in nature "the figure of a disguised man" and notes that "the world may be reeled off from any Idea like a ball of yarn." They were sufficiently pervasive that Thoreau could describe Walden Pond as earth's eye, as well as God's drop, because the water reflected the viewer to himself and the heavens beyond; that Whitman could reduce the whole of life to a blade of grass and could say of his work, "Camarado, this is no book,/Who touches this touches a man."

Melville's art shows in gradual development a technique of using Transcendental symbols that would compress a total view of nature into a restricted image. In *Mardi*, he imagined a cluster of islands surrounded by a coral reef as his symbol of the world. But since Taji turns away from this world, it is not a mirror of his mind: nor does it reflect any other character to himself. In *Redburn* and *White-Jacket*, however, Melville reduces his vision of the world to a ship, although in *Redburn* he further concentrates it into the symbol of a single work of art, a glass model ship, which the narrator identifies with as a child, long before he goes to sea.

Melville described *Redburn* to his friend Richard Henry Dana as "a little nursery tale of mine" (L, 93). As such it parallels *Typee*, which portrays the initiation of a young sailor into primitive nature. Like Tommo, Wellingborough Redburn is motivated to seek basic experience. But unlike all of Melville's earlier narrators, Redburn has a clearly defined angle of vision. The world, as he sees it first in his home, is like a fragile "old-fashioned glass ship, about eighteen inches long, and of French manufacture, which his father, some thirty years before, had brought

from Hamburgh [sic] as a present to a great-uncle."⁵ Kept in a glass case
on a "little claw-footed Dutch tea-table in one corner of the sitting room,"
this international ship named *La Reine*, or The Queen, is "the wonder and
delight of all the people of the village" (7). The youth tries "to peep in at
the portholes," to discover its dark mystery and "perhaps some gold
guineas." On one occasion he feels "a sort of insane desire to be the death
of the glass ship, case and all, in order to come at the plunder" (8).

In the image of the ship, with its tiny glass sailors portrayed as
performing their duties and its captain as "leaning against the bulwark,
with one hand to his head; perhaps he was unwell, for he looked very
glassy out of the eyes," Melville humorously foreshadows the characters,
action, and social criticism to follow. He also hints at the fragility of the
human condition by referring to the dust "like down" that had worked
through the joints of the ship model's case "so as to cover all the sea with
a light dash of white," which resembled "foam and froth raised by the
terrible gale the good Queen was battling against" (9).

Melville devotes more space to describing the appearance of the glass
ship than he does to the real ship on which Redburn sails. The episodes
in the novel unravel like Emerson's ball of yarn as Redburn adjusts his
inner vision to outer realities. He sees only with the eyes of innocence
when he first steps aboard the merchantman *Highlander* in New York
harbor. Characteristically, his first impression is not of the ship as a
whole—because he is not whole—but of the captain's cabin, where he is
impressed by the handsome furnishings. Similarly, his initial view of the
skipper is one that later proves to be incomplete and misleading. Captain
Riga appears to the youth as "a fine looking man, about forty, splendidly
dressed, with very black whiskers, and very white teeth, and what I took
to be a free, frank look out of a large hazel eye" (15). What the boy sees
is the facade the captain puts on in port. The whole truth about the
captain and also the ship corresponds to the glass model.

The progression from partial to whole vision is metaphorically from
darkness to light. Redburn's first lesson aboard the *Highlander* destroys
his romantic illusions and sense of wonder. The first sailor he meets sends
him forward to the forecastle, which resembles a cave. When the youth
asks for a light, the sailor replies, "Strike your eyes together and make
one. We don't have any lights here." Beginning his life as a sailor in the
darkness of his own ignorance, Redburn gradually becomes aware of the
shabby realities of the seafarer's life. He perceives he is in a "smoky looking

place" with wooden boxes or bunks suggesting coffins around the sides (25).

This cave, his home at sea, is more Emersonian than Platonic, since the light in Plato's metaphor is that of ignorance, which projects its shadows on the wall. By contrast, light for Emerson is from the self, in the power of the eye to see, as it is for Redburn. What he sees wears the colors of his glum spirit. Similarly, in his first view of the ocean, the details reflect his loneliness:

> At last we got as far as the Narrows, which everybody knows is the entrance to New York Harbor from the sea; and it may well be called the Narrows, for when you go in or out, it seems like going in or out of a door-way; and when you go out of these Narrows on a long voyage like this of mine, it seems like going out into the broad highway, where not a soul is to be seen. For far away and away, stretches the great Atlantic Ocean; and all you can see beyond is where the sea comes down to the water. It looks lonely and desolate enough, and I could hardly believe, as I gazed around me, that there could be land beyond, or any place like Europe or England or Liverpool in the great wide world. (34)

The contrast between this view and the composite picture of the sea Melville gives in the early pages of *Typee*, discussed in Chapter 4, shows the artist's new tendency to match external reality to the inward attitude of the perceiver.

During the voyage, Redburn's varied individual impressions contribute to his growing awareness of human misery and depravity perpetuated by custom and what Melville describes as "the cold charities" of civilized man. The youth's initiation has three broad stages that correspond to the legs of the journey. On the outward passage to Liverpool, Redburn is reduced to the animal level of experience but endures. "Miserable dog's life is this of the sea!" he says, "commanded like a slave and set to work like an ass!" Then in Liverpool, he discovers the realities of slums and the starving poor that contrast with the romantic descriptions in his father's guidebook. On the homeward trip, he witnesses the suffering of hundreds of emigrants, roped off from cabin passengers and reduced by famine and disease to animalism.

Redburn's disillusionment, however, is not so extensive as to include the ultimate scheme of creation. Despite evidences of degradation aboard ship and ashore, he develops a sense of spiritual brotherhood with sailors and perceives them as saviors. Though outcasts, they are "the *primum mobile* of all commerce" (139). He notes also that each Liverpool dock "is a small archipelago, an epitome of the world, where all the nations of Christendom, and even those of Heathendom, are represented" (165). In an expansive mood, he perceives America as a nation of nations, in a passage that reflects Emerson's idea of the whole in the part and also looks ahead to Whitman:

> You can not spill a drop of American blood without spilling the blood of the whole world. . . . We are not a nation, so much as a world; for unless we may claim all the world for our sire, like Melchisedec, we are without father or mother.[6]

Redburn's identification with the sailor's life in particular and the American experience in general links him to three characters representing the principal kinds of evil aboard Melville's first world-ship. In Captain Riga, Melville portrays the evil of authority perpetuated by a heartlessly materialistic code. Polite in port but a petty tyrant at sea, the skipper of the *Highlander* conforms to the conventions of the merchant marine, in which people have value only as commodities to be used or transported for profit. He is Emerson's partial man, "metamorphosed into a thing," who functions according to routines which form his sole basis for judging the worth of an individual (W, I, 83).

Melville implies Riga's crudeness through Redburn's description of the clothes the captain wears once the *Highlander* leaves port: "old-fashioned snuff-colored coats, with high collars and short waists; and faded, short-legged pantaloons, very tight about the knees; and vests, that did not conceal his waistbands, owing to their being so short, just like a little boy's." His hats were "all caved in, and battered, as if they had been knocked about in a cellar; and his boots were sadly patched" (71). In short, he is a tramp at sea.

In this satirical description, Melville's narrator, whose own role is identified by his hunting jacket, is something of a clothes philosopher in a manner that parodies Carlyle's Professor Diogenes Teufelsdröckh in *Sartor Resartus* (1833). The irony of Redburn's conclusion that Riga is "some sort of impostor" suggests Carlyle's point:

> What thou seest is not there on its own account; strictly taken, is not there at all: Matter exists only spiritually, and to represent some Idea, and *body* it forth. Hence Clothes, as despicable as we think them, are so unspeakably significant.[7]

For Carlyle and also for Emerson, clothes correspond to external nature, which both writers describe as the garment of God. Melville's focus, however, is on dress as an outer sign of the inner self.

In contrast to the coarse skipper, who personifies the shabby code of the merchant marine, is Redburn's overly refined friend Harry Bolton, whom he meets in Liverpool. This pathetically ineffective son of a gentleman is so debilitated by the conventions of polite English society that he is unable to establish his manhood. Harry embodies the Emersonian notion of the victim of civilization. In his character, Melville has provided a nautical equivalent of the idea in "Self-Reliance" that the "civilized man has built himself a coach but lost the use of his feet." For Harry cannot climb the rigging and thereby fails to gain the respect of the common sailor. "His levity of manner," Redburn observes, "and sanguine assurance, coupled with the constant sight of his most unseamanlike person—more suited to the Queen's drawing-room than a ship's forecastle—bred many misgivings in my mind" (220). Melville suggests Harry's lack of self-reliance by having him wear false whiskers and mustache to deceive his friends.

In an episode that reflects Carlyle's attack on worldly pleasures in *Sartor Resartus*, Harry takes Redburn to a mysterious and decadent "semi-public place of opulent entertainment" in London, where the wealthy patrons "seemed exceedingly animated about concerns of their own."[8] Harry leaves the innocent Redburn for a period and returns with his face flushed from some sensual excess. The novel concludes with an afterword on the fate of this youth, the narrator's foil who can "sing like a bird" but is unfit for the rigorous existence of sailor. While serving years later as a crewman on the whaler *Huntress*, Harry is crushed to death by a whale jammed against the side of the ship.

Melville's most significant portrait of depravity in *Redburn* is the diabolical sailor Jackson, at war not only with society represented by the crew, but also with nature. Jackson anticipates the character of Ahab as an embodiment of human perversity.[9] Redburn fears his evil eye and observes: "He seemed to be full of hatred and gall against everything and everybody in the world; as if all the world was one person, and had done him some dreadful harm, that was rankling and festering in his heart" (61). As unlikely as it may seem, Melville's picture of "Cain afloat" reflects Emerson's notion of "cracked nature": "His nose had broken down in the middle, and he squinted with one eye, and did not look very straight out of the other" (56).

Jackson's spiritual isolation, even among sailor outcasts who "only go *round* the world, without going *into* it," also is implied by his clothes. As Melville says, "He dressed a good deal like a Bowery boy, for he despised the ordinary sailor-rig" and wore "over-all blue trousers, fastened with suspenders, and three red woolen shirts, one over the other" and "a large white wool hat, with a broad rolling brim" (56). So clad in red, white, and blue, Jackson stands out in ironic opposition to the idea of spiritual nature. "Don't talk of heaven to me," he cries. "It's a lie—I know it—and they are all fools that believe in it" (104).

Jackson's death fall from the main-topsail-yard provides a dramatic illustration of Emerson's notion of compensation: "Curses always recoil on the head of him who imprecates them" (W, II, 109). Riding the yard-arm end in a storm, Jackson utters "a blasphemous cry" and then, Melville writes, "his hands dropped to his side, and the bellying sail was spattered with a torrent of blood from his lungs" (296). Jackson's blood spattering on the crew as well recalls Redburn's meditation, "You can not spill a drop of American blood without spilling the blood of the whole world" (169). In Jackson, a relative of Andrew Jackson, Melville provides an ironic counterstatement to Redburn's view that "our blood is as the flood of the Amazon, made up of a thousand noble currents all pouring into one" (ibid.).

Jackson's plunge, which contrasts also with the symbolic life-saving fall of the narrator from the main-top in *White-Jacket*, is merely a striking episode rather than the thematic climax of the novel. Despite the incidental nature of the effect, it anticipates Ahab's tragic death moment in *Moby-Dick*, in which Ahab, like Jackson, is subject to the law of compensation and is destroyed, as if through the recoil of his own curses.

Even though Redburn is intimidated by Jackson, led into a house of sinful pleasure by Harry Bolton, and finessed out of his wages by Captain Riga, he retains his integrity and establishes himself as a good shipmate, loyal friend, and sensitive observer of the human condition. Redburn evolves in the Emersonian mold of "The American Scholar," nurtured primarily by nature and action through his deckhand experiences and willingness to go aloft in all weather and share the risks of seamanship. For him, book learning, particularly the traditional lore in his father's guidebook, is of little use, a "dear delusion" of the kind that led Emerson to say, "Books are for the scholar's idle times." Ultimately, Redburn learns to see relations beneath the surface appearances of things and enlarges both his self-knowledge and his sense of involvement with mankind. He misses the crew whose hardships he shared, but Harry, lacking this growth, expresses relief when the voyage is over:

> As, after shaking our hands, our shipmates departed, Harry and I stood on the corner awhile, till we saw the last man disappear.
> "They are gone," said I.
> "Thank heaven!" said Harry.

If *Redburn* marks Melville's first attempt to unite "visible truth" with symbols that define the title character's angle of vision toward the world, *White-Jacket* amounts to an elaborate restatement of the theme of self-realization with symbols of even greater complexity suggesting the changing relationships between the individual, society, and nature. A substantially longer novel than *Redburn*, it provides a remarkable mixture of richly textured narrative and philosophical speculation that builds suspense without the sustained dramatic conflict which later characterizes *Moby-Dick*. Melville's controlling idea is suggested in the sub-title, "The World of a Man of War," and made explicit in the concluding chapter. "As a man-of-war that sails through the sea," he writes:

> so this earth that sails through the air. We mortals are all on board a fast-sailing, never-sinking, world-frigate, of which God was the shipwright; and she is but one craft in a Milky-Way fleet, of which God is the Lord High Admiral. The port we sail from is forever astern. And though far out of sight of land, and for ages and ages we continue to sail with sealed orders, and our last destination remains a secret to ourselves and our officers; yet our final haven was predestinated ere we slipped from the stocks of creation. (398)

The idea is as expansive as anything in *Mardi*, or for that matter in Emerson's writings. Melville returns to the notion of questing for an unattainable secret in nature by presenting a ship sailing under sealed orders, in which "we ourselves are the repositories of the secret packet," for "there are no mysteries out of ourselves" (398). His Ideal Man's role is taken over by the noble nonconformists among the crew—men like Mad Jack, Jack Chase, and Old Ushant—who sail the *Neversink* through storms in nature and the spirit. White-Jacket, the sailor narrator, identifies with these natural aristocrats rather than with the ranking officers, who represent to him various kinds of incompetence. In the rhapsodic concluding paragraph of the novel, Melville reflects the Emersonian ethic that the individual is responsible for his own welfare:

> Our gun-deck is full of complaints. In vain from Lieutenants do we appeal to the Captain; in vain—while on board our world-frigate—to the indefinite Navy Commissioners, so far out of sight aloft. Yet the worst of our evils we blindly inflict on ourselves; our officers cannot remove them, even if they would. From the last ills no being can save another; therein each man must be his own savior. (399-400)

But where Emerson sees a connection of the self to the Over-Soul, Melville notes the remoteness of the Navy Commissioners, supreme beings in a sailor's world, from the individual seaman.

In *White-Jacket,* Melville explores in detail the artificial barriers and compartments that dehumanize society aboard a warship. He expresses his outrage against flogging, a common practice that he witnessed on 163 occasions during his service aboard the *United States.*[10] But his decision to make an issue of flogging can be viewed as a timely response to a vigorous editorial attack directed at his ship in the March 3, 1849, issue of *The Boston Republican.* It is probable that he read the article, entitled "Flogging in the Navy," since on that day he was in Boston writing his letter on hearing Emerson lecture to Evert Duyckinck. The article begins:

> The U.S. Frigate 'United States' arrived at Norfolk recently from the Mediterranean,—days at sea, 457, days in port, 530. During the cruise she visited the coast of Africa, as far south as the equator, most of the ports in the Mediterranean west of Italy, also Cadiz and Tangier. She lost 14 men, 4 by accident, 8 by coast fever, and 2 from chronic diseases; *served out the number of 8172 lashes, being an average of 22 lashes to each man.* [Italics added.] (2)

The article continues with an editorial condemnation of flogging that suggests the hard line Melville was to take in his book:

> The account seems from the hand of an officer. It smacks of professional narrative. How quietly he recites the facts, like the log book. Served out! So the United States serve out lashes and rations to the men who represent the life of the nation on the sea. Shame and confusion upon the officers of this frigate, from the head, (whether named captain or commodore) down to the youngest midshipman on board; persons so little noble, that they could not impress their characters upon the men under their command, but must fall to the barbarism of enforcing respect and order by the scourge. The story is a shameful commentary upon the character of the officers. (2)

Though Melville's criticism lies parallel with the current of public indignation reflected in this article, we should note that the sailors who are flogged in *White-Jacket* include noble nonconformists like Ushant, who would take lashes rather than give up his beard, as though Melville had in mind Emerson's metaphor on flogging, "For nonconformity the world whips you with its displeasure" (W, II, 55–56).

The enduring significance of this novel lies in the extraordinary richness of Transcendental symbolism linking the mind to nature. In no other novel before *Moby-Dick* has Melville produced episodes which suggest a sense of movement, or undulation as Emerson calls it, in terms of characters, action, and setting interrelated into the metaphor of life as journey: "Whoever afflict us, whatever surround, Life is a voyage that's homeward bound" (400).

The fictitious journey begins for the narrator in Callao on the coast of Peru, the last Pacific port of call for the *Neversink* on its homeward voyage to Norfolk. It is there the youth makes a sailor's surtout, the white-jacket of the title, which serves as a Carlylian symbol of the self. Like the emblematic shooting jacket worn by Redburn, the white jacket is appropriate to the character of its inquisitive wearer. It was a self-made white duck frock with "a Quakerish amplitude about the skirts," indicating tolerance. It had "an inform, tumble-down collar," suggesting the narrator's humility and nonconformity, and "a clumsy fullness about the wristbands" for freedom to work and to grow. Further, the lining consisting of "many odds and ends of patches—old socks, old trouser-legs, and the like" implies an eclectic, spontaneous nature. In effect, it was a cocoon that seemed to absorb the weather, as much as offer protection from it. The narrator adds, "And my shroud it afterward came very near proving" (3). Wearing this eccentric garment, White-Jacket is symbolically clothed for his role in the novel of absorbing experience and growing into manhood.

Shortly before the *Neversink* arrives at its destination, the narrator loses the jacket in an episode that dramatizes his spiritual death and rebirth.[11] Melville suggests that the crucial event is part of the larger scheme of nature interacting with instinct, as White-Jacket falls into the sea from the main-top. It offers a seafaring example of the kind of relation that Emerson had described in accounting for the education of the American scholar. As the narrator is busy working at the end of the "weather-top-gallant yard-arm" the ship plunges "in the sudden swells of the calm sea." As the skirts of the jacket pitch over the narrator's head, he instinctively reaches for them with both hands, thinking he is grabbing sail for support. Thus holding on to himself, he falls into the sea (392).

In this manner, Melville represents the impact of external nature on the self, which leads to the experience of death and rebirth. White-Jacket descends vertically "toward the infallible center of this terraqueous globe" where "some fashionless form brushed my side—some inert, coiled fish of the sea" (ibid.). Melville then expands the moment to suggest its Transcendental significance:

> For one instant an agonizing revulsion came over me as I found myself utterly sinking. Next moment the force of my fall was expended; and there I hung, vibrating in the mid-deep. What wild sound then rang in my ear! One was a soft moaning, as of low waves on the beach; the other wild and heartlessly jubilant, as of the sea in the height of the tempest. Oh soul! thou then heardest life and death: as he who stands upon the Corinthian shore hears both the Ionian and the Aegean waves. The Life-and-death poise soon passed; and then I found myself slowly ascending, and caught a dim glimmering of light. (393)

In this passage, White-Jacket is like Emerson's Ideal Man, who learns "that in going down into the secrets of his own mind he has descended into the secrets of all minds" (W, I, 103). The world-ship itself participates in the physical and spiritual movement, in which the youth must demonstrate complete self-reliance. "I had fallen in a line with the main-mast," White-Jacket says:

I found myself nearly abreast of the mizzen-mast, the frigate slowly gliding by like a black world in the water. Her vast hull loomed out of the night, showing hundreds of seamen in the hammock nettings, some tossing over ropes, others madly flinging overboard the hammocks; but I was too far out from them immediately to reach what they threw. (393-394)

Beyond help from others, White-Jacket must cut himself out of his cocoon, which is dragging him under, and swim for the ship. Melville presents the image of rebirth: "I whipped out my knife, that was tucked in my belt, and ripped my jacket straight up and down, as if I were ripping open myself" (394). As soon as he is brought aboard the ship, he climbs into the rigging to continue his job like any other full-fledged member of the world-ship's crew.

In contrast to the death plunge of Jackson in *Redburn*, White-Jacket's fall provides a thematic climax for the novel. Melville describes the jacket, the ship, and the sea as interrelated facts, in which each trifle, as Emerson prescribes in "The American Scholar," bristles "with the polarity that ranges it instantly on an eternal law" (W, I, 111).

Within the scope of this comprehensive portrait of the self in relation to the world, Melville delineates characters who represent all levels of shipboard society, which he divides into the broad Transcendental categories of nonconformist and conformist:

> Oppressed by illiberal laws, and partly oppressed by themselves many of our people are wicked, unhappy, inefficient. We have skulkers and idlers all round, and brow-beaten wasters, who for a pittance, do our craft's shabby work. Nevertheless, among our people we have gallant fore, main, and mizzentop men aloft, who, well treated or ill, still trim our craft to the blast. (373)

Melville's nonconformists break the rules that govern shipboard society when these threaten to compromise their integrity or endanger the world-ship. Foremost among these men of instinct, who refuse, as Emerson said in "Self-Reliance," to "capitulate to badges and names, to large societies and dead institutions" is Jack Chase, the first captain of the main top. Jack's Carlylian sense of duty enables him to accept naval discipline afloat; yet ashore, Melville observes, "he was a stickler for the Rights of Man and the liberties of the world" (17). Melville portrays Jack as the kind of successful individualist whom Emerson describes as being able "to carry himself in the presence of all opposition as if every thing were titular and ephemeral but he" (W, II, 51). "Loved by seaman and admired by officers," Jack has "a high conceit of his profession" (13).

If Jack Chase is an idealized portrait of the man who lives by instinct, Mad Jack, a heavy-drinking officer, is a realistic conception of the individualist who disobeys orders to get things done in a crisis. He is a man of action who displays an intuitive understanding of the primitive forces of nature. In the stormy rounding of Cape Horn, he countermands the captain's order in a dramatic confrontation:

> "Hard *up* the helm!" shouted Captain Claret, bursting from his cabin like a ghost, in his nightdress.
> "Damn you!" raged Mad Jack to the quarter-masters; "hard *down*—hard *down*, I say, and be damned with you!" (106)

These two orders, Melville explains, given by the captain and his subordinate exactly contrast their characters: The captain's "*hard up*" was "for *scudding*; that is, for flying away from the gale." Mad Jack's "*hard down*" was "for running the ship into its teeth." Melville observes that "the latter step, though attended with more appalling appearances, is, in reality the safer of the two" (110). His additional comment, "But, sailor or landsman, there is some sort of a Cape Horn for all," suggests Emerson's statement in "The American Scholar" on the value of facing nature, with its attractions and dangers, rather than running away from it:

> So much of life as I know by experience, so much of the wilderness have I vanquished and planted, or so far have I extended my being, my dominion. (W, I, 95)

Opposing these men, yet envying them, are the conformists in the highly stratified society aboard the *Neversink*. To a man, they display what Emerson described in "Self-Reliance" as the "foolish consistency" which is "the hobgoblin of little minds. Although Melville recognizes the need for discipline and an orderly division of duties among the five hundred men in a man-of-war's crew, he attacks "the immutable ceremonies," "iron etiquette," "spiked barriers" separating ranks, "delegated absolutism of authority on all hands" and "the impossibility, on the part of the common seaman, of appeal from incidental abuses." Such conventions of Navy life, he comments, debase the individual. Melville's basic target is the inflexible *Articles of War*, which gives the captain the power of a despot to inflict cruel punishments on his crew. Melville's attack is similar to Thoreau's more general criticism of law in "Civil Disobedience," published in 1849. "Law never made men a whit more just," Thoreau said, "and, by means of their respect for it, even the well-disposed are daily made the agents of injustice."[12] Melville underscores the inhumanity of flogging:

> Let us have the charity to believe them—as we do—when some captains in the Navy say, that the thing of all others most repulsive to them in the routine of what they consider their duty, is the administration of corporeal punishment upon the crew; for, surely, not to be scarified to the quick at these scenes would argue a man but a beast. (138)

Unlike the individualists, who preserve their integrity by breaking the rules, the conformists aboard the *Neversink* readily submit to the stereotyped patterns of behavior, which ultimately serve to exalt the officers or "sea lords" over the crewmen or "sea commoners." Melville points up the superficiality of all ritual in this satirical description of the captain boarding the ship:

> The Captain then slowly mounted the ladder, and gravely marching through a lane of "side boys," so-called—all in their best bibs and tuckers, and who stood making sly faces behind his back—was received by all the lieutenants in a body, their hats in their hands, and making a prodigious scraping an bowing, as if they had just graduated at a French dancing-school. Meanwhile, preserving an erect, inflexible, and ramrod carriage, and slightly touching his chapeau, the captain made his ceremonious way to the cabin, disappearing behind the scenes,like the pasteboard ghost in *Hamlet*. (163)

Presented here as a ghost, rather than as a man, Captain Claret is king of the world-ship, a heartless administrator of rules that cover every convention, including that of telling time. On the other hand, despite his absolute authority, which he sustains by means of flogging and other inhumane punishments, he is not intrinsically evil. "What he was," Melville says, "the usages of the Navy had made him. Had he been a mere landsman—a merchant, say—he would no doubt have been considered a kind-hearted man" (367). The idea, which derives from Melville's first-hand experience, nonetheless applies Emerson's argument on the evils of conformity.

Melville's satire against the pretentiousness and cruelty of Navy conventions has neoclassical overtones with its emphasis on easily-recognizable character types. The little commodore with eyes like musket balls sustains the dignity of his rank by remaining aloof aboard the ship, seldom speaking. "I have serious doubts," White-Jacket comments, "whether, for the most part, he was not dumb" (21). Officers of lesser rank also have appearances that distinguish them according to rank. First lieutenants, for example, walk with one shoulder "disproportionately drooped" because they wear only one epaulet (48). The "barons of the gun room," who include lieutenants, purser, marine officers, and sailing master, are "gentlemen of stiff upper lips and aristocratic noses" (ibid.). As to the crew, those most likely to thrive on a man-of-war are "the Happy Jacks," fellows "without shame, without a soul, so dead to the least dignity of manhood" that any one of them "could hardly be called a man." All that a sailor needs besides a healthy body, Melville says, is "a good memory, and the more of an arithmetician he is, the better" (11).

Melville's criticism of types is extended to include the professions, which he satirizes on the basis of their heartless attention to empty ceremony and form. In passages that echo the caricatures of Smollett and Dickens, Melville describes how Surgeon Cuticle, the senile senior medical officer, demonstrates the procedures for amputating the leg of an injured sailor, who dies. The surgeon is himself a form, rather than a man, having prepared himself by removing his wig, glass eye, and false teeth to stand before the horrified patient and assembled junior officers as an emblem of death.

Melville is less severe with the clergy, which he represents in the character of the ship's chaplain, who "had drunk at the mystic fountain of Plato; his head had been turned by the Germans; and this I will say, that White-Jacket himself saw him with Coleridge's Biographia Literaria in his hand" (155). Melville's description of this "transcendental divine" addressing "five hundred salt-sea sinners upon the psychological phenomena of the soul" suggests his own religious skepticism. The minister, however, is characterized primarily in terms of the class he represents, rather than as an individual or as a Transcendentalist. "Of all the noble lords in the wardroom," White-Jacket says, "this lord-spiritual with the exception of the purser, was in the highest favor with the commodore, who frequently conversed with him in a close and confidential manner" (156).

The evils which Melville perceives in the forms of civilized behavior are embodied in the character of Bland, the master-at-arms, whose diabolism anticipates the malevolence of Claggart in *Billy-Budd*. As chief of police on the world-ship, Bland sees that orders are obeyed and arrests those who break regulations. Like Jackson in *Redburn*, Bland is cast in the mold of "an organic and irreclaimable scoundrel, who did wicked deeds as the cattle browse the herbage, because wicked deeds seemed the legitimate operation of his whole infernal organization" (188). But unlike Jackson, whose cracked nature is suggested in his physical appearance, Bland is a "neat and gentlemanly villain, and broke his biscuit with a dainty hand" (187). Bland "never swore, and chiefly abounded in passing puns and witticisms, varied with humorous contrasts between ship and shore life, and many agreeable and racy anecdotes, very tastefully narrated" (ibid.). If Jackson represents the will at war with nature, Bland portrays Melville's conception of a man completely lacking in moral sensitivity; he is the epitome of conformity. White-Jacket rates him next to Jack Chase as the most entertaining, if not the most companionable man in the mess. Though Bland is suspended for smuggling, Captain Claret reinstates him in a public ceremony, perhaps, as the narrator suggests, as an act of gratitude for a favor.

Portrayed in this manner as forms, rather than as men, none of the conformists aboard the *Neversink* has the stature of Melville's natural aristocrats, his gallant nonconformists. On the other hand, such characters as Jack Chase and Mad Jack, despite their self-reliance, lack the fullness of conception of either the epic or tragic hero. Sailing as they are, under secret orders, they are ignorant of their destination and none the wiser for their experiences. White-Jacket alone grows inwardly; his development toward wholeness of vision, however, is at times secondary to his role as observer and commentator on social evils.

In *Redburn* and *White-Jacket,* Melville not only regained his popularity as a novelist, but also discovered ways to compress the world into symbols derived from the visible truths of characters, setting, and action. His perception in these works of nature as a varied metaphor of the mind and his division of humanity into the heroically self-reliant and the debased, often incompetent conformists are more than reactions to experience. As the evidence in the two novels indicates, they also are responses to the stimuli of Emerson in 1849. Encouraged by the successful application of Transcendental ideals linking the inner man to sensory perception, Melville again concentrates his vision of the world in the image of a ship in his next novel, *Moby-Dick*. In the sinking of the *Pequod* as a consequence of Ahab's tragic quest for total knowledge, Melville fulfills the promise implicit in the glass ship in *Redburn* and the ironically-named *Neversink* in *White-Jacket*: the destruction of a conforming society and the shipwreck of the soul.

CHAPTER 7

TRANSCENDENTALISM AND TRAGIC VISION IN *MOBY-DICK*

1. Creative Confluence: Instinct and Craft

"Great geniuses are parts of the times," Melville wrote in the summer of 1850; "they themselves are the times, and possess a correspondent coloring."[1] His comment in the essay, "Hawthorne and His Mosses," which he wrote while working on *Moby-Dick*, reflects a leading idea in Emerson's *Representative Men*, published early in 1850. Emerson had written that although a great man "inhabits a higher sphere of thought, into which other men rise with labor and difficulty," such a unique individual "must be related to us, and our life receive from him some promise of explanation" (W, IV, 6). He continued, "But the great are near" (7), and "the key to the power of the greatest men" is that "their spirit diffuses itself" (33).

Melville's essay, a tribute to Hawthorne purportedly written "by a Virginian Spending July in Vermont," is phrased in language that recalls Emerson's statements on genius and his pleas for independence in literary matters. "No American writer," Melville said, "should write like an Englishman, or a Frenchman; let him write like a man, for then he will write like an American" (413). The idea echoes the call for independence in "The American Scholar," which was republished in a volume with *Nature* and other early addresses in 1849 and then easily accessible to Melville. For Melville, as for Emerson, the scholar or poet must stand indomitably on instinct as a whole man engaged in thinking or writing.

133

In his essay, Melville suggests his own recovery of equilibrium after the failure of *Mardi*. "But it is better to fail in originality than to succeed in imitation," he writes. "He who has never failed somewhere, that man cannot be great. Failure is the true test of greatness" (413). He also lauds Hawthorne's darkness because it "gives more effect to the ever-moving dawn, that forever advances through it, and circumnavigates the world" (406). These notions of failure as a requirement for success and of idealism enhanced by a sense of evil restate Emerson's argument in "Compensation" that every action invites a reaction, since all nature consists of polarities in delicate balance. Emerson's prefatory lines of poetry provide the key images:

> The wings of time are black and white,
> Pied with morning and with night.
> Mountain tall and ocean deep
> Trembling balance duly keep.

These affinities of Melville to Emerson's thought suggest the pervasiveness of Emerson's influence on him in 1850. That *Moby-Dick* presents in the characters of Ishmael, Ahab, the mates, and the primitive harpooners aboard the *Pequod* a gallery of representative men sailing on a world ship is evidence of Melville's timely response to Emersonian ideas. For unlike the crew of the *Neversink*, whom Melville divides into types of conformists and nonconformists, the characters in Melville's new novel embody individual aspects of the self that illuminate the human condition as a whole. Each one develops a distinct though limited angle of vision toward nature as symbolized by the white whale, which reflects each man to himself. In this way, the whale represents Emerson's notion of nature as a disguised man.

But *Moby-Dick*, the first American novel to present a comprehensive world view with tragic plot, also is a response to Hawthorne's genius. From the intense relationship which Melville cultivated with Hawthorne beginning in the summer of 1850, Melville apparently learned lessons in the craft of fiction, including refinements in the art of characterization, plotting in the traditional sense of building up a dramatic conflict to a crisis and resolution, and also the foreshadowing of great climaxes. Melville's stress on the dark side of human nature in both *Redburn* and *White-Jacket*, along with hints of the diabolic in *Typee*, suggests that he had little to learn from Hawthorne on the nature of evil. Instead, he matches an awareness of Hawthorne's sense of dramatic structure with its tragic peripeties and discoveries to his knowledge of Emerson's instinctive symbolistic view of nature as a reflector of the self. In effect, Melville resolves in *Moby-Dick* his artist's dilemma over the relative demands of instinct and craft, which he represented first in *Typee* in terms of his separate portraits of artists in the natural state: Marnoo, the primitive social critic, and Karky, the tattooist. The resolution is individualistic; for Melville's drama is primarily the product of his own creative drive, which builds on influence but ultimately is accountable to itself.

2. *The Lightness of Darkness*

Transcendentalism and tragic vision would seem to be incompatible ingredients in a work of art; yet the influences of Emerson and Hawthorne on *Moby-Dick* lend themselves readily to a merger. For the underside of optimism, which Emerson implies but seldom mentions, is a compensatory pessimism, like the kick of a gun or the backwash of a great wave. The rotation of his circle requires forces at each end of a diameter to thrust in opposing directions. This contrast is part of Emerson's theory of polarity despite Emerson's stress on positive values in his lectures, which he often delivered in the midst of hard times. As a man of belief, Emerson could tolerate, even admire, the skeptic; his impulse to "affirm and yet affirm" was his response to a practical world beset by doubt. But Emerson, too, had his moments of doubt, which could enable him to deny even the values of nonconformity and self-trust. His poem, "Grace," shows a side of his disposition that he chose largely to conceal. The poem appeared in *The Dial* in 1842, but he omitted it from his collected *Poems* (1847):

> How much, preventing God, how much I owe
> To the defenses thou has round me set;
> Example, custom, fear, occasion slow,—
> These scorned bondmen were my parapet.
> I dare not peep over this parapet
> To gauge with glance the roaring gulf below,
> The depths of sin to which I had descended,
> Had not these me against myself defended.

On the other hand, Hawthorne's dark view of the human condition that Melville professed to admire was not without its idealistic overtones, which were especially noticeable to his contemporaries who associated him with the Transcendentalists.[2] In Hawthorne, Melville found an example of a self-reliant author who had overcome early failure to succeed. *The Scarlet Letter*, published early in 1850, was a best-seller of the day, establishing Hawthorne's reputation as a novelist possessing a profound insight into what he later called "the truth of the human heart."[3] If Melville needed views on art from a writer of fiction, rather than from a lecturer-poet such as Emerson, it was available to him in the following passage from "The Artist of the Beautiful" in *Mosses from an Old Manse*:

> It is requisite for the ideal artist to possess a force of character that seems hardly compatible with its delicacy; he must keep his faith in himself, while the incredulous world assails him with its utter disbelief; he must stand up against mankind and be his own sole disciple, both as respects his genius, and the objects to which it is directed.[4]

Melville triple-scored this sentence in his copy of Hawthorne's *Mosses*, which he received from his Aunt May Melville on July 18, 1850, one month before the first installment of his review of the book appeared in *The New York Literary World* (Log, I, 379, 389). B. R. McElderry, Jr. notes, however, that had Melville desired, he could easily have found a parallel passage in Emerson's "The Poet," which appeared in *Essays* (Second Series) in 1844, the same year that Hawthorne wrote his story on art.[5] Emerson also stresses the artist's need to keep faith with himself in the face of public indifference:

> O poet! a new nobility is conferred in groves and pastures, and not in castles or by swordblade any longer. The conditions are hard, but equal . . . The world is full of renunciations and apprenticeships, and this is thine; thou must pass for a fool and a churl for a long season. . . . And this is the reward; that the ideal shall be real to thee, and the impressions of the actual world shall fall like the summer rain, copious but not troublesome to thy invulnerable essence. (W, III, 41–42)

The conclusion of Hawthorne's story, in which the artist, Owen War-land, spiritually triumphs even though he sees the destruction of his mechanical butterfly, so impressed Melville that he alluded to it in the opening lines of "Hawthorne and his Mosses."

These links of Hawthorne and Melville to Emerson's thought suggest that the friendship which developed between the two novelists was based at least in part on their unacknowledged though genuine appreciation of Emerson's aesthetic views. The blackness Melville saw in Hawthorne and also in Shakespeare furnishes the background for "those occasional flashings-forth of the intuitive Truth," in which darkness is illuminated by the light of the mind. Though Melville identified with Hawthorne's Calvinistic strain, it is through Hawthorne that Melville had his most important personal access to New England Transcendentalism. Hawthorne, who was fifteen years older than Melville, was married to a younger sister of Elizabeth Peabody, a prominent member of the Transcendental Club. Further, despite Hawthorne's satirical treatment of Transcendentalism in "The Celestial Railroad," he and his wife Sophia had a long-standing business and personal relationship with Emerson, as well as with Bronson Alcott and other Transcendentalists. In addition to residing briefly at Brook Farm in 1841 and even serving in the offices of Trustee and Chairman of the Committee on Finance, Hawthorne had rented the "Old Manse" in Concord for three years with Emerson as a landlord.

In the fall of 1850, when Hawthorne, then living in Lenox, and Melville in nearby Pittsfield began exchanging neighborly visits, Sophia Hawthorne reported in a letter to her mother not only that Melville "shut himself into the boudoir" one morning "and read Mr. Emerson's essays," but also that Melville described her husband's features in a manner suggesting Emerson's characterization of the Transcendental poet:

> [Melville] said Mr. Hawthorne was the first person whose physical being appeared to him wholly in harmony with the intellectual and spiritual . . . "the gleam—the shadow—and the peace supreme" all were in exact response to the high, calm intellect, the glowing, deep heart—the purity of actual and spiritual life.[6]

Similarly, in "The Poet," Emerson refers to the poet as one who "stands among partial men for the complete man." He is

> the person in whom these powers are in balance, the man without impediment, who sees and handles that which others dream of, traverses the whole

scale of experience, and is representative of man, in virtue of being the largest
power to receive and to impart. (W, III, 6–7)

During these visits, Hawthorne was completing *The House of Seven
Gables*, which he regarded as his favorite work. In it, he offsets the
blackness of his thought with a portrait of a cheerful Transcendental
heroine, self-reliant Phoebe, who helps to dispel evil influences of the past
that have haunted the old Pyncheon home. But Melville in his letter to
Hawthorne, dated April 16, 1851, commented especially on the novel's
tragic overtones. He called it "a fine old chamber, abundantly, but still
judiciously furnished . . . There are rich hangings, wherein are braided
scenes from the tragedies" (L, 123–124). Melville praised the character of
Clifford and observed in a postscript that the marriage of Phoebe with the
daguerreotypist "is a fine stroke, because of his turning out to be a *Maule*"
(124). Melville's comment suggests his awakening interest in the relation
of setting and character to plot, with its sustained dramatic conflict and
possibilities for ironic resolution. These very qualities distinguish *Moby-
Dick* from Melville's five preceding novels.

In addition to the mixture of Calvinism and Transcendentalism that
Melville admired, Hawthorne's art reflects an almost neoclassical interest
in symmetry of form, which contrasts sharply with Melville's characteristic
digressiveness. As one novelist writing about another, Hawthorne
summed up his attitude towards Melville's art in a letter to Evert Duyckinck on August 29, 1850. Hawthorne had read Melville's work "with a
progressive appreciation of the author," and comments:

> No writer ever put the reality before the eyes of his reader more unflinchingly
> than he does in 'Redburn' and 'White-Jacket.' 'Mardi' is a rich book, with
> depths here and there that compel a man to swim for his life. It is so good
> one scarcely pardons the writer for not having brooded long over it, so as to
> make it a great deal better. (Log, I, 391)

Hawthorne's interest in craftsmanship, evident in this remark, is probably his most important contribution to Melville's artistic development. In
contrast to Melville's continuing struggle to integrate varied materials
drawn from experience and reading into some recognizable form, Hawthorne typically began with a moral equation and strove to invent details
of character, setting, and action that would give it substance. Edgar Allan
Poe had identified Hawthorne's method of composition in his review of

Hawthorne's *Twice Told Tales*: "In the whole composition there should be no word written, in which the tendency, direct or indirect, is not to the one preestablished design."[7] Unlike Melville, whose capacity to absorb a great amount of information from his reading is well-recognized, Hawthorne kept notebooks as memory banks, not only for ideas, but also for intriguing details that he could later use in his stories. In his *American Notebooks* for 1837 his brief statement of the idea of "The Birthmark" illustrates his method:

> A person to be in possession of something as perfect as mortal man has a right to demand; he tries to make it better, ruins it entirely.[8]

The Calvinistic severity of this theme, in effect the fall of man through egotism, is representative of Hawthorne's sense of blackness, as Melville describes it. Characteristically, Hawthorne modified the design of his story before he wrote it. In 1840 he entered in his notebook a second statement of the theme with an added Transcendental note of comfort and forgiveness for an attempt to achieve the ideal:

> A person to be the death of his beloved in trying to raise her to more than mortal perfection; yet this should be a comfort to him for having aimed so highly and holily. (210)

The finished story, first published in 1843, closely follows the revised plan. But Melville in his own copy of *Mosses* checked and underscored this passage in the story that suggests his contrasting method of composition:

> [Aylmer's] most splendid successes were almost invariably failures, if compared with the ideal at which he aimed. . . . [Aylmer's journal] was the sad confession and continual exemplification, of the short-comings of the composite man—the spirit burthened with clay and working in matter; and of *the despair that assails the higher nature* [Melville's scoring], at finding itself so miserably thwarted by the earthly part. Perhaps every man of genius, in whatever sphere, might recognize the image of his own experience in Aylmer's journal. (Log, I, 380)

Melville in this example works inductively from a direct impression which he reacts to in his own art, rather than from abstract statements of story ideas or images such as Hawthorne recorded in his notebooks. Even so, Hawthorne's shadowy portrait of a "composite man," reflecting the

Emersonian aesthetic ideal of representing a total view of man's estate, also anticipates Melville's far more dynamic Captain Ahab, whose exalted despair, however, is over his own moral imperfection.

Despite their underlying similarity, Aylmer and Ahab illustrate the essential difference in the art of the two writers. If Melville's need as an artist was to achieve a feeling for design, Hawthorne's basic problem was to infuse an abstract idea with the flesh and blood of concrete reality. The charm of "The Birthmark" and most of Hawthorne's fiction lies in an evanescent dream-like quality, an otherworldliness which is typical of allegory. Hawthorne was aware of a lack of vigor characterizing many of his stories. In the Preface to the 1851 edition of *Twice-Told Tales*, which he composed at the time Melville was working nearby on *Moby-Dick*, Hawthorne commented that his stories "have the pale tint of flowers that blossomed in too retired a shade—the coolness of a meditative habit, which diffuses itself through the feeling and observation of every sketch."[9]

Far from pointing out Hawthorne's deficiencies, or offering advice on how he might enrich the texture of his fiction, Melville in his letters to Hawthorne at this time showed an increasing preoccupation with his own problems of design. In a letter to Hawthorne dated June 1, 1851, for example, Melville echoed Hawthorne's Preface to *Twice-Told Tales* in commenting that "the calm, the coolness, the silent grass-growing mood in which a man ought always to compose,—that, I fear can seldom be mine" (L, 128). He followed this complaint with a vigorous criticism of his own work: "Dollars damn me. . . . What I feel most moved to write, that is banned,—it will not pay. Yet, altogether, write the *other* way I cannot. So the product is a final hash, and all my books are botches" (128). Again, in November, after Hawthorne had read *Moby-Dick*, Melville wrote to him about the imperfections in the design of his new book: "You were archangel enough to despise the imperfect body, and embrace the soul," he said. "Once you hugged the ugly Socrates because you say the flame in the mouth, and heard the rushing of the demon,—the familiar,—and recognized the sound; for you have heard it in your own solitude" (142).

This new self-consciousness over form, evolving from Melville's association with Hawthorne, is an advance over the earlier supposed "chartless voyaging" of *Mardi*. The evidence is clear that Melville modified his oversimplified view of the artist who works at random following instinct, probably because he found in Hawthorne a model of an established writer whose strength lay in his mastery of preconceived effects.

As a result of Melville's fortunate association with Hawthorne during the critical years 1850 and 1851, *Moby-Dick* is Melville's most carefully constructed novel. Though critics have noticed several minor anomalies in the text that suggest his processes of revision, the work has a remarkable unity of effect based, as we shall demonstrate, on the interrelatedness of its parts in a complex symbolic design.[10] The two-fold source of this power is in Hawthorne's influence on the form, which intensifies Emersonian elements that Melville already had absorbed. In the central dramatic confrontation between Ahab and the white whale, Melville points up the conflict between mortal man questing for ultimate values and primal powers of creation that exceed human understanding. By comparison, even Hawthorne's masterpiece, *The Scarlet Letter*, though more symmetrical in structure than any of Melville's novels, is far more restricted in scope than the all-encompassing panorama of experience presented in *Moby-Dick*. While gaining from Hawthorne's example of craftsmanship, Melville retained a breadth of vision that characterizes his writings from *Mardi* onward and that has its most significant and timely antecedents in the example of Emerson.

3. The Shipwreck of the Soul

The germ of *Moby-Dick*, as most readers know, is the true story of the ramming and sinking of the whaleship *Essex* from Nantucket by a sperm whale, which attacked the vessel twice on November 20, 1820, about two thousand miles west of the Galapagos Islands. Melville heard about this event in 1841 as a sailor aboard the whaler *Acushnet*, where he said it was occasionally a topic of forecastle conversation on the long voyage from Fairhaven around Cape Horn to the South Seas fishery. In July of that year, during a gam or visit on the high seas of the *Acushnet* with the whaler *Lima* from Nantucket, he met the sixteen-year-old son of Owen Chase, the first mate of the *Essex* who had written an account of the shipwreck and the ordeal of survival for the crew that followed. The youth, William Henry Chase, produced for Melville a printed copy of his father's narrative. Melville later reminisces: "The reading of this wondrous story upon the landless sea, and close to the very latitude of the shipwreck had a surprising effect on me."[11]

Though Owen Chase's account is devoted largely to the harrowing experience of Captain George Pollard and his crew of the *Essex*, who drifted in open boats nearly 3000 miles for nearly three months and resorted to cannibalism before the last survivors were rescued, Melville's interest centered on the shipwreck; for this provides his materials for the climax of *Moby-Dick*. Of all Melville's novels to this point in his career, this is the only work in which the climax is both dramatic and preconceived. That Melville chose to brood over the story for nearly nine years, while composing five other novels, suggests that he was keeping it in reserve until he felt ready to work on it.

We can estimate the challenge of this episode to an impressionable mind disposed to perceive life in terms of symbols. In the beginning, Melville was attracted by the idea of the power and malice of the whale in purposefully sinking a whaleship. To an inexperienced deckhand, the story must have combined qualities of myth and apocalyptic vision of the destruction of a fragile world similar to that of the *Acushnet*. Melville's sailor awareness of Nantucket as the principal whaling center for New England, with one hundred ships as opposed to about twenty in New Bedford and Fairhaven, must soon have directed his interest to probably the most important names associated with whaling on that island, and certainly the most colorful—Joseph Starbuck and Jared Coffin. They were wealthy merchants and ship owners, whose relatives were in many ways connected with the lore of whaling. A David Starbuck, for example, was killed by a whale in 1827; and an Owen Coffin, the cabin boy aboard the *Essex* and nephew of Captain Pollard, consented to let himself be eaten by members of the crew, so that they might survive the ordeal.[12] But the names alone suggest the polarities of spiritual aspiration and mortality that intrigued Melville. Had he visited Nantucket, although there is no evidence that he did before completing *Moby-Dick* in late summer of 1851, he would have found Captain Pollard's modest frame house, where he lived in retirement, across the street from the large brick Coffin House, an inn since 1845, and a few blocks away from the three adjoining Starbuck houses, also of brick. There within a short walk would be convenient reminders for a story on whaling: a survivor of the frightening attack on a ship and symbolic names associated with the precarious venture of hunting the sperm whale.

It is conceivable that in the early stages of his thinking Melville imagined a tragic contest between a star-bucking captain and a whale which turns his ship into a coffin. But his thought, nourished by his reading and especially by ideas from Emerson in 1849 and Hawthorne in 1850 and after, expanded into a complex symbolic drama of the mind at war with nature. In the novel, Melville ironically gives the name, Starbuck, to the prudent first mate aboard the doomed *Pequod* and sums up the idea of the defiant mind in Captain Ahab and the symbol of nature in the legendary white whale of the South Seas fishery.[13] Melville uses the Coffin name in a variety of ways. In the opening paragraph of the novel, Ishmael finds himself standing before "coffin warehouses," such as would recall those of Jared Coffin as well as indicate Ishmael depressed state of mind. Later, the proprietor of the Spouter Inn is Peter Coffin, whose function in the novel is to bring together Ishmael, the meditative outcast narrator, and Quee-queg, the primitive harpooner who becomes Ishmael's bosom friend. Near the end, the *Pequod* fulfills the Parsee's prophesy and becomes a hearse, or carrier of coffins, as it sinks; and Ishmael floats to safety on a coffin made by Queequeg. We can sense in these details the play of Melville's imagina-tion as he considers the problems of survival and annihilation in nature.

In Chapter 3, we observed how these problems correspond to the central issue that Emerson addressed in his Boston lecture series, "Mind and Manners," early in 1849 and repeated in substance the following year in New York. Emerson's Ideal Man then was portrayed as a "man diver" seeking a "commanding insight" while facing the danger of "shipwreck" or "ruin" of the inquiring mind on the vices of egotism, fatalism, and practicality. Emerson's familiar "line," as the *Boston Post* described it, probably was close to matching Melville's own thought based on his memory of the *Essex* disaster story when he heard Emerson lecture. Certainly what Melville heard of Emerson's comprehensive view of man, with its connected notions of cracked nature, the whole existing in the part, identity, and life as an angle of vision, would provide powerful stimuli to his imagination, even if Melville was naturally skeptical of Emerson's religious beliefs transcending the visible truths on which he concentrated his art. Granting that to him the underlying secret in nature was ungraspable, Melville obviously was attracted by Emerson's image of nature as a mirror which from every angle reflects a disguised man. He admired Emerson, too, for the energy of his quest for a Transcendental absolute. In the lecture series, then, Emerson made current the basic ideas that Melville incorporated into his masterpiece.

In the vastness and complexity of *Moby-Dick*, most readers can identify five interlocking interests that prepare for the climactic three-day battle of

Captain Ahab and the *Pequod* with the white whale: Ishmael's survival; Ahab's annihilation; the resulting disaster of the *Pequod*; the white whale as symbol of nature, and the digressions on whaling including the nine gams or meetings of whaleships that the *Pequod* encounters on the way to its rendezvous with the white whale. The unifying focus for all of these interests is of course the white whale, which Melville first refers to as "a grand hooded phantom," as it rises in Ishmael's imagination at the end of "Loomings" (Chapter 1) and as "a tremendous apparition," as it literally surfaces before Ahab in "The Chase: First Day" (Chapter 133). In each of these lines of interest, Emerson's notion of nature as a symbol of spirit prevails. With this idea as his basis, Melville reflects attendant ethical and aesthetic views on the self in relation to nature and society that derive in large part from Emerson.

First is the story of Ishmael, whose character evolves from his initial sense of death, the feeling of "November in my soul," to the final image in the novel of his rebirth at Easter time as he floats on a coffin-life buoy, the lone survivor of the adventure. In the haunting opening sentence of the narrative, "Call me Ishmael," Melville identifies him as an outcast seafaring Everyman. The reader is to think of what his name means rather than who he is, for the "I" in this novel is not Herman Melville or some other identifiable person. Ishmael is a larger than life representation of the self questing for commanding insight. He establishes his intention early to do some thought diving by observing that the sea and meditation "are wedded forever" (2). The events in which he participates amount to a series of tests that define his angle of vision and morally justify his survival.

At the Spouter Inn, Ishmael meets his first test in his encounter with Queequeg, a tattooed cannibal. Though presented with much humor, it has the serious purpose of setting forth Ishmael's capacity to accept his fellow man, as he is. Ishmael passes this basic test in human relations through the friendship that develops between the two. It has its reward, for in the end, the coffin Queequeg builds turns out to be Ishmael's life saver.

This bonding recalls Emerson's statement of the purpose of friendship as "a commerce of the most strict and homely that can be joined" for "aid and comfort through all the relations and passages of life and death" (W, II, 205–206). So with Ishmael and Queequeg. The relation between these two contrasting types of characters is much more than that of traveling companions, which characterize the narrators' closest associations in the earlier novels. It embodies Melville's most comprehensive treatment of the value of friendship as a means for survival. This friendship has, in Emersonian terms, the quality of "entireness, a total magnanimity and trust" (W, II, 217).

Beyond demonstrating the capacity for friendship, Ishmael learns from Father Mapple's sermon at the Seamen's Bethel both the stern law of obedience to divine will through its retelling of the story of Jonah, and the limitation of human knowledge as the preacher describes his mission. In a follow up to his sailor version of the Old Testament story, Father Mapple gives what amounts to a second sermon, in which he violates the New Testament admonition to "turn the other cheek" and ignores the doctrine of Christian love. Instead, the "far, far upward, and inward delight" that Father Mapple predicts for the man "who against the proud gods and commodores of this earth, ever stands forth his own inexorable self" is not from Scriptures, which teach humility and obedience to divine will (48). Rather, the message reflects the error of Father Mapple's vision, for his comment ironically foreshadows the hapless plight of the whaler *Delight*, the last ship Ahab sees before encountering the white whale. For all his eloquence and spiritual aspiration, the preacher does not see life whole. The self-reliance he advocates is a species of defiance directed at worldliness. He "acknowledges no law or lord" among men and is "only a patriot to heaven" (48). As an ironic counterpoint to this religious enthusiasm verging on fanaticism, Ishmael in an act of friendship and religious tolerance joins Queequeg in worshiping the cannibal's wooden idol.

Aboard the *Pequod*, Ishmael's essentially idealistic tendencies are balanced against the realism of his mast-head meditation, in which he warns of the "sunken-eyed young Platonist" who "will tow you ten wakes round the world, and never make you one pint of sperm the richer." He describes the Pantheistic sailor dreaming aloft, losing his identity by taking "the mystic ocean at his feet for the visible image of that deep, blue, bottomless soul, pervading mankind and nature." But "slip your hold at all; and your identity comes back in horror. Over Descartian vortices you hover," he says. "And perhaps, at midday, in the fairest weather, with one half-throttled shriek you drop through that transparent air into the summer sea, no more to rise for ever. Heed it well, ye Pantheists" (157)!

Here Ishmael's attack on idealism detached from visible truth is really a criticism of extremes and the expression of an intellect questing for moral equilibrium. He would be "the balanced soul," even as Emerson said of Plato, who combined in his brain "the unity of Asia and detail of Europe; the infinitude of the Asiatic soul and defining, result-loving, machine-making, surface-seeking, opera-going Europe" (W, IV, 53–54). Ishmael also rejects the idea of complete innocence and benignity in nature. In his meditation on the whiteness of the whale, the conventional association of white with purity, as in the bridal gown, is overmatched for him by its connotation of fear, as suggested in the iceberg, the polar bear, and the albino Moby Dick.

But in the mat-maker scene, Ishmael demonstrates his capacity for an integrated moral vision in his description of the relation of necessity, free will, and chance in terms of their "interweavingly working together" as he with the assistance of Queequeg makes a mat. Ishmael's "commanding insight" is one of balance:

> The straight warp of necessity, not to be swerved from its ultimate course—its every alternating vibration, indeed, only tending to that; free will still free to ply her shuttle between given threads; and chance, though restrained in its play within the right lines of necessity, and sideways in its motion directed by free will, though thus prescribed to both, chance by turns rules either, and had the last featuring blow at events. (213)

Ishmael's sense of equilibrium of the self with nature is a Melvillean application of the Emersonian ideal of interrelatedness: "We can no more halve things and get the sensual good, by itself, than we can get an inside that shall have no outside, or a light without a shadow" (W, II, 105). Of necessity, Melville's "straight warp," Emerson has no illusions. "Life invests itself with inevitable conditions," he says,

> which the unwise seek to dodge, which one and another brags that he does not know, that they do not touch him;—but the brag is on his lips, the conditions are in his soul. (W, II, 105)

These conditions are as severe as Melville's, since both Emerson and Melville have their roots in the Puritan tradition with its notion of the divine predestination of events. Of free will, Melville's shuttle, Emerson's teachings on self-reliance are the obvious source, though Melville has Ishmael perceive this faculty as restricted, in comparison to Emerson's sense of the infinitude of the private man. Of chance, "the last featuring blow at events," Melville does not attempt to explain it; Emerson perceives it as the seemingly random physical evidence of the mysterious divine purpose.

Because Ishmael is able to achieve the "trembling balance" of opposite forces that Emerson advocated, and is a Melvillean equivalent of "the balanced soul," he finds himself at the end of the novel buoyed up by his coffin life raft in a state of harmony with primal forces: "The unharming sharks, they glided as if with padlocks on their mouths; the savage sea-hawks sailed with sheathed beaks." He is picked up by the humanitarian crew of the whaler *Rachel* that "in her retracing search after her missing children only found another orphan" (567).

Ishmael's story of survival, which provides the frame for the narrative, contrasts with the main story, which concerns Ahab's annihilation. This is the second of the five interrelated interests in the novel. The complexity of Ahab's character continues to intrigue readers, who recognize that he is much more than a composite of a variety of sources drawn from Melville's reading and experience. Though he has been described as a Promethean hero, a Yankee Lucifer, an unreformed Jonah, King Lear at sea, and so on, his essential role, which begins and ends on a note of hate, is that of a quester motivated to battle the hidden powers of creation to the death. He would buck a star: "I'd strike the sun if it insulted me," he tells Starbuck, who murmurs, "God keep me!—keep us all" (162). (We can appreciate Melville's discretion in not assigning the Starbuck family name to the role of a God-defying whaling captain.) Ahab's belligerency is in opposition to Emerson's overriding conception of the active soul seeking harmony with the forces that created him. To Emerson, who believed in celestial circuits of energy, a star is for hitching one's wagon.[14]

Ahab's vice that leads to his destruction and that of his ship is egotism, which for Hawthorne is the bosom serpent and cause of Original Sin.[15] For Emerson in 1849, it is the source of ruin for the questing mind because it upsets the balance between man and nature through a dissociation of the inward and outward senses. It is the schism that runs under the world, the crack that Melville, in hearing Emerson lecture, applied to thought divers like Emerson and proceeded to mold into Ahab's character. This egotism is not Emersonian self-reliance, which is in effect God-reliance, comprehending all virtues and committed to inspire and ennoble through creative activities. That is more the role of Ishmael, who finds checks and balances in himself and in nature that keep him afloat.

As Ahab's character unfolds, it undergoes subtle changes that mark stages in withdrawal, disorientation to reality, and ultimate self-delusion. Melville's genius is to endow his tragic hero with a self-contained personality that stands against the primal forces of creation, as he like everyone else aboard the *Pequod* is subject to the law of compensation.

The first direct reference to Ahab in the novel keynotes both the splits in his temperament and his epic stature. Captain Peleg describes him to Ishmael as one neither sick nor well who "keeps close inside the house," a "queer man" but "a good one." These details hint at a psychological disturbance, but Peleg proceeds to describe the skipper in heroic terms: Ahab is "a grand, ungodly, godlike man" who is "above the common." He has "been in colleges, as well as 'mong the cannibals" and "been used to deeper wonders than the waves." He has "fixed his fiery lance in mightier stranger foes than whales" (79). This lance, which Ahab forges himself, defines his angle of vision, since it attaches to the line that ends with his "eye splice" (565).

The dissociation in Ahab's temperament, corresponding to Emerson's concept of cracked nature, is physically represented by his loss of a leg from an earlier encounter with Moby Dick and the lightning-caused scar running like a seam down his body. This dramatic schism is further reflected in the layered view of nature which he sets forth in the quarter-deck scene, as he announces his intention to pursue the white whale. Standing with slouch hat and sullen eye, though Melville also describes him as wearing the crucifixion in his face, Ahab speaks of the evil he perceives behind the apparently benign surfaces of experience:

> "Hark ye yet again,—the little lower layer. All visible objects, man, are but as pasteboard masks. But in each event—in the living act, the undoubted deed—there, some unknown but still unreasoning thing put forth the mouldings of its features from the unreasoning mask." (161)

The irony in the passage is that in Ahab's view it is nature, not he, that is cracked. He would strike through the mask with his lance, or, shifting his metaphor, through the wall of his mortality, to reach what he believes is the "inscrutable malice" behind it (162). That is what he hates, he tells the astonished Starbuck, whose prudence prevents him from effectively responding.

Having presented Ahab's distorted inward view, Melville proceeds to develop it and finally to portray nature, as represented by the white whale, matching it—malice for malice. In the chapter, "Moby Dick," Ahab becomes a tragic hero of epic stature, as the image of the whale swims in his imagination "as the monomaniac incarnation of all those malicious agencies which some deep men feel eating in them, till they are left living on with half a heart and half a lung" (181). With his thought so polarized, Ahab is at this stage enslaved by his hatred that consumes him internally like a fire burning inside a lightning-struck tree.[16] His fixed will does not allow him to hold in mind a compensatory idea about either the whale or nature, such as Ishmael succeeds in doing in his meditations on the whiteness of the whale and on making mats. As a result, Ahab has condemned himself to find in the real white whale only the evil he has heaped on the image in his mind.

As his hatred burns, Ahab assumes a surface calm that he projects like a mask. But occasionally a spark escapes. In "The Doubloon," a meditative chapter that occurs late in the narrative, Ahab sees himself reflected in all nature as he studies the gold coin nailed to the mast. Since in Emerson's words, this fisherman follows fish "because *he* was *fish*," Melville here prepares for the final encounter between Ahab as the white whale and the whale as Ahab. In "The Candles," the fire in Ahab's mind asserts itself to the crew, who regard the phenomenon of St. Elmo's fire that illumines the three masts "God's burning finger" laid on the *Pequod*. Ahab alludes to his having been struck by lightning in worshiping fire and notes "in the sacramental act so burned by thee that to this hour I bear the scar." For this reason, he continues, "I now know thee, thou clear spirit, and I now know that thy right worship is defiance." Acknowledging that "to neither love nor reverence wilt thou be kind," he proceeds to overmatch the stand of the other defiant old man, Father Mapple, who would stand forth "his own inexorable self." But where Mapple preached about obedience to God's will, Ahab declares his own complete self mastery:

No fearless fool now fronts thee. I own thy speechless placeless power; but to the last gasp of my earthquake life will dispute its unconditional, uninte-gral mastery in me. In the midst of the personified impersonal, a personality stands here. Though but a point at best; whencesoe'er I came; wherese'er I go; yet while I earthly live, the queenly personality lives in me, and feels her royal rights. (500)

The significance of this passage to Ahab's character development is that the skipper here rips off the mask to utter what Melville admired in the frantic speeches of King Lear as "the sane madness of vital truth."[17] The truth that Melville presents, however, is that of Ahab's total spiritual isolation and his tragic destiny. Melville embellishes that scene with stage directions calling for repeated flashes of lightning that cause the St. Elmo's fires to leap to three times their height and Ahab to press his hand over his eyes as if blinded.

From this symbolic display of the human ego at war with spiritual forces acting through nature, readers might conclude that Ahab's character is completely drawn as a representation of the will in rebellion. But Melville presents a final stage of Ahab's deterioration, his hero's spiritual annihilation. In "The Symphony," the most willful character in the novel denies that he has any power over himself:

> Is Ahab, Ahab? Is it I, God, or who, that lifts this arm? But if the great sun move not of himself; but by some invisible power; how then can this one small heart beat; this one small brain think thoughts; unless God does that beating, does that thinking, does that living, and not I. By heaven, man, we are turned round and round in this world, like yonder windlass, and Fate is the handspike. (536)

As a man of will turned fatalist, Ahab, who had declared himself a whole person in "The Candles," is split as a personality before he encounters the white whale. In "Mind and Manners in the Nineteenth Century," Emerson characterized the times as divisive: "It is the age of severance, of dissociation, of freedom, of analysis, of detachment" with "every man for himself" (M, 9). His criticism applies to the generality of men: "The new race is stiff, heady, and rebellious. They are fanatics in freedom: they have tolls, taxes, turnpikes, banks, hierarchies, governors, yes, almost all laws" (10). They turn "not to the cheerful world full of work, and the fraternity of a thousand laborers, but inward, and farther inward, to revolve the matter overmuch. Men are sick, ocular, vain, and vagabond" (20). Hearing arguments like these from Emerson in 1849, Melville reacted, embodying them in Ahab, a representative of the mind whose quest leads to self-deception and tragic failure. "Who's to doom,"

Ahab asks Starbuck, "when the judge himself is dragged to the bar" (536)? In Ahab's final act of defiance, he hurls the self-forged lance of his thought at the white whale and becomes strangled in his own line, which is attached to his nemesis. The whale dives, dragging the voiceless skipper out of his whaleboat to the bar.

The third major interest in the novel, that of the *Pequod* shipwreck with the loss of the entire crew except for Ishmael, is interwoven with Ahab's story, since the ship is his kingdom and the crew his hierarchy of "knights," who are the mates, "squires," the harpooners, and "commons," sailors forming "an Anacharsis Clootz deputation from all the isles of the sea, and all the ends of the earth." They are accompanying "Old Ahab in the Pequod to lay the world's grievances before that bar from which not very many of them ever come back" (119).

In developing this part of the plot, Melville departs significantly from the *Essex* narrative, in which all hands successfully abandon ship. It is conceivable that in the early stages of Melville's thinking, he could have envisioned Ishmael escaping with Queequeg or some other companion, for Owen Chase's narrative offers a factual account of how prompt emergency measures aboard the *Essex* saved lives.[18] But dramatic considerations overruled literalness, and no such example of competence occurs aboard the *Pequod* in its moment of truth with the white whale.

Melville portrays the *Pequod* as a symbol of a decadent world that Emerson had described with its stress on ritual, tradition, and customary practices. The crew represents various aspects of the self in isolation in this world. Each man, Melville says, is an "*Isolato* living on a separate continent of his own" (118). Though all are efficient in the various routines of whaling, none are able to transcend their habitual modes of thinking and acting in a transcendent crisis. Their ship, appropriately named after the Pequod Indian tribe that was destroyed in 1637, is "of the old school" with "an old fashioned claw-footed look about her." She is "a thing of trophies," "a Cannibal of a craft" decked out "in the chased bones of her enemies," sperm whales. This exotic vessel has sailed "in typhoons and calms of all four oceans," her hull "darkened like a French grenadier's, who has alike fought in Egypt and Siberia," her masts "cut somewhere on the coast of Japan" and standing "stiffly up like the spines of the three old kings of Cologne," and her decks "worn and wrinkled, like the pilgrim-worshipped flag-stone in Canterbury Cathedral where

Becket bled." Ishmael sees her as "a noble craft, but somehow a most melancholy" and observes, "All noble things are touched with that" (68–69).

The crew has a corresponding nobility and melancholy, befitting a romance of the whaling industry, which at the time Melville was writing was declining. The three mates—Starbuck, Stubb, and Flask—represent the ordinary competencies of ship officers, but they lack the commanding insight that would enable them to break with custom and routine, either to face up to Captain Ahab or to respond effectively to save the ship or their lives. In Emerson's terms, they represent the pitfalls of thought-diving that he pointed out in his lectures—egotism, fatalism, and practicality. None are self-reliant. Their deficiencies show up most clearly in the final encounter between the *Pequod* and Moby Dick.

As the whale attacks the ship, Starbuck, who represents on the surface such values as prudence, orthodoxy, respect for authority, is overcome by fear for himself, a species of egotism that differs sharply from Ahab's assertiveness:

> Oh, all ye sweet powers of air, now hug me close! Let not Starbuck die, if die he must, in a woman's fainting fit. Up helm, I say—ye fools, the jaw! the jaw! Is this the end of all my bursting prayers? all my life-long fidelities? (564)

This surprising faint-hearted speech contrasts also with Mad Jack's self-reliant countermanding of Captain Claret's order during the Cape Horner episode in *White-Jacket*. At bottom, Starbuck's conduct is governed by self-doubt, the need to protect his ego from uncertainties that threaten his existence. His fidelities are to conventional modes of belief and behavior, which, as Emerson repeatedly shows, cannot prepare him for exceptional conditions of living. The jaw that Starbuck sees mirrors his own fear of death.

Though Starbuck has "inward presentiments" that describe a fearful future, Stubb has none. His hedonism covers an underlying fatalism that allows him to take "perils as they come with an indifferent air." His "good-humored, easy, and careless" manner, however social, is for his own comfort. As the whale draws near in its fatal charge, he, too, is unable to save the ship. His comment, "I grin at thee, thou grinning whale," suggests his lack of insight into the nature of the encounter. As a fatalist, he wishes for a mattress stuffed with brushwood for floating and "one red cherry ere we die" (564)! On the other hand, Flask, who sums up practicality, worries about how much money his mother will be left, "for the voyage is up" (ibid.). These self-revealing speeches together comprise an apocalyptic nightmare dramatizing the failures of conventional civilized attitudes that both Emerson and Melville believed would bring to ruin whatever is noble in the human heart.

The primitive harpooners and crewmen, though closer to elemental nature than the mates, are also unable to act in the crisis, since they, too, are creatures of routine. Melville describes how they "hung inactive; hammers, bits of plank, lances, and harpoons, mechanically retained in their hands" as they turned "all enchanted eyes intent upon the whale" (564). The harpooners in the rigging were still looking for whales: "Like dislodged trucks, the heads of the harpooneers aloft shook on their bull-like necks" (565).

Despite their general inability to think for themselves, Melville gives them noble attributes: Queequeg represents essential human nature as one of nature's noblemen; Daggoo, a huge black, embodies physical strength; Tashtego, the Indian, primitive spirituality; and Ahab's personal harpooner, Fedallah (his name suggests faithful to Allah), the essential mystery of the primitive. With his white hair wrapped in a turban like Mohammed's, he is nonetheless a Parsee, or Zoroastrian priest, who had functioned as Ahab's religious counselor. The richness and suggestiveness of Melville's details even in representing minor characters such as these serve to magnify the tragedy as a comprehensive portrait of the human condition.

The actual sinking of the *Pequod* coincides with Ahab's death moment. As in the *Essex* narrative, the whale rams the vessel and runs "quivering along its keel." Then turning under water, it appears "far off the other bow, but within a few yards of Ahab's boat, where, for a time, he lay quiescent" (565). When Ahab hurls his lance, the tranced crew in his boat see both the skipper and ship disappear. To them, the *Pequod* is a "fading phantom, as in the gaseous Fata Morgana; only the uppermost masts out of water." Melville then describes "concentric circles" that seize "the lone boat itself, and all its crew, and each floating oar, and every lance-pole, and spinning, animate and inanimate, all round and round in one vortex, carried the smallest chip of the *Pequod* out of sight" (566). Characteristically, Tashtego at the top of the mainmast is nailing Ahab's flag, the emblem of his kingdom, to the spar as his head goes underwater. His hammer fastens a skyhawk to the mast, as an emblem of the shipwreck of the soul:

> so the bird of heaven, with archangelic shrieks, and his imperial beak thrust upward, and his whole captive form folded in the flag of Ahab, went down with his ship, which, like Satan, would not sink to hell till she had dragged a living part of heaven along with her, and helmeted herself with it. (566)

The consistent symmetry of design expressing the duality of spiritual aspiration and mortal limitations reflected through the entire narrative, but brought into sharpest focus in this concluding image, suggests the influence of Hawthorne, to whom Melville inscribed the novel in "admiration or his genius." Then, too, the comprehensiveness of Melville's vision, with its ordering principle of compensatory forces uniting external nature with the human mind in an almost perfect match, derives from Melville's appreciation of Emerson's insights, especially those that were current at the time he was writing. But the extraordinary richness of texture, with every detail of visible reality having significance as part of a massive symbolic drama, is the sine qua non of Melville's creativity, amply demonstrated in these three story interests.

Emerson's concept of the each as related to the all, or, as he put it in 1849, the idea that reels off the world like a ball of yarn, offers a useful perspective on the fourth and fifth interests in *Moby-Dick*—the white whale and the inserted chapters on whaling, including the meeting of the *Pequod* with nine whaleships. So far, we have observed that in the whale, Melville sums up these forces in nature that define individual perspective. But it is apparent that no one in the novel, not even Ishmael, fully comprehends Moby Dick, which at the end is as much "the ungraspable phantom of life" as is the image in the water he describes in the beginning. The whiteness of the whale, for example, transcends Ishmael's meditation on its beauty and terror. Reflecting all color in the spectrum, white suggests nature in its totality, including human nature. The color is represented in the whale-bone fittings on the *Pequod*, in Ahab's livid scar and the artificial leg of whale-bone that set off his bronzed complexion, in dark Fedallah's turban of white braided hair resembling a second moon when he is aloft at night searching for the whale. It is in the waves shining in the calm moonlit sea like silver scrolls, in the white fire of stormy waters at the time of the first lowering, in the mysterious lightness of the squid, in the pallid glow of St. Elmo's fire that illuminates the masts, in the sun that brightens the sea during the climactic days of struggle with the whale, and finally in the creamy pool of foam that marks where the *Pequod* sinks.

The color had attractions for Melville from the beginning of his writing career, but in the early novels its significance is limited. White in *Typee*, for example, is characteristic of the natives' thatched huts and of the sacred tappa cloth which Fayaway wears. In *Mardi*, Taji is accompanied by the blond Viking Jarl, but later is haunted by the image of the fair-haired Yillah. In *Redburn* with its allusions to Carlylean clothes philosophy, the evil Jackson wears a white hat; and in *White-Jacket*, the narrator's self-made white garment absorbs weather like a sponge in the beginning and almost becomes a shroud at the end.

In *Moby-Dick*, this pervasive color becomes a unifying force, suggesting the omnipresence of the white whale, though it appears to Ahab and his crew only in the last three chapters. Until then, it exists as images in the minds of characters, not only aboard the *Pequod*, but also on the whalers she meets. One after another, in responding to Ahab's probing questions about the whale, the sailors of all levels of humanity indicate their limited angles of vision toward nature. It is really Ahab's deranged cabin boy Pip, who speaks the sane madness of vital truth about the meaning of the whale, and the problem of human perception, as he runs about the deck at the end of the chapter "The Doubloon" saying, "I look, you look, he looks; we look, ye look, they look" (432). The whale is Melville's "each" that is related to the "all," and embodies the all—physical, moral, and spiritual. When it finally appears and acts on its own, first by swimming away from its persistent attackers, then by turning when provoked and destroying them, it plays the dramatic role of nemesis. In its totality, however, the whale is best comprehended in terms of Emerson's sense of nature, or any item in nature, as "a chamber lined with mirrors" in which "the image of man comes throbbing back to us" (II, A, 2).

Melville's description of the whale's "predestinating head" as it rushes with malice toward the *Pequod* suggests a Calvinistic idea that he shared with Hawthorne and that is a part of the meaning of the final attack.[19] But if Hawthorne had any single piece of advice to offer Melville in writing his first novel with a preconceived dramatic climax, it probably would be that every event must prepare for the big moment. Each occurrence must seem to the reader as though it were predestined to occur. In *Moby-Dick*, the whale's destruction of the *Pequod* and the events leading up to it have the quality of inevitability, starting in the first chapter with Ishmael's determination that his decision to go to sea is part of "the grand programme of Providence that was drawn up a long time ago" (5).

The fifth and concluding interest contributing to the shape of the novel consists of the digressions. The chapters on the lore of whaling function like the wake of the white whale, providing insights and information that enhance the image of Melville's central symbol for nature; the nine gams of the *Pequod* are like islands along the way, as in *Mardi*, each with a separate story offering a perspective on nature, ranging from ignorance or indifference to partial knowledge. But whatever Melville says of whaling in explanatory essays halting the main action or through dramatic interludes, the effect is to suggest an aspect of the whole, including its ultimate mystery, in the part. "At the outset," he writes in "Cetology," "it is but well to attend to a matter almost indispensable to a thorough appreciative understanding of the more special leviathanic revelations and allusions of all sorts which are to follow" (129). Each aspect of whaling, each part of the whale's body, adds a dimension to the story. In "The Sphynx," for example, Ahab meditates on the "black and hooded head" that hangs "in the midst of so intense a calm, it seemed the Sphinx's in the desert" and ironically discloses his own dark vision. "O head!" he says, "thou has seen enough to split the planets and make an infidel of Abraham, and not one syllable is thine" (310)! In "The Tail," Melville points out that the trunk tapers "to about the girth of a man" and then describes the beauty and power inherent in its structure, suggesting the role of the whale in the novel, a tale that also encompasses man.

The episodes of the gams serve not only to offer clues in Ahab's search for Moby Dick and suspense-building warnings about its outcome, but also to show the stages in Ahab's separation from the world outside the *Pequod*. In the meeting with the phantom-like *Albatross*, the first ship encountered, the "strange captain, leaning over the pallid bulwarks" drops his speaking trumpet into the sea and is unable to reply to Ahab's inevitable question, "Have ye seen the White Whale?" Though the *Pequod* manages to communicate with the other ships, none give Ahab an answer that satisfies him. He does not hear the *Town Ho's* story of the white whale administering divine justice by destroying the evil mate Radney; he shows no interest in encounters with three ships that have no knowledge of Moby Dick; and he rejects advice and pleas for assistance from the other ships that suffered losses in encounters with this unbeatable adversary.

Through the gams, as most readers know, Melville satirizes attitudes associated with religion, philosophy, and European civilization; but his focus always is on whales. The last meeting with the ironically named *Delight*, a battered ship which is burying its dead at sea after an encounter with Moby Dick, offers a tragic vision that Ahab looks at but does not see. To his question comes this response:

> "Look!" replied the hollow-cheeked captain from his taffrail; and with his trumpet he pointed to the wreck. (531)

Uncomprehending, Ahab orders the *Pequod* to continue toward its own rendezvous.

The gams and interpolated essays on whaling interlocking with one another and with the other parts of the novel provide a gigantic illustration of Emerson's idea, that a work of art is "an abstract or epitome of the world" (W, I, 23). This view often expressed in Emerson's essays, reiterated in "Mind and Manners in the Nineteenth Century," is part of Emerson's commanding insight into the compensatory tension uniting all images and ideas. Though Emerson's view of God as "the all-fair" creator of everything contrasts with Melville's tragic vision with its implied doubt, it is Emerson's stimulus more than any other outside influence that gives *Moby-Dick* its cosmic scope. As Emerson said, art represents the whole of nature "passed through the alembic of man" (24). In Melville's masterpiece, the idea comes to life.

CHAPTER 8

THE LONG DARDENELLES:
MELVILLE'S LATER FICTION

1. *Attack on the Sentimental Novel:* Pierre

Creative connections among artists—whether overt or covert, formal or informal, reciprocal or one-sided—tend to be transitional, even though their impact on art may have great significance. With few exceptions, as in the enduring relation of Emerson and Carlyle, these fragile associations or affinities quickly build and may just as quickly dissolve, so that the "partners in the labor of thought" one day may become opponents the next. With Melville, the evidence in letters, reviews, and especially his novels following *Moby-Dick* points to a loss of rapport with Hawthorne that contributed to a rebellion against the literary establishment then dominated by Emerson.

Certainly Melville's talent alone was not sufficient to account for the shape and texture of *Moby-Dick*. As we have seen, responsiveness had been an important contributor to his achievement. But his reliance on his own instinct and experience would give him freedom to change course and to seek new methods of expression. "Leviathan is not the biggest fish," he wrote to Hawthorne after completing *Moby-Dick*. "I have heard of Krakens" (L, 143).

With *Moby-Dick*, Melville had hoped to gain economic security, to delight readers by challenging them to think and to feel, and to acquire a reputation befitting his awareness of his own great talent. Because his expectations were high, the moderate success of this work, as compared to, say, the popularity of Hawthorne's sentimental novel, *The House of the Seven Gables*, came as a disappointment. Though some reviewers, like the Transcendentalist George Ripley, praised Melville's artistry, most of them responded with mixed approval and disapproval.[1] Even Evert Duyckinck, who had lauded *Mardi*, was sharply critical about portions of the new book. "The intense Captain Ahab is too long drawn out," he said. "If we had as much of Hamlet or Macbeth as Mr. Melville gives us of Ahab, we should be tired even of their sublime company" (Log, I, 437). He qualifies his criticism, however, by noting that "Ahab is a striking conception, firmly planted on the wild deck of the *Pequod*—a dark disturbed soul arraying itself with every ingenuity of material resources for a conflict at once natural and supernatural in his eye" (437). He sees the whale as "the most dangerous extant physical monster of the earth, embodying, in strongly drawn lines of mental association, the vaster moral evil of the world" (ibid.). But his objections ironically extend to the influence of Emerson:

> This piratical running down of creeds and opinions, the conceited indifferentism of Emerson, or the run-a-muck style of Carlyle is, we will not say dangerous in such cases, for there are various forces at work to meet more powerful onslaught, but is out of place and uncomfortable. We do not like to see what under my view, must be to the world the most sacred associations of life violated and defaced . . . (437)

This slap from an influential friend Melville might have borne philosophically if the book had sold well. But sensing from such criticism that it was not destined to be a financial success, and worried about the slow recovery of Elizabeth following the birth of the couple's second child, Stanwix, on October 22, 1851, he plunged with some resentment into writing his seventh novel, *Pierre; or, the Ambiguities*. He completed it in approximately five months, as compared to the year and a half he had spent working on *Moby-Dick*. "Yet he must go on writing," his granddaughter, Eleanor Metcalf, comments, "Where else will bread and butter come from" (135)?

To complicate matters, on November 21 the Hawthornes moved away from "the Red House" in Lenox, suddenly, it appears, since there is no reference to such a move in Melville's letter to Hawthorne on November 17. This letter, which is effusively laudatory, is phrased in Transcendental references to immortality and even the *One*, which Melville describes as the unity of his and Hawthorne's genius. In a hyperbolic postscript, Melville writes:

> If the world was entirely made up of Magians, I'll tell you what I should do. I should have a paper-mill established at one end of the house, and so have an endless riband of foolscap rolling in upon my desk; and upon that endless riband I should write a thousand—a million—billion thoughts, all in the form of a letter to you. (L, 143–144)

Whatever Hawthorne's motive for moving—Randall Stewart among others cites his dislike of the climate, the inconveniences of the house, which was rented, and his desire to rejoin his Concord friends—Melville's reaction to the move was one of correct politeness and detachment, covering disappointment over a severed relationship.[2] After the letter of November 17, Melville apparently did not write again directly to Hawthorne for eight months. In his next known communication on July 17, 1852, approximately three months after completing *Pierre*, Melville acknowledged receipt of Hawthorne's new novel, *The Blithedale Romance*, and turned down an invitation to visit Hawthorne in Concord. Beneath the formal courtesy, there is a hint of the bittersweet:

> Said my lady-wife, "there is Mr. Hawthorne's new book, come by mail." And this morning, lo! on my table a little note, subscribed by Hawthorne again.— Well, the Hawthorne is a sweet flower; may it flourish in every hedge.
>
> I am sorry, but I can not at present come to see you at Concord as you propose.—I am but just returned from a two weeks' absence; and for the last three months and more I have been an utter idler and a savage—out of doors all the time. So, the hour has come for me to sit down again. (L, 152–153)

Actually, it was Sophia Hawthorne who first wrote to Melville one month after the Hawthorne's moved from Lenox. In her letter to Melville dated December 29, 1851, she praised *Moby-Dick*. Melville's reply to her on January 8, 1852, was cordial, but surprisingly fatalistic, in contrast to his earlier reference to the Transcendental *One*. Though he admitted that his novel was "susceptible of an allegoric construction" which Hawthorne apparently had recognized, Melville denied that he had meant to spiritualize nature (L, 146). "We can't help ourselves," he says, in an apparent defense of his tendency to heap praise on Hawthorne. "Life is a long Dardenelles, My Dear Madam," he concludes:

> the shores whereof are bright with flowers, which we want to pluck, but the bank is too high; and so we float on and on, hoping to come to a landing place at last—but swoop! we launch into the great sea! Yet the geographers say, even then we must not despair, because across the great sea, however desolate and vacant it may look, lie all Persia and the delicious lands roundabout Damascus.
> So wishing you a pleasant voyage at last to that sweet and far countree— (L, 147)

Except for the complimentary wish at the end, perhaps a belated farewell to his departed friends, Melville's letter suggests both his disappointment over the separation and disillusionment with the New England literary establishment—the bank is too high for him to reach. But the reference to finding Persia offers a hint at his own literary aspirations.

In *Pierre*, Melville's rebellion against custom, which characterizes all of his fiction to date, extends to include the conventions of the sentimental romance, especially as exemplified by *The House of the Seven Gables*. For its unrelieved pessimism, *Pierre* stands in relation to *Moby-Dick* almost as Mark Twain's "The Mysterious Stranger" to *Huckleberry Finn*. Though in recent years critical readers have come to appreciate the new novel as being much more than a "prodigious by-blow of genius," as Henry A. Murray had described it, its effect does have an important overlooked source in its parody of Hawthorne's novel.[3]

Pierre, stripped of its copious autobiographical references to the febrile struggles of an immature author, amounts to an ironic inversion of the structure of *The House of the Seven Gables*. Where the affairs of the leading actors, a young artist and a Transcendental heroine whose name in each book means light, move from darkness to light in Hawthorne's narrative, they progress from light to darkness in Melville's. Both novels turn on the identical theme of the sins of the fathers, Original Sin represented in terms of its effects on the present. Hawthorne's statement in the preface to *The House of the Seven Gables* suggests the thematic axis of both works: "the wrong-doing of one generation lives into the successive ones, and, divesting itself of every temporary advantage, becomes a pure and uncontrollable mischief."[4] But where Hawthorne dramatizes the power of self-reliance and love in overcoming the evils of tradition, Melville presents the insufficiency of these ideal virtues in an ambiguous contest with fate.

Melville's interest in *The House of the Seven Gables* dates from his letter to Hawthorne on April 16, 1851, praising its "braided scenes from tragedies" (L, 124). Though most readers have noted Hawthorne's humor and geniality that are part of the total effect of his novel, Melville focuses on Hawthorne's ability to say "NO! in thunder," a tendency that would better serve as a description of *Pierre*. In Melville's novel, the wrong-doing of the past is the sin of Pierre's father, whose supposed illegitimate daughter, Isabel, suddenly disrupts the youthful artist's Platonic and exaggeratedly sentimental romance with his fiancee, Lucy, in the Eden-like setting of Saddle Meadows. Acting on impulse alone, Pierre breaks off the relationship with Lucy to shelter Isabel, whom he accepts as his half sister. The parody develops as Pierre and Isabel move from the country into a bizarre Melvillean equivalent of the House of the Seven Gables. It is a seven-storied office and apartment building constructed in the yard of the former Church of the Apostles. Melville mimics Hawthorne's style in describing the setting. Like the Pyncheon home, which Hawthorne portrays as a "weatherbeaten edifice," an emblem of the past standing "half-way down a by-street" of a New England town, the Apostles complex is "a rather singular and ancient edifice, a relic of the more primitive time," situated "in the lower old-fashioned part of the city, in a narrow street—almost a lane—once filled with demure looking dwellings."[5] In contrast to the quaintness of Hawthorne's structure, with "an elm tree of wide circumference" near the door is the drabness of the Apostles, surrounded by the "immense lofty warehouses" of an "encroaching city."[6]

Into these relics of tradition come the Transcendental heroines motivated by their idealism. In Hawthorne's novel, Phoebe's sudden arrival at the old Pyncheon home is a victory for the powers of light and maidenly charm:

> What was precisely Phoebe's process we find it impossible to say. She appeared to have no preliminary design, but gave a touch here and another there; brought some articles of furniture to light and dragged others into the shadow; looped up or let down a window-curtain; and, in the course of half an hour, had fully succeeded in throwing a kindly and hospitable smile over the apartment.[7]

"You will find me a cheerful little body," she tells her elderly relative, Hepzibah, who would have her return to the country. "Ah! Phoebe," Hepzibah sighs, "your knowledge would do but little for you here! And then it is a wretched thought that you should fling away your young days in a place like this" (97). But Phoebe and the genteel conventions of the sentimental novel prevail. In staying, she makes herself invaluable caring for the feeble Clifford, Hepzibah's brother, and wins the love of Holgrave, a daguerreotypist who lives at the house. Through her marriage to the young man, the evil of tradition is expiated, since he turns out to be descended from the rightful owner of the old mansion.

In Melville's novel, by contrast, Lucy's arrival at the Apostles is disastrous. Her intuitional knowledge does little for her, and she flings herself away in attempting to be a live-in servant for Pierre and Isabel, who she mistakenly believes are married. Like Phoebe, Lucy would play the role of country cousin. In a letter, she informs Pierre to prepare a nook for "thy resolved and immovable nun-like cousin, vowed to dwell with thee forever; to serve thee and her, to guard thee and her without end" (366).

Lucy's actual arrival is announced with her cry for help. Pierre rushes from his apartment to the hall and finds her struggling to meet him, "clinging to the baluster" as two young men "were vainly seeking to remove the two thin white hands without hurting them" (382). Pierre rescues her from her brother and suitor, who want to take her back to the country; but in Melville's novel the Platonic motives of the hero and heroine lead to tragic ends: Lucy dies of grief; Pierre kills her suitor, and Pierre and Isabel take their own lives in prison. This is the outcome of Melville's narrative that begins where Hawthorne's ends, in a great mansion in a beautiful country setting.

One target of Melville's strange drama, in which nothing turns out right for the main characters, is the falsification of life depicted in the sentimental novel, in which heroes and heroines and even their relatives relate to one another as brothers and sisters and after much tribulation live happily ever after. Two years later in *Walden*, Thoreau would ridicule such provender, as he called it, saying of the tastes of readers:

> They read the nine thousandth tale about Zebulon and Sephronia, and how they loved as none had ever loved before, and neither did the course of their true love run smooth,—at any rate how it did run and stumble, and get up again and go on! (105)

Hawthorne, of course, elevated the form; Melville sought to demolish it.

If Melville's responsiveness led him to give a reverse twist to conventional story elements found in *The House of the Seven Gables*, his desire to be innovative led to what critics have described as the "flawed grandeur" of *Pierre*.[8] Even though Emersonian optimism is the antithesis of the view that Melville dramatizes, his spectacle of human disaster derives in part from ideas that he assimilated from Emerson. Like the *Pequod*, the Apostles is a microcosm of the world, the whole in the part, but also a setting in which characters test their fictional values. Pierre himself, as Murray has suggested, is a combination of hero types drawn from fiction and tradition, including Oedipus, Romeo, Hamlet, Memnon, Orestes, Timon, Manfred, Cain, Christ, Satan, and Melville's own Ishmael.[9] He transcends parody as a composite portrait of a fallen angel. The conditions of life Pierre finds at the Apostles reflect the Emersonian crack in nature, which Melville presents in terms of individual characteristics, interpersonal relations, and philosophical argument. On the surface, Pierre's two romantic interests, Lucy and Isabel, dramatize the polarities of spirit and flesh, innocence and guilt, frailty and strength—traditional oppositions set forth in sentimental novels. On a deeper level, Isabel, to whom Pierre turns, is both half-sister and half-lover in his mind, since he would protect her reputation by the extreme measure of posing with her as man and wife, but he soon becomes attracted by her charms. Ultimately, Pierre finds it impossible to reconcile the spiritual and sensual drives in his own nature.

The idea of cracked nature, however, has its most memorable representation in the character of Plotinus Plinlimmon, a resident in the old church tower and Grand Master of the Mystic Society of the Apostles. He is a satiric portrait of the intellectual establishment, embodying features of both Hawthorne and Emerson. Plinlimmon, like Hawthorne, is a detached observer, sheltered from reality by the window glass through which he constantly watches the other occupants of the Apostles complex.[10] He is both cheerful and unapproachable. But like Emerson, he has a reputation of being a successful lecturer with an enthusiastic following. His lecture, "Chronometricals and Horologicals," a portion of which Pierre reads during his journey from the country to the city with Isabel, is antithetical to Emerson's lectures in the Boston series that Melville heard with their persistent emphasis on the unity underlying the schism in nature. It also clashes with Father Mapple's sermon celebrating the delight of the faithful in *Moby-Dick*. In essence, Plinlimmon reasons by false analogy that ideal virtue, like Greenwich time, is unsuited to the rest of the world, which must abide by the practical conditions of experience, represented by local time. "Bacon's brains," he says, "were mere watch-maker's brains; but Christ was a chronometer" (248).

Plinlimmon develops his chronometrical and horological analogy, which should be read tongue-in-cheek, to prove

> that in things terrestrial (horological) a man must not be governed by ideas celestial (chronometrical); that certain minor self-renunciations in this life his own mere instinct for his own every-day general well-being will teach him to make, but he must by no means make a complete unconditional sacrifice of himself in behalf of any other being, or any cause or any conceit. (251)

Since the argument is itself a conceit, Plinlimmon has built into it a total disclaimer. What Pierre reads is a torn copy ending on the words, "Moreover: if—" that suggests the ambiguous nature of the message that renounces the idealistic foundation of sentimental fiction.

Melville portrays the optimistic Plinlimmon as dehumanized by his philosophy of splitting off Transcendental notions from everyday practicalities:

> The whole countenance of this man, the whole air and look of this man, expressed a cheerful content. Cheerful is the adjective, for it was the contrary of gloom; content—perhaps acquiescence—is the substantive, for it was not Happiness or Delight. But while the personal look and air of this man were thus winning, there was still something latently visible in him which repelled. That something may best be characterized as non-Benevolence. Non-Benevolence seems the best word, for it was neither Malice nor Ill-will; but something passive. (341)

Such passivity and cheery non-benevolence are probably the traits Melville felt best represented the unapproachable and unmovable establishment he was rebelling against in *Pierre*.

Beyond the motive of satire and at the deepest level of significance lies Melville's repudiation of the idea of compensation, which Emerson perceived as the means for mending the crack in nature and keeping the polarities of mind and experience in delicate balance. In *Pierre*, Melville replaces this governing principle, in which the self becomes identified with nature, with the notion of the self as cipher, an insoluble puzzle that no angle of vision is capable of penetrating, certainly not Plinlimmon's, which has no provision for either love or hate in a lifestyle governed wholly by expediency and practicality. The chief cipher in this novel of human enigmas is Pierre himself. His exhaustive probing of motives and his behavior based on imperfect perceptions of the outer world lead to the melodramatic death scene and his epitaph, gasped by the dying Isabel: "All's oer, and ye know him not" (427). This is Melville's answer not only to the smug certainties of sentimental fiction, but also to the whole issue of individual identity. Whatever the defects of *Pierre*, its nobility lies in its complexity.

2. *The Experimental Muse: "Bartleby" to* The Confidence-Man

After *Pierre*, Melville may be described as a writer detached from the creative community of New England intellectuals that provided him with ideas, as well as from the reading public. Critics having rejected his novel as outrageous and incomprehensible, he set about experimenting with different kinds of subject matter and literary forms in an attempt to keep his career alive.[11] From 1853 to 1857, his remaining years as a professional writer of fiction, he composed two novels and fifteen short stories, which include some of his most innovative work, though he made very little money from it. In this phase, Emersonian ideas occasionally are central to the narrative, as in the ethical criticism of slavery in "Benito Cereno," which corresponds to arguments Emerson makes in his address on "The Fugitive Slave Law" in New York City. But more obvious, at least to readers in our day, is the parody of Emersonian self-reliance in "Bartleby, the Scrivener" and the caricature of Emerson himself in *The Confidence-Man*.

Among Melville's works during this period, the image that best suggests his sense of isolation is conveyed in the short story "I and My Chimney," published in 1856. The chimney at Arrowhead, his farmhouse in Pittsfield, is the symbol of his creative imagination. A huge, smoky, stone structure taking up the center of the house, it is much in the way; and the wife, as represented in this story, would have it removed. To the charge that the chimney is so heavy that it is settling, the embattled narrator responds:

I, too, am settling, you know, in my gait. I and my chimney are settling together, and shall keep settling, too, till as in a great feather-bed, we shall both have settled away clean out of sight.[12]

· If Melville felt his career were sinking—like an overweight chimney, if not a ship—he was determined to go down with it in grand style. His subjects, even in short stories, are comprehensive in their view of the human condition. From the world apartment building in *Pierre*, he moves to a world office on Wall Street in "Bartleby, the Scrivener" with its skylight, its window that faces a wall, and its partition separating the employer from his workers. In this suggestive setting, Melville examines once again the problem of the individual in a compartmentalized society. This, too, was a continuing concern into the 1850's for Emerson and also Thoreau in *Walden*. But in Melville's story, Bartleby, the only character identified by name, represents the Emersonian idea of self-reliance carried to an intolerable extreme. For not only would he "prefer not to" perform the routines of his scrivener's job, as his debased, nicknamed co-workers Turkey and Nippers do, but he also would prefer not to participate in the other routines necessary to living, including eating. He would be totally independent. Where Emerson's "man diver" is an activist, Bartleby is a motionless young man. His compassionate employer, the narrator, tries to compensate for Bartleby's individualism, even to the extent of moving out of the office when Bartleby refuses to leave; but in the end Bartleby wastes away and dies, though the business continues. There is more to this many-faceted story, but it is essentially an ironic counterpoint to the Emersonian notion of the unlimited power of instinct.[13]

The evidence in Melville's *The Piazza Tales*, a collection of stories published in 1856, indicates not so much his rejection of Emerson's ideas as his ability to play with them, as if to test their artistic potential. For in contrast to the ironic challenge to Emersonian self-reliance in "Bartleby", "The Lightning Rod Man" takes a defiant stand in favor of it. Here the narrator rejects the intimidating pitch of the lightning rod salesman, who travels in storm time selling his wares. "Your rod rusts, or breaks," the narrator says to the peddler,

and where are you? Who has empowered you, you Tetzel, to peddle round your indulgences from divine ordinations? The hairs of our heads are numbered, and the days of our lives. In thunder as in sunshine, I stand at ease in the hands of my God. False negotiator, away! (124)

Emerson would have agreed with this stance that illustrates what he must have meant in an early description of Transcendentalism as the "Saturnalia or excess of Faith" (W, I, 338).

Of all Melville's short stories, however, the one that most clearly indicates a timely reaction to a challenging Emersonian idea is "Benito Cereno," which first appeared in *Putnam's Monthly Magazine* for October, November, and December, 1855. Captain Delano's inability to comprehend the degradation of slavery in contrast to Benito Cereno's tragic awareness of what it means to be a slave has a striking parallel in Emerson's address, "The Fugitive Slave Law," delivered at the tabernacle in New York City, March 4, 1854.[14] In a vigorous, well-publicized attack on Daniel Webster for backing the Law, Emerson points out the difference between innocence and experience in relation to the evil of slavery:

> I have lived all my life without suffering any known inconveniences from American Slavery. I never saw it; I never heard the whip; I never felt the check on my free speech and action, until, the other day, when Mr. Webster, by his personal influence, brought the Fugitive Slave Law on the country. (W, XI, 219)

It is essentially this difference which separates Delano, skipper of a trading ship from Massachusetts, from Cereno, Spanish captain of a slave ship captured by slaves, though he retains his symbols of authority. Of the malignant principle in slavery that enslaves the masters, Emerson observes:

> The new Bill made it operative, required me to hunt slaves, and it found citizens in Massachusetts willing to act as judges and captors. Moreover, it discloses the secret of the new times, that Slavery was no longer mendicant, but has become aggressive and dangerous. (W, XI, 228–229)

Melville, too, would be interested in the secret of the new times.

Emerson's awareness of evil, which motivated him to participate in the abolitionist movement during the 1850's, is implicit in his notion of compensation, which permeates his writings. In this speech, he points to the danger of slavery in terms of this principle:

> A man who commits a crime defeats the end of his existence. He was created for benefit, and he exists for harm; and as well-doing makes power and wisdom, ill-doing takes them away. A man who steals another man's labor steals away his own faculties; his integrity, his humanity is flowing away from

him. The habit of oppression cuts out the moral eyes, and, though the intellect goes on stimulating the moral as before, its sanity is gradually destroyed. (W, XI, 237)

In this passage is the master design of Cereno's failure and its consequence. The Spanish captain, his integrity compromised through participation in the slave trade, meets his nemesis in Babo, the ringleader of the slaves, who becomes his master. Though Cereno is rescued by Captain Delano, Cereno dies as a result of a self-consuming vision of evil:

> "You are saved," cried Captain Delano, more and more astonished and pained; "you are saved: what has cast such a shadow upon you?"
> "The negro."
> There was silence, while the moody man sat, slowly and unconsciously gathering his mantle about him, as if it were a pall. (In *The Piazza Tales*, 116)

Through this ironic exchange Melville gives dramatic form to a timely Emersonian idea.

As in his other writings of this era, Melville expands the scope of his narrative to suggest the underlying relation of idealism to experience in an evil world. The main action occurs aboard the slaver *San Dominick*, which represents both the particular timely evil of slavery and the general evils of tradition and conformity. The enslaved Cereno, debased by his experience, is forced into total conformity, with the trappings of rank and privilege that he retains serving the purposes of his captors. Babo, on the surface his slave but truly his master, represents that element of diabolism that Melville saw in evil institutions, and that Emerson pointed out in his reference to the mendacity of slavery. On the other hand, the victorious Delano, who does not comprehend the evil he has not experienced, is self-reliant, naive, and outgoing. Though he is emotionally blind even at the end, he alone is untouched, as though his instinct were a sufficient shield for the evil of the world.

Despite the harmony between Melville's drama and Emerson's argument in "The Fugitive Slave Law," the story did not win back the enthusiastic following of readers who had enjoyed the romantic escapades of Tommo nearly ten years earlier in *Typee*. Melville's collection of stories, *The Piazza Tales*, received brief critical reviews, some of them favorable, but nothing to stir the public imagination.

Two novels he wrote during these years are in part responses to growing public indifference. *Israel Potter: His Fifty Years of Exile* (1855) is a plotless historical novel based on an anonymous life of the title character published in 1824. The book calls attention to the plight of a Revolutionary War hero and exile who was refused a pension in his old age "by certain caprices of law" and died in poverty. At the end of his fifty years of exile, the old veteran returns home an outcast in a changed society, but unlike Washington Irving's Rip Van Winkle, no one recognizes him or takes him in. As Melville concludes, "His scars proved his only medals" (169). The bitterness under the surface in this story would appear to have little to do with Emerson and much to do with Melville's own estimate of an unappreciative society. Even so, his attack on the literary establishment that began with *Pierre* expands in this novel with the insertion of a gallery of satiric portraits of historical figures, including George III, Benjamin Franklin, John Paul Jones, and Ethan Allen that affords the opportunity for mild ridicule. This work, which was initially published serially in *Putnam's Monthly* magazine before it appeared in book form in 1855, received generally favorable reviews, but it also failed to win back the reading audience he had offended in *Pierre*.

In *The Confidence-Man: His Masquerade* (1857), Melville's targets Emerson and his values, but not his concept of art as an abstract or epitome of the world. This work, the last fiction that Melville had published during his lifetime, may be described as a *Titanic* of a novel which presents a comprehensive criticism of the optimism of the mid-1850's. Its setting, the ironically named Mississippi steamboat *Fidèle*, is yet another world ship, appropriately white-washed as though to cover up the flaws in society. In effect, it carries the public that had ignored him through shallow muddy waters from St. Louis, a bustling trading center, to New Orleans, renowned in those days for its slave market.

The idea of a natural aristocracy that Melville assimilated probably from Emerson's 1849 lectures in Boston becomes the essential principle of structure, but in reverse. Melville presents an unnatural hierarchy of deceitful humanity, ranging from a mysterious Scripture-inscribing deaf mute who boards the *Fidèle* on April Fool's Day to Frank Goodman, the Cosmopolitan, the author's version of Mr. Worldly Wiseman. All of the passengers are alike in their promotion of confidence schemes based on false hope, misdirected or denied trust, and the total absence of charity, although the word dominates the book from the first chapter.

Melville's most experimental work of fiction is not a novel in the usual sense. It has no plot building to a dramatic crisis; its characters appear in an interlocking sequence that suggests they are avatars of one confidence man, who is most likely the Cosmopolitan. He stands as the antithesis of Emerson's ideal man who is dedicated to questing for nature's inner truth. He and the other passengers aboard the *Fidèle*, whom Melville playfully likens to Canterbury pilgrims, are hunters of a different sort:

> Natives of all sorts, and foreigners; men of business and men of pleasure; parlor men and backwoodsmen; farm-hunters; heiress-hunters, gold-hunters, buffalo-hunters, bee-hunters, happiness-hunters, truth-hunters, and still keener hunters after all these hunters. (13)

They represent the varied faces of humanity, lacking heart. Modern readers acquainted with the writings of Joseph Campbell can view Melville's design as an inversion of the mythic vision of the hero with a thousand faces.

Both Emerson's idea of one man and Melville's counterpoint of one confidence man have a source in St. Paul's First Epistle to the Corinthians, from which the deaf mute derives his Scriptural passages. In Chapter 12 of Paul's letter, the apostle argues by analogy that the different parts of the body of the Church represent different spiritual gifts, each contributing to the whole, which represents Christ. "If the whole body were an eye," he asks, "where were the hearing? If the whole were hearing, where were the smelling" (verse 17)? With Emerson, in "The American Scholar," the various faculties, skills, and occupations coalesce, so that "you must take the whole society to find the whole man" (W, I, 82).

Melville's idea is more directly related to Paul's teaching than to Emerson's, for Paul denies the validity of any gift that is not motivated by charity. In fact, the theme of Melville's novel is suggested in Paul's admonition to the Corinthians in the opening verse of Chapter 13:

> Though I speak with the tongues of men and of angels, and have not charity, I am become as sounding brass, or a tinkling cymbal.

Melville begins with the description of a deaf mute scribbling passages on charity from this chapter on a placard while the passengers ignore him and his message, as the *Fidèle* starts its journey. The novel proceeds to report for its entire length on the conversations of men, if not angels, as the sounding brass and tinkling cymbals of deceit.

In developing his theme, Melville turns to Paul's description of the worthlessness of any gift not imbued with love:

> And though I have the gift of prophecy (i.e., preaching), and understand all mysteries, and all knowledge; and though I have all faith, so that I could remove mountains, and have not charity, I am nothing. And though I bestow all my goods to feed the poor, and though I give my body to be burned, and have not charity, it profiteth me nothing. (1 Cor. 13.2–3)

These valueless gifts correspond to several avatars of the confidence man—preachers, philosophers, businessmen, philanthropists, soldiers, and so on. As examples, the transfer agent of the Black Rapids Coal Company has the business of removing mountains; Thomas Fry, a member of the Devil's Regiment, may be said to offer his body to be burned.

Against this background, the mute's phrases describing the qualities of charity, or Christian love, serve to identify what the passengers lack. Where Paul is advocating a community united by love, Melville presents a satiric portrait of a world totally lacking it.

This distinction between the ideal of charity and its absence in the world forms the basis of Melville's criticism of Emerson in this period of disillusionment. Emerson's whole man, as Melville viewed him at that time, is not motivated by love. In the character of Winsome, a mystic modeled on Emerson, Melville draws another portrait of non-benevolence reminiscent of Plotinus Plinlimmon, the lecturer in *Pierre*. This masquerader is

> a blue-eyed man, sandy-haired, and Saxon-looking; perhaps five and forty [Emerson in the mid-1850's was in his early fifties]; tall, and, but for a certain angularity, well made; little touch of the drawing room about him, but a look of plain propriety of a Puritan sort, with a kind of farmer dignity. (265)

Melville notes also that his brow was "placidly thoughtful" and his ruddy cheek "coolly fresh, like a red clover-blossom at coolish dawn—the color of warmth preserved by the virtue of chill." He is a mixture of "shrewdness and mythiness, strangely jumbled," a cross between "a Yankee peddler and a Tartar priest, though it seemed as if, at the pinch, the first would not in all probability play second fiddle to the last" (265).

These contrasting traits recall Lowell's well-known description of Emerson in "A Fable for Critics" (1848):

> A Greek head on right Yankee shoulders, whose range Has Olympus for one pole, for t'other the Exchange.

In conversing with the Cosmopolitan, another type of heartless humanity, Winsome comments on the beauty of the rattlesnake and asks: ". . . did it never occur to you to change personalities with him? to feel what it was to be a snake? to glide unsuspected in grass? to sting, to kill at a touch" (267)? The question parodies the Emersonian idea of identity, which Melville had successfully applied in yoking Ahab to his counterpart in nature, the white whale, in *Moby-Dick*.

In response, the Cosmopolitan smoothly declines to be identified with a rattlesnake on the grounds that "there would be no such thing as being genial with men," who would fear him (267). This demurer fits his character as a mixer with the other passengers. The Cosmopolitan's rejection of the philosophy of Winsome and his protege, a caricature of Thoreau called Egbert, is on the basis of its lack of heart, a deficiency in his own nature. He is not genial in his comment to Egbert:

> Apt disciple! Why wrinkle the brow, and waste the oil both of life and the lamp, only to turn out a head kept cool by the under ice of the heart? What your illustrious magian has taught you, any poor, old, broken-down, heart-shrunken dandy might have lisped. Pray, leave me, and with you take the last dregs of your philosophy" (p. 311).

In the end, the Cosmopolitan turns out to be a freeloader in persuading the ship's barber to take down his sign, "No Trust," making a loan agreement with him, and then refusing to pay. "Look to your agreement," the Cosmopolitan says. "You must trust" (327).

Melville's own rejection of Emersonian ideas at this time is part of his larger rejection of art itself as a sham. Passages on creating literature fit into the book as observations of the ultimate masquerader, the author himself. The last sentence of the book, "Something further may follow of this Masquerade," is the final false promise, since it is the novel's end, and Melville turned to other means than fiction writing to earn his living.

3. *Emerson's Ideal Man in the World of* Billy Budd

In retrospect, we can view Melville's professional career as a writer of prose fiction through 1857 as passing through four distinctive stages in relation to his creative response to Emersonian ideas:

1845–1846: early agreement with Emerson's idea of self-reliance and criticism of social conformity in *Typee* and *Omoo*, but no evidence that Melville was reading Emerson at this time;

1847–1848: discovery of Emerson's aesthetic ideas through reviews in the literary journals and initial experiments with them in *Mardi*;

1849–1851: intense study or thought-diving into Emerson's ideas with timely messages in Emerson's lectures counterbalancing Hawthorne's influence on craft since 1850 and accounting for the progressively complex symbolic texture and world views in *Redburn*, *White-Jacket*, and *Moby-Dick*;

1852–1857: after the failure of most reviewers and the public to fully appreciate *Moby-Dick*, some repudiation of both Emerson and Hawthorne and criticism of the tastes of the reading public through 1857, when Melville ceased attempting to make a living from his writing.

Though Melville in later years wrote considerable poetry, he did not return to prose fiction until near the end of 1888, when at the age of sixty-nine he began working on the short novel *Billy Budd*, published posthumously in 1924. This last work, which was not altogether finished at the time of his death in 1891, has been appropriately described as Melville's valedictory to Emerson; but few readers have appreciated the nature and extent of Melville's mature assimilation of Emerson's thought.[15]

In *Billy Budd*, Melville takes a long view of Emerson and works into his symbolic drama four strands of thought that have their source in ideas from the great period of 1849–1851. They are the ascendancy of natural aristocracy over social hierarchy, the primacy of instinct over logic, cracked nature as it applies to the divided mind of modern man, and the principle of moral compensation. These account for the complex world view which Melville presents, an "inside narrative" as much concerned with the ideas of transcendence and the schism that runs under the world as with the outer circumstances of a threatened mutiny aboard a warship, which is ironically resolved by the hanging of an innocent man.

The first strand, the contrast Melville draws between natural aristocracy and social hierarchy, is the basis for the conflict. Emerson cites this distinction in his lecture series in Boston in 1849, the announced topic of his final lecture being "Aristocracy."[16] But the idea permeates Emerson's writings, and Melville could not have missed the concept of the ideal man as "the lover of nature" who has "retained the spirit of infancy even into the era of manhood" (W, I, 9). To Emerson, such a child of nature, if he should appear, would be like Adam before the fall, a free spirit unburdened by Original Sin, spontaneous in thought and behavior, instinctive in his faith: his natural aristocrat would be a Transcendentalist. But Emerson, whose "thought too bold" was deliberately beyond the reach of his practical-minded audiences, qualifies his description: "There is no pure Transcendentalist," for "all who by strong bias of nature have leaned to the spiritual side in doctrine have stopped short of their goal" (W, I, 338). Without an historical example of a man who "has leaned entirely on his character," Emerson points to "the instinct of the lower animals" for "the suggestion of the methods of it [Transcendentalism], and something higher than our understanding" (338).

In the character of Billy Budd, however, Melville embodies the ideal of a pure Transcendentalist, such as the world has not yet known, and places him aboard an English man-of-war in the late 1790's, when England was at war with France. He is, as R.W.B. Lewis has noted, "not of any world but of the New World."[17] The conflict between this natural aristocrat and men of rank dedicated to maintaining discipline aboard ship has tragic consequences, dramatically offset by the transfiguration of Billy. His spirituality transcends the real world of the warship, with his death providing an image of radiance and blessedness.

In the opening lines, Melville introduces the idea of aristocracy by describing the type of the Handsome Sailor, who moves among sailors like "some superior figure of their own class." He has the "offhand unaffectedness of natural regality" (43). Billy is such a natural leader, whose appearance aboard the *H.M.S. Bellipotent* (Melville also considered the name *Indomitable*) resembles "that of a rustic beauty transplanted from the provinces and brought into competition with the highborn dames of the court" (51).

Billy, however, is more than just a Handsome Sailor, a recognizable type occasionally observed along the docks of any sizable seaport surrounded with an entourage of admirers. Jack Chase of *White-Jacket*, to whom Melville dedicated *Billy Budd*, was such a sailor. Billy is not only self-reliant and outgoing, but morally innocent. To his shipmates, he is welkin-eyed "Baby Budd," a sailor motivated by love and trust of his fellow man, "a sort of upright barbarian, much such as Adam presumably might have been ere the Serpent wriggled himself into his company" (52). This blending of beauty and virtue in his character is in harmony with Emerson's ideal view, "Beauty is the mark God sets upon virtue" (W, I, 19).

The contrast between Billy's natural nobility and the social hierarchy aboard a warship is at once apparent as Billy is being impressed from an English merchantman appropriately named the *Rights of Man* for service aboard the *Bellipotent* on the high seas. When Billy waves to his former ship, saying "And good-bye to you too, old *Rights of Man*," the naval officer taking him, a Lieutenant Ratcliffe (for high rat), shouts, "Down, sir!" The lieutenant, who has acquired the wisdom of the serpent that Billy lacks, is unable to perceive Billy's innocence: "This [Billy's remark] he rather took as meant to convey a covert sally on the new recruit's part" (49). The incident sets up the governing confrontation between Billy's innocent good nature and the urbane wisdom of superior officers, protected by the Articles of War and the rigid code of naval discipline.

Aboard the *Bellipotent*, Billy, an illiterate foundling who does not know where he came from ("God knows, sir," he says), does not comprehend the natural depravity of John Claggart, the master-at-arms, who knows his origins but keeps them to himself. In contrast to Billy, Claggart is an educated conformist, who has risen in rank, Melville notes ironically, through his "constitutional sobriety, an ingratiating deference to superiors, together with a peculiar ferreting genius" and "a certain austere patriotism" that "abruptly advanced him" to his rank (67). But like Billy, Claggart is the perfection of a type. His diabolism recalls the characters of Jackson, Bland, and Babo, as well as Melville's criticism of cold intellectuality, as in his remark to Hawthorne, "To the dogs with the head! I stand for the heart" (L, 129). Claggart's even temper and discreet bearing amount to a disguise that conceals a predatory nature. As Melville describes it:

> Civilization, especially if of the austerer sort, is auspicious to it. It folds itself in the mantle of respectability. It has its certain negative virtues serving as silent auxiliaries. It never allows wine to get within its guard. It is not going

too far to say that it is without vices or small sins. There is a phenomenal pride in it that excludes them. It is never mercenary or avaricious. In short, the depravity here meant partakes nothing of the sordid or sensual. It is serious, but free from acerbity. Though no flatterer of mankind it never speaks ill of it. (75–76).

As a law enforcer, Claggart manipulates rules at times to achieve an aim "which in wantonness of atrocity would seem to partake of the insane," and yet he "will direct a cool judgment sagacious and sound" that "to the average mind is "not distinguishable from sanity" (76).

Though Emerson rarely uses the word *evil* in his published writings (For him the meaning is carried in words like *conformity* and *consistency*), in his journals, which were not intended for publication, he approaches Melville's conception as embodied in the character of Claggart:

> The existence of evil and malignant men does not depend on themselves or on men; it indicates the virulence that still remains uncured in the universe, and uncured and corrupting, and hurling out these pestilent rats and tigers, and men rat-like and wolf-like. (*Journals*, vol. 8, 452)

At the top of the social hierarchy aboard the *Bellipotent*, Captain Edward Fairfax Vere is another exceptional man, who represents in the extreme the naval version of civilized conformity. Though he has a deceptive "unobtrusive demeanor" and at times "a certain dreaminess of mood" that leads fellow officers to call him "Starry Vere," he becomes resolute and practical in making decisions, "never tolerating an infraction to discipline" (60–61). Appropriately, his last name, in nautical terms, means to swing around by facing the stern to the wind, as though to scud from a storm, as Captain Claret wanted to do during the Cape Horner aboard the *Neversink*.[18]

Though Vere's fellow officers praise him to one another as comparing to Lord Nelson in seamanship and fighting qualities, they also rate him "a dry and bookish gentleman" with "a queer streak of the pedantic running through him" (63). He is no barbarian, such as Melville portrayed in the character of John Paul Jones, who made his own rules in *Israel Potter*.[19] A modern sailor would recognize Vere as the type of officer who runs his ship and fights "by the book." His forte is book learning: "his bias was toward those books to which every serious mind of superior order occupying any active post of authority in the world naturally inclines."

These include "history, biography, and unconventional writers like Montaigne," who "philosophize upon realities." There is no place in his reading for poetry and books on moral values, which would throw light on the mystery of the self. The effect of his reading is to confirm his convictions. Vere's books were "as a dike against those invading waters of novel opinion social, political, and otherwise, which carried away as in a torrent no few minds in those days" (62).

In the drama aboard the *Bellipotent* that pits Vere's urbane angle of vision against Billy's moral innocence, the captain emerges as Melville's most realistic tragic character. As a conformist dealing with extraordinary circumstances, he finds himself the virtual prisoner of his book knowledge, in particular the Articles of War and the Mutiny Act, which form the legal underpinning of the social order aboard the man-of-war.

The second strand of thought that Melville derives essentially from Emerson, the higher value of instinct over logic, internalizes this conflict between natural aristocracy and social hierarchy. These faculties, which Emerson refers to in *Nature* as Reason and Understanding, comprise the world of the mind and justify Melville's subtitle "An Inside Narrative." Billy is the child of Reason; Vere, of Understanding.

For wholeness of vision, Emerson had perceived the American scholar or poet as influenced primarily by nature, which nourishes the instinct, and secondarily by book learning and action, which cultivate logic and its adjuncts of habit and experience. Billy, as a representative of Emerson's "unhandselled savage nature," is untouched by book learning, though he composes his own songs. Relying wholly on instinct, he quickly asserts natural leadership over the crew of the *Bellipotent* as a Handsome Sailor. By contrast, Vere, a man of books and action who suppresses his instinct, makes decisions essentially according to the letter of the law, practicality, and his sense of traditional order. Claggart's presence in this dualistic world dramatizes the evil that logic is capable of harboring.

The third idea that Melville derives from Emerson, the notion of a schism that runs under the world, enlarges the drama aboard the *Bellipotent* into a portrait of the human condition. The crack in nature is for Emerson, as for Melville, the mark of mortality. No one is immune. Even Billy, as an embodiment of moral innocence, is not entirely pure. His speech impediment, which is apparent when he is under great emotional stress, is a calling card from "the envious marplot of Eden," who "still has more or less to do with every human consignment to this planet of Earth"

(53). Emerson in "Spiritual Laws," an essay Melville read, repeats the idea using the term *marplot*, in which he describes the selfish motives that interfere with the higher law of instinct:

> If we would not be *mar-plots with our miserable interferences* [italics added], the work, the society, the letters, arts, science, religion of men would go on far better than now, and the heaven predicted from the beginning of the world, and still predicted from the bottom of the heart, would organize itself, as do now the rose and the air and the sun. (W, II, 139–140)

It may be coincidental that at Billy's execution, after he says "God bless Captain Vere!" with no sign of the marplot in his speech, he is hanged, ascending into "the full rose of the dawn" (124). What is not coincidental is that in death, Billy through his final act of forgiveness dramatizes the power of instinct to heal the crack in nature. This is the promise of "Spiritual Laws" that underlies all of Emerson's writings, the ideal that transcends logic, practicality, and the wisdom of the serpent.

As for the other major participants, Melville portrays them in terms of striking dualities. Though Claggart's surface respectability masks inner malice, his character is all the more demonic because of its civilized appearance. Though Vere suppresses his private conscience in favor of an unbending public demeanor, his agony of spirit intensifies his role as a Melvillean model of the organizational man at sea. These divisions within characters occur in the larger context of social disintegration, represented in the war between Britain and France and the continuing threat of mutiny aboard the *Bellipotent*. In this manner, *Billy Budd* dramatizes at every level the cracked condition in the heart of man; and in Billy's benediction, "syllables too delivered in the clear melody of a singing bird on the point of launching from the twig," an image of perfection.

The fourth idea that Melville assimilated from Emerson, moral compensation, governs the narrative structure of *Billy Budd*, as it did in *Moby-Dick* and "Benito Cereno." In Melville's last novel, unlike its predecessors, the architecture approaches the symmetry of design in Hawthorne's best work. The opposing forces are in precise balance, with decisions matched by consequences, as though Melville had in mind an underlying moral equation. Early in the narrative, Billy matches Claggart, his first opponent among the ship's officers, face for face and light for light:

> That Claggart's figure was not amiss, and his face, save the chin well molded, has already been said. Of these favorable points he seemed not insensible for

he was not only neat but careful in his dress. But the form of Billy Budd was heroic; and his face was without the intellectual look of the pallid Claggart's, not the less was it lit, like his from within, though from a different source. The bonfire in his heart made luminous the rose-tan in his cheek. (77)

In the crucial action, these two representatives of good and evil, love and hate, heart and head are ordered to the captain's cabin, where in Vere's presence, they clash, with Vere very much a part the battle because of his own spiritual struggle. The dramatic sequence of events justifies close examination: After Claggart falsely accuses Billy of fomenting a mutiny, Billy tries to speak but cannot. Suddenly aware of Billy's speech impediment, the captain, "laying a soothing hand on his shoulder" and speaking in a fatherly tone, tells him to take his time in answering (99). In response, Billy struggles unsuccessfully for words, then impulsively strikes Claggart in the forehead. So the heart battles the head. The master-at-arms falls to the deck, gasps, and dies. Then Vere "with one hand covering his face stood to all appearance as impassive as the object at his feet" (ibid.), Melville asks, "Was he absorbed in taking in all the bearings of the event and what was best not only now at once to be done, but also in the sequel" (ibid.)? Apparently he was, for true to a sailor's view of his name, Vere quickly veers from instinct to logic, from Billy's fatherly supporter to Billy's judge. He detaches himself from the situation that his words and his touch had inadvertently abetted and morally involved him in the consequences. To the ship's surgeon, he exclaims, "Struck dead by an angel of God! Yet the angel must hang" (101).

At Billy's court-martial, the captain argues for Billy's conviction on grounds of practicality: "But for us here, acting not as casuists or moralists, it is a case practical, and under martial law practically to be dealt with" (110). In this manner suppressing his private conscience, his instinctive awareness of Billy's moral innocence, and also his private knowledge of his own personal involvement in the youth's predicament, Vere stands on logic: "Let not warm hearts betray heads that should be cool" (111). This advice, which is contrary to Melville's own beliefs in the truths of the heart, as well as Emerson's stand on the primacy of instinct, leads to Billy's sentence to death by hanging.

Vere changes course again, as he gives Billy the news of the verdict in a confrontation that Melville alludes to but does not describe. Again, Melville matches the participants, not so much as sailor to captain or

prisoner to captor, but as son to father, child to man. Of Vere's relation
to Billy, Melville writes:

> He was old enough to have been Billy's father. The austere devotee of military
> duty, letting himself melt back into what remains primeval in our formalized
> humanity, may in the end have caught Billy to his heart, even as Abraham
> may have caught young Isaac on the brink of resolutely offering him up in
> obedience to the exacting behest. (115)

Melville's irony should not be overlooked: Abraham was obeying God;
Vere, the Mutiny Act.

At its deepest level, Vere's tragedy is that of modern man, torn between
his spiritual aspirations and the facts of life. Vere's middle name, "Fairfax,"
indicates his bias. Shortly after Billy's death, the *Bellipotent* engages the
French warship *Atheist*; in the resulting battle, Vere is mortally wounded
"by a musket ball from a porthole of the enemy's main cabin" (129). This
compensatory event suggests a governing principle for the worlds of the
Bellipotent and of the mind: when head overcomes heart, when logic
suppresses instinct, the result is the loss of faith and a sense of the spiritual
nature of man. Of the name *Atheist* for Vere's nemesis, Melville called it
"the aptest name ever given a warship" (20).

In this tragedy of limited vision and the mind divided against itself,
wholeness of vision to the extent that it is possible in the real world is best
represented in the character of the Dansker, an old sailor from the tragic
warship *Agamemnon*. He is the "salt seer," whom Melville describes as
"long anglicized in the service, of few words, many wrinkles, and some
honorable scars" (69). Of all Billy's associates aboard the *Bellipotent*, he
alone is able to keep the "trembling balance" that Emerson described as
essential for survival. Like Ahab, the Dansker has a crack in his nature
represented by "a long pale scar like a streak of dawn's light falling athwart
the dark visage"; but he has not lost his perspective on either the inner or
the outer world. In contrast to Billy, an unscarred young Saxon, the
Dansker has a knowledge of evil derived from experience which enables
him to keep out of Claggart's way and also to warn Billy, "*Jemmy Legs* is
down on you" (71). In contrast to Vere, the Dansker retains his individuality and essential humanity while doing his duty despite the pressures of
the conforming society aboard the warship. Young crewmen regard him
as an eccentric; Billy reveres him as a "salt hero." His post as "mainmast-

man in his watch" suggests his role in the drama. Though the Dansker takes no active role in the conflict of exceptional forces, it is he, not Claggart, not Billy, not Vere, who is the center of stability and clear vision aboard Melville's embattled world ship. Melville describes his manner as "a pithy guarded cynicism" (p. 71). This is the antithesis of optimism, but it reflects the instinct to survive.

In *Billy Budd* perhaps better than any other of Melville's novels, we can sense the responsiveness of Melville's genius to Emerson's complex vision. In this last work, written eight years after Emerson's death, the four dominant strains of Emersonian ideas woven into it have the enrichment of memory, for Melville had tried them all in his other fiction. Readers who perceive him as rejecting Emerson's optimism may have underestimated both the comprehensiveness of Emerson's view of man, which makes room even for the skepticism of Montaigne, and the capacity of Melville to create in his divided world of the mind an image of almost perfect spirituality in Billy. Unlike in religious outlook and temperament, Melville and Emerson find common ground at the highest level of creativity. The light which for Emerson "flashes across his mind from within" ignites in Melville the white fire of imagination.

CHAPTER 9

EPILOGUE

To the question, What makes a man a man? the traditional scientific answer is heredity and environment, or as the late Nobel laureate Jacques Monod put it, "partially his genome and partially his culture."[1] If we ask, What makes Melville Melville? the answer must lie in his native ability and his reaction to his life experiences, which include the pressure of the personalities that define his culture.

Among American writers of Melville's era, Emerson best fits his own description of the poet as a "liberating god." But in a materialistic age, his vocabulary of inspiration, symbol, and myth has diminished appeal to readers inclined to self-analysis and the quantification of experience, tendencies suggesting the retrospective cast of mind Emerson rebelled against. So he was not taken seriously in his own time, nor is he in ours—except by other rebels against conforming usages and excesses of logical thinking. Writers like Melville, Hawthorne, Thoreau, and Whitman were such protesters in the mid-nineteenth century literary milieu. Emerson's liberating influence affected each of them. As the chief advocate for self-reliance in art as well as life, he was the one writer they could not ignore. They responded to him because the ideas and images he articulated with stunning eloquence were reminders of what they already knew from their observation and reading. In effect, it was Emerson's power of selection and articulation that made traditional materials timely, enlarging the sense of the present moment, so that a writer like Melville could say, as though he had first thought of the idea himself, "For genius, all over the world,

185

stands hand in hand, and one shock of recognition runs the whole circle round."[2]

In this survey of Melville's creative responses in prose fiction to Emerson's expansive vision, we have observed the growth of a consummate artist in relation to the most important mentor in American literature. If Hawthorne taught Melville lessons in dramatic form, it was Emerson who transmitted to Melville the basis for a world view, with the self as its center. Even if we concede that Melville rejected Emerson's Transcendental religious faith, reflecting in part critical opinions in the press, we nevertheless can see how he received from Emerson an expansionist view of art as epitome of the whole of creation, of symbol as the link between the self and total nature, of self as determined by angle of vision, of nature as essentially moral, and of individual integrity rather than imitation as the way of the artist. These are marks of Melville's genius, just as surely as they characterize Emerson's. The evidence indicates that they overmatch the conventional discrimination between Emerson's optimism and Melville's pessimism, and they suggest the value of the social dimension of artistic achievement that transcends individual differences.

The idea of this study has been to indicate the responsiveness of Melville to Emerson's genius and to explain the significance of this influence. In a more general sense, our examination has demonstrated how it was possible for a writer of extraordinary talent and originality to discover the treasury of his own mind and art through clues embedded in the sentences of a writer whom he did not personally know, but who served as spokesman and advocate for the ideas of his time. "Art," Emerson said, "is the path of the creator to his work." The sentences in his lectures, essays and poems, like beams of light, enhanced Melville's capacity to *see*, even though the path Melville took was his own.

NOTES

Chapter 1

1. *Stimulating Creativity* (New York: Academic Press, 1974) 251.

2. Sealts asserts, "There is no mention of Melville either in Emerson's published works or in his journals, letters, and lectures." In "Melville and Emerson's Rainbow," *Pursuing Melville: 1940–1980* (Madison, WS: U of Wisconsin P, 1982) 254.

3. In "Emerson—Golden Impossibility, Representative Man," *Emerson Society Quarterly* 21 (1975): 241–259.

4. *Virginia Quarterly Review* 20 (1953): 564, 575.

5. *PMLA* 94 (October 1979): 915.

6. In "Melville and Emerson's Rainbow," Sealts seeks "to assemble all the evidence concerning Melville's response to Emerson" (254). But Sealts does not consider popular reactions to Emerson in the periodicals, which swayed Melville even before he heard Emerson lecture. In arguing the influence of Plato on *Mardi*, Sealts takes Melville at his word as not knowing Emerson before hearing him lecture in 1849 (See 279). Evidence presented in Chapter 5, however, points to Melville's discovery of Emerson as early as 1847, during the composition of *Mardi*. Melville could not have missed the popular opinions, supported by extensive quotations from Emerson, expressed in *The New York Literary World* at that time.

7. W, I, 26. Emerson also stresses the identity of the mind and nature in the lecture series, "Mind and Manners," which he delivered in Boston early in 1849, when Melville heard him speak. See Chapter 3 for details of the contents.

8. (New York: Hendricks House, 1952) 310.

9. In *American Renaissance* (New York: Oxford UP, 1941) vii, Matthiessen lists these works produced between 1850 and 1855 as masterpieces: Emerson's *Representative Men* (1850), Hawthorne's *The Scarlet Letter* (1850) and *The House of the Seven Gables* (1851), Melville's *Moby-Dick* (1851) and *Pierre* (1852), Tho-

reau's *Walden* (1854), and Whitman's *Leaves of Grass* (1855). Of their quality, Matthiessen comments: "You might search all the rest of American literature without being able to collect a group of books equal to these in imaginative vitality."

10. From an article by Lowell in *Nation*, quoted in W, VII, 342.

11. *Classic Americans* (New York: Harcourt, Brace, 1931) 160.

12. "Emerson the Lecturer," *My Study Windows* (1871); rpt. in *The Recognition of Ralph Waldo Emerson*, ed. Milton R. Konvitz (Ann Arbor: U of Michigan P, 1972) 45.

13. In "Eloquence," W, VII, 64. Edward Waldo Emerson notes, "In February, 1847, Mr. Emerson gave a lecture on Eloquence before the Boston Mercantile Library Association. It seems to have been much the same as the present essay" (364).

14. *American Literature*, 9 (November 1937): 318.

15. Matthiessen 185–186.

16. Sealts notes (258) that Wallace Williams, who is editing an edition of Emerson's lecture manuscripts, suggests that "The Superlative" is "almost as likely" the one Melville heard. I find it difficult to accept either Sealts' or Wallace Williams' view, since Melville's images in his letter of March 3, 1849 point to other lectures in the series. As an innovator who ad libbed, Emerson possibly rearranged the contents of his lectures, even without changing the announced titles. It is conceivable that he recapitulated ideas from earlier lectures before beginning a new one for the benefit of newcomers in his audience like Melville. The evidence of layer on layer of revision in Emerson's lecture manuscripts has led Stephen E. Whicher and Robert E. Spiller to remark: "One cannot be sure that any folder represents Emerson's choice of material, or that the material is ordered as Emerson left it." (See *The Early Lectures of Ralph Waldo Emerson* (Cambridge: Harvard UP, 1959) I: xiii-xiv.)

17. In Genesis 4.15, the familiar "mark of Cain" is presented as a divine protective sign, not a mark of weakness: "And the Lord set a mark upon Cain, lest any finding him should kill him." In *Paradise Lost*, Milton describes Satan: "his face / Deep scars of thunder had entrenched" (I.600–601). Henry F. Pommer notes the similarity to Ahab's scar in *Milton and Melville* (Pittsburgh: U of Pittsburgh P, 1950) 92. The connection of the Pittsfield elm, damaged by lightning, to the description of Ahab was first noted by Melville's friend, J. E. A. Smith, as Howard Vincent observes in *The Trying Out of Moby-Dick* (Carbondale: Southern Illinois UP, 1949) 111–112.

18. Conrad observes, "Literature seems to me a collaborative—almost a familial—activity, marrying the past with the present and from that union generating the future." In *The History of English Literature* (Philadelphia: U of Pennsylvania P, 1985) vii.

19. *The Echoing Green* (Princeton: Princeton UP, 1984) 4.

20. (Princeton: Princeton UP, 1975) 93–100. Since the principles in this text are expressed as formulae (e.g., *X influences Y with respect to a*), I have reworded

those that are appropriate to the discussion of Emerson's influence on Melville in sentence statements.

21. See *The Anxiety of Influence* (New York: Oxford UP, 1973). Bloom's theory of how a "strong poet" wrestles with his "strong precursor" focuses on the relation of the individual writer to a predecessor in the tradition. It does not take into account the idea of a creative community which facilitates a sharing of consciousness among contemporaries. Bloom, however, does make exceptions to his theory. He notes that Emerson apparently did not feel the anxiety of influence (50), nor did Shakespeare, whose work towers over that of his precursor, Marlow (11). By comparison, though Melville wrestled mightily with ideas and feelings, the evidence of his extensive borrowings suggests that his conscience also was not disturbed by influence.

22. *Literary Essays of Ezra Pound*, ed T. S. Eliot (New York: New Directions, 1935) 5.

23. *The Portable Melville*, ed. Jay Leyda (New York: Viking, 1952) 406.

24. *The Portable Melville* 742.

Chapter 2

1. Bliss Perry, "Emerson's Most Famous Speech," *The Praise of Folly and Other Papers* (Boston: Houghton Mifflin, 1923) 86. In his reconstruction of the occasion, Perry writes, "Among the Fellows of the Harvard Corporation, you will note two of the foremost lawyers of the Commonwealth, Joseph Story and Lemuel Shaw."

2. Ralph L. Rusk, *The Life of Ralph Waldo Emerson* (New York: Charles Scribner's Sons, 1949) 54. See also Oliver Wendell Holmes, *Ralph Waldo Emerson* (Boston: Houghton Mifflin, 1912) 43. Though Gay Wilson Allen has titled his biography of Emerson *Waldo Emerson*, he observes that the family called Emerson as a boy Ralph. See (New York: Viking, 1981) vii.

3. Perry 97–99.

4. The phrase is from *Moby-Dick* 110. In an autobiographical reference, Melville has his narrator, Ishmael, comment: "If, at my death, my executors, or more properly my creditors, find any precious MSS, in my desk, then here I prospectively ascribe all the honor and glory to whaling; for a whale-ship was my Yale College and my Harvard." The whaler *Pequod* in the novel is based on Melville's experiences sailing on three whalers—*Acushnet*, *Lucy Ann*, and *Charles and Henry*—during the years 1841–1844. Melville returned to Boston from his travels as a sailor aboard the frigate *U.S.S. United States*, which he boarded in Hawaii.

5. The phrase "*organicism* in an American setting" is from Porte's *Representative Man: Ralph Waldo Emerson in His Time* (New York: Oxford UP, 1979) vii.

6. William R. Hutchinson, *The Transcendental Ministers* (New Haven: Yale UP, 1959) 30–31. Hutchinson points out that the elder statesmen of Unitarianism—

James Walker, Nathaniel Frothingham, and Dr. Channing—were invited but did not become regular members of the Transcendental Club.

7. See Perry Miller, "From Edwards to Emerson," in *Errand into the Wilderness* (New York: Harper and Row, 1964) 184–203, for a detailed discussion of the relation of Emerson to the Puritan tradition.

8. Hutchinson 29.

9. Quoted from Harold Clarke Goddard, *Studies in New England Transcendentalism* (New York: Hilary House, 1960) 165.

10. For the discussion of German sources of New England Transcendentalism, I have relied primarily on Vogel's *German Influences on the American Transcendentalists* (New Haven: Yale UP, 1955) and the first three chapters of Frothingham's *Transcendentalism in New England* (New York: Harper and Brothers, 1959). Leon Chai's *The Romantic Foundations of the American Renaissance* (Ithaca, NY: Cornell UP, 1987) is a helpful supplement which focuses on reactions of American writers to these sources.

11. Kenneth W. Cameron, *Ralph Waldo Emerson's Reading* (Raleigh, NC: Thistle Press, 1941) 18, 23, 47. See also, Vogel 173–175.

12. In *The Complete Works of Samuel Taylor Coleridge*, ed. W. G. T. Shedd, vol. 3 (New York: Harper, 1854) 374.

13. The reference to Emerson's "Merlin" is from W, IX, 122. For Melville's similar statement on art, see *The Portable Melville* 742.

14. See listings in *Melville's Reading: A Check-List of Books Owned and Borrowed* (Madison, WI: U of Wisconsin P, 1966). All references to Melville's reading are from this source.

15. *Journal of a Visit to London and the Continent, 1849–1850*, ed. Eleanor Melville Metcalf (London: Cohen and West, 1949) 11.

16. For Marovitz's analysis of the Adler-Melville relation, see "More Chartless Voyaging: Melville and Adler at Sea," *Studies in the American Renaissance: 1986*, ed. Joel Myerson (Charlottesville: UP of Virginia, 1986) 373–384.

17. The letter, written on May 21, 1840 is quoted from *The Transcendentalists*, ed. Perry Miller (Cambridge, MA: Harvard UP, 1950) 255.

18. *Journals of Ralph Waldo Emerson*, eds. Edward Waldo Emerson and Waldo Emerson Forbes, vol. 7 (Boston: Houghton, Mifflin, 1912) 532–533.

19. *The American Puritans*, ed. Perry Miller (Garden City, NY: Doubleday, 1956) 158–159.

Chapter 3

1. "To Nathaniel Hawthorne," June 1, 1851, L, 130. Melville is referring to the year 1844, but he wrote the letter six years later while he was working on *Moby-Dick*.

2. "The Records of Melville's Reading," *Melville's Reading: A Check-List of books Owned and Borrowed* 3–26 discusses Melville's reading habits.

3. "Melville and Emerson's Rainbow," in *Pursuing Melville: 1940–1980* 263–267.

4. *Melville's Reading: A Checklist of Books Owned and Borrowed* 59.

5. Foreword to vol. 11, *The Journals of Ralph Waldo Emerson*, ed. A. W. Plumstead, et al., vol. 11 (Cambridge: Harvard UP, 1975) xx-xxi.

6. *A Memoir of Ralph Waldo Emerson*, vol. 2, 753.

7. Bredahl 1–2. The quotation from Emerson's *Nature* (1836) is as follows: "Nature is made to conspire with the spirit to emancipate us. Certain mechanical changes, a small alteration in our local position, apprises us of a dualism. We are strangely affected by seeing the shore from a moving ship, from a balloon, or through the tints of an unusual sky. The least change in our point of view gives the whole world a pictorial air. A man who seldom rides, needs only to get into a coach and traverse his own town, to turn the street into a puppet-show. The men, the women, talking, running, bartering, fighting—the earnest mechanic, the lounger, the beggar, the boys, the dogs, are unrealized at once, or, at least, wholly detached from all relations to the observer, and seen as apparent, not substantial beings" (W, I, 50–51).

The quotation from Melville's journal entry for December 13, 1856 reads: "Started alone for Constantinople and after a terrible long walk, found myself back where I started. Just like getting lost in a wood. No plan to streets. Pocket-compass. Perfect labryth [labyrinth]. Narrow. Close, shut in. If one could but get *up* aloft, it would be easy to see one's way out. If you could get up into a tree. Soar out of the maze. But no. No names to the streets no more than to natural allies among the groves. No numbers. No anything." See *Journal of a Visit to Europe and the Levant: October 11, 1856–May 6, 1857*, ed. Howard C. Horsford (Princeton: Princeton UP, 1955) 79.

8. See reviews of *Mardi* in *The Recognition of Herman Melville* 14–17. Melville's own estimate is contained in *Pierre* 332–334.

9. L 130. In a note to this letter, the editors refer to an experiment by G. P. R. James at Stockbridge, MA of planting some wheat seed taken from the inside of an Egyptian mummy case. See also S. M. Ellis, *The Solitary Horseman, or The Life and Adventures of G.P.R. James*, cited in *American Notes and Queries*, 7 (December 1947): 41.

10. See "The Hemispheric Processes of the Brain" in *The Human Brain*, ed. M. C. Wittrock et al. (Englewood Cliffs: Prentice Hall, 1977) 87–130 for summaries of recent research relating to split-brain theories. Robert D. Nebes' "Man's So-called Minor Hemisphere" (97–106) describes the right cerebral hemisphere's functions in processing information synthetically rather than analytically.

Chapter 4

1. *Influence and Art in Literature* 98–99.

2. James Baird correctly views Melville's tendency toward polarity as a basic

feature of Melville's art from *Typee* on. See *Ishmael: A Study of the Symbolic Mode of Primitivism* (New York: Harper, 1956) 189. But in developing his argument on the uniqueness of Melville's symbols, Baird asserts, "I cannot see, despite Feidelson's excellent account of Melville, that Melville was an inheritor of Emerson during the major period of his productivity" (xvii). This view apparently does not take into account the Emersonian ideas and images on polarity available to Melville in newspapers and periodicals at the time he was writing.

3. See Charles R. Anderson, *Melville in the South Seas* (New York: Morningside Heights, 1939) 149.

4. Note in particular, "To John Murray," 2 September 1846 and 29 January 1847 in L, 44–47, 52–54.

5. R. W. B. Lewis in *The American Adam* (Chicago: U of Chicago P, 1955) 135 notes parallels of Melville's sojourn among the Typees to Thoreau's stay at Walden Pond. The argument could be extended to include Emerson's views on an original relation to the universe in *Nature*.

Chapter 5

1. See listings for Byron, Keats, and Shelley in Sealts, *Melville's Reading: A Check-List of Books Owned and Borrowed* 45-46, 72, 94.

2. The evidence presented here of Melville's access to Emerson through *The New York Literary World* challenges the view of Sealts that Melville's knowledge of Plato "antedated his knowledge of Emerson, beginning in 1848 and constituting a major influence on both *Mardi* and *Moby-Dick*." ("Melville and the Platonic Tradition" in *Pursuing Melville: 1940–1980* 278.) Though Platonic elements undoubtedly enrich *Mardi* and later works, as Sealts has shown, Emerson's influence was that of a contemporary; his ideas on individualism, the life of the mind, and art were widely disseminated in periodicals and newspapers and set the literary standards for that era. Melville could not have missed them; nor could he have failed to be impressed as a successful young writer in 1847 in search of a literary reputation. For these reasons, Emersonian elements, more than any other, account for Melville's expanded vision and also for the structural defects in *Mardi*.

3. *The Portable Melville* 601.

4. *The Recognition of Herman Melville* 12.

5. *Melville's Reading* lists no works of Plato that Melville owned or has been known to have borrowed. Sealts points out, however, that in *Pierre* the title character "specifically remembers the appearance of his father's set of the works of Plato," and adds, "It is by no means unlikely that in these passages Melville drew upon recollections of his own boyhood, either at home or in the Albany library of his mother's brother Peter Gansevoort, as Henry A. Murray has suggested" (8). Since the reference is to fiction, it seems more likely that Melville is using Plato as a metaphor for books that reflect idealistic philosophies. In the "Historical Note" to *Mardi*, Elizabeth S. Foster says, for example, that Babbalanja's "gibberish"

about "Adyta, the Monads, and the Hyparxes; the Dianoias, the Unical Hyposta-
ses" and Doxodox's "esoteric jargon" are from Thomas Taylor's translation of *The
Six Books of Proclus on the Theology of Plato* (London, 1816) 673–674. Plato is a
convenient label that could apply to any number of books on Transcendental
topics.

6. Merrell R. Davis explains the *Parki* episode as evidence of Melville's random
or "chartless" methods of building the novel in *Melville's Mardi: A Chartless Voyage*
(New Haven: Yale University Press, 1952).

7. Dorothee Metlitsky Finkelstein points out that Yillah's name resembles the
Mohammedan word for God, Allah, particularly the invocation of faith, "La ilaha
illa-llah." See her *Melville's Orienda* (New Haven: Yale University Press, 1961) 204.

8. Jarl and Samoa, Taji's companions in his adventures before he reaches the
Mardian isles, drop out of the narrative to make way for these allegorical figures.

Chapter 6

1. Melville uses the term "visible truth" in a letter to Hawthorne in April 1851
(See quotation on pp. 77–78). Since Melville had boldly turned away from
representing the real world in his excursion into romantic fantasy in *Mardi*, a book
which he considered a failure, his use of the term indicates his recovery of respect
for details drawn from actuality. It is these which he endows with symbolic value.
From 1849 on, visible truth to Melville refers to the writer's perception of natural
objects as metaphors of the mind. He presents this idea most succinctly in *Pierre*:
"All great books in the world are but the mutilated shadowings-forth of invisible
and eternally unembodied images in the soul; so that they are but the mirrors,
distortedly reflecting to us our own things; and never mind what the mirror may
be, if we would see the object, we must look at the object itself, and not at its
reflection" (334). The statement strongly suggests the connection of Melville's
focus on the object and Emerson's sense of the object as a mirror reflecting the
self.

2. "Melville and Emerson's Rainbow," *Pursuing Melville: 1940–1980* (Madison, WI: U of Wisconsin P, 1982) 250–277. Though we cannot be certain which
essays Melville read of Emerson in 1849, the evidence in *Redburn* and *White-Jacket*
indicates his familiarity with "Self-Reliance" and "Compensation."

3. See William H. Gilman, *Melville's Early Life and Redburn* (New York: New
York University Press, 1951).

4. Robert E. Spiller, et al., *Literary History of the United States* (New York:
Macmillan, 1953) 447.

5. *Redburn*, eds. Harrison Hayford, Hershel Parker, and G. Thomas Tanselle
(Chicago: Northwestern UP, 1969) 7.

6. Compare this quotation at the end of Chapter 33 with its counterpart in
Whitman's Preface to the 1855 edition of *Leaves of Grass*: "The Americans of all
nations at any time upon the earth have probably the fullest poetical nature. The

United States themselves are essentially the greatest poem. . . . Here at last is something in the doings of man that corresponds with the broadcast doings of the day and night. Here is not merely a nation but a teeming nation of nations." Ed. Emory Holloway (New York: Doubleday, Page, 1924) 448.

7. *The Works of Thomas Carlyle*, vol. 1 (New York: Scribner's 1896) 57.

8. *Redburn* 228. In *Sartor Resartus*, Carlyle refers to Teufelsdröckh's "Temptations in the Wilderness," which in "an Atheistic Century" is "the populous moral Desert of selfishness and baseness." See *The Works of Thomas Carlyle*, vol. 1: 146–154.

9. For a detailed comparison, see Gilman 272–273.

10. Howard P. Vincent, *The Tailoring of Melville's White-Jacket* (Evanston: Northwestern UP, 1970) 90. Vincent notes that Melville supplemented his memories of flogging episodes with materials drawn from books, in particular Samuel Leech's *Thirty Years from Home*. See pp. 86–106 for Melville's use of Leech and other literary sources in developing his attack on flogging.

11. Melville did not himself fall from the maintop. As Spiller says, "Melville coolly lifted" the episode from Nathaniel Ames' *A Mariner's Sketches* (*The Literary History of the United States* 447).

12. *The Writings of Henry David Thoreau*, ed. H. E. Scudder, vol. 10 (Boston: Houghton, Mifflin, 1893) 134.

Chapter 7

1. "Hawthorne and His Mosses," in *The Portable Melville* 410. The essay was published in Evert Duyckinck's *The New York Literary World*, August 17 and 24, 1850.

2. See "Hawthorne and the Transcendentalists" in Marjorie J. Elder's *Nathaniel Hawthorne: Transcendental Symbolist* (Athens, OH: Ohio UP, 1969) 3–14.

3. The phrase is in Hawthorne's preface to *The House of the Seven Gables*, in *The Complete Works of Nathaniel Hawthorne*, vol. 3 (New York: Houghton, Mifflin, 1882) 13.

4. *The Complete Works of Nathaniel Hawthorne*, vol. 2, 512.

5. B. R. McElderry, Jr., "The Transcendental Hawthorne," *Midwest Quarterly* 2 (Summer 1961): 318–319 notes this similarity.

6. Eleanor Melville Metcalf, *Herman Melville: Cycle and Epicycle* (Cambridge, MA: Harvard UP, 1953) 91.

7. In *The Works of Edgar Allan Poe*, vol. 3 (New York: Redfield, 1859) 198.

8. *The Complete Works of Nathaniel Hawthorne*, vol. 9, 106. Melville marked four passages from the story in his copy of Hawthorne's *Mosses* (Log, I, 380).

9. *The Complete Works of Hawthorne*, vol. 1, 16.

10. James Barbour and Harrison Hayford have concisely summarized current theories concerning Melville's processes of composition and revision in "The Composition of *Moby-Dick* in *Melville Society Extracts*, September 1980: 2–3.

Evidence for these theories largely concerns such textual irregularities as "unnecessary duplicates," the unexplained disappearance of Bulkington from the story and hints that Peleg may have been the original pegleg captain of the *Pequod*. Barbour and Hayford observe that "the book was extensively rethought and revised in the process of composition, but perhaps not radically altered nor surgically severed and joined as the theory of 'The Two *Moby-Dicks*' would suggest."

11. B. R. McElderry, Jr., "Introduction" to *Shipwreck of the Whaleship Essex* by Owen Chase (New York: Corinth Books, 1963) vii-xix. The quotation of Melville is on p. 138 in the transcript of notes he made in his copy of the narrative, which is not at Harvard. Melville received this copy in April 1851 from his father-in-law, Judge Lemuel Shaw.

12. For the reference to David Starbuck, see explanatory note in *Moby-Dick* 663. The story of Owen Coffin is in Captain Pollard's narrative of the *Essex* sinking included in McElderry's edition of Chase's account, p. 101.

13. Melville probably heard by word of mouth or read Jeramiah N. Reynolds, "Mocha Dick: or the White Whale of the Pacific," *Knickerbocker Magazine*, May 1839: 377–393, which describes "a renowned monster" and victor in "a hundred fights with pursuers" that "was as white as wool." See excerpts from the article and discussion of Mocha Dick as a source of Melville's whale in the explanatory notes in *Moby-Dick* 691–695.

14. Emerson's aphorism, "Hitch your wagon to a star," is part of an argument on developing moral and spiritual energies in the individual. "If we can thus ride in Olympian chariots by putting our works in the path of celestial circuits," he says, "we can harness also evil agents, the powers of darkness, and force them to serve against their will the ends of wisdom and virtue." (In "Civilization," W, VII, 30.)

15. Melville refers to Hawthorne's story, "Egotism: or, The bosom Serpent," in his discussion of Original Sin in "Hawthorne and His Mosses," *The Portable Melville* 406. Ahab's vice, then, is representative of the general condition of men.

16. Melville describes Ahab's scar as resembling "that perpendicular seam sometimes made in the straight, lofty trunk of a great tree, with; the upper lightning tearingly darts down it, and without wrenching a single twig, peels and grooves out the bark from top to bottom, ere running off into the soil, leaving the tree still greenly alive, but branded" (120–121).

17. In "Hawthorne and His Mosses," *The Portable Melville* 407.

18. *Shipwreck of the Whaleship Essex* 22.

19. Melville's Calvinistic attitudes are explored in T. Walker Herbert, Jr., *Moby-Dick and Calvinism* (New Brunswick, NJ: Rutgers UP, 1977). As artists, both Hawthorne and Melville probably would consider the aesthetic uses of the doctrine of predestination as a means of justifying story events and building suspense.

Chapter 8

1. Ripley's perceptive review, printed in *Harper's*, December 1851, has this comment: "Beneath the whole story, the subtle, imaginative reader may perhaps

find a pregnant allegory, intended to illustrate the mystery of human life. Certain it is that the rapid, pointed hints which are often thrown out, with the keenness and velocity of a harpoon, penetrate deep into the heart of things, showing that the genius of the author for moral analysis is scarcely surpassed by his wizard power of description." Quoted in *The Recognition of Herman Melville* 43.

2. Randall Stewart, *Nathaniel Hawthorne: A Biography* (New Haven: Yale UP, 1948) 118–119. For other views of Melville's reaction to Hawthorne's move, see Charles N. Watson, Jr., "The Estrangement of Hawthorne and Melville," *New England Quarterly* 46 (1973): 380–402, also Edwin H. Miller, *Melville* (New York: Persea Books, 1975) 220–224.

3. "Introduction" to *Pierre* (New York: Hendricks House, 1949) xciii. Critics appear to have underestimated Melville's attempt at parody of Hawthorne's *The House of the Seven Gables*. Edward H. Rosenberry in *Melville and the Comic Spirit* (Cambridge MA: Harvard UP, 1955) perceives Melville's endeavor to satirize sentimental fiction in *Pierre* (159–161), but he does not identify *The House of the Seven Gables* as Melville's specific target. Rosenberry and others have pointed out the ridicule of transcendentalism in references to Plotinus Plinlimmon and the satire on the New York literary establishment in the digression on "Young America in Literature." Still others taking a serious view of Melville's novel have noted his indebtedness to Hawthorne. Matthiessen, for example, observes that *The House of the Seven Gables* may have suggested "the change in *Pierre* from the aristocratic past to the democratic present" (468). Edwin Haviland Miller among others records similarities between *Pierre* and *The Blithedale Romance*, written at about the same time (240–241). Critics also have pointed out allusions to Hawthorne in certain characters in Melville's novel. Murray notes the resemblance of Plotinus Plinlimmon to Hawthorne (lxxviii–lxxix). Charles N. Watson, Jr. observes that the relation of Pierre to Glen Stanley, which progresses from early intimacy to estrangement, corresponds to the Melville-Hawthorne association (395). Richard H. Gamble also investigates the Pierre-Glen Stanley parallels in "Reflections of the Hawthorne-Melville Relationship in *Pierre*," *American Literature* 47 (January 1976): 629–632. None of these studies, however, indicates the precision and comprehensiveness of Melville's parody of *The House of the Seven Gables*.

4. *Complete Works of Hawthorne*, vol. 3, 14.

5. See *Complete Works of Hawthorne*, vol. 3, 17; *Pierre* 311.

6. Ibid. Melville's parody is partly concealed, possibly for the benefit of a thorough reader like Hawthorne. Where Hawthorne's novel begins with a stately description of the old house, Melville holds off his description of the Apostles until a chapter that he labels "Book XIX."

7. *Complete Works of Hawthorne*, vol. 3, 94.

8. See Brian Higgins and Hershel Parker, "The Flawed Grandeur of Melville's *Pierre*," *Perspectives on Melville*, ed. Faith Pullen (Kent, OH: Kent State UP, 1978) 162–196. Higgins and Parker make an interesting observation: "In *Pierre* itself two books were also written, the one up through Book IV (and intermittently thereafter) which examined the growth of a deluded by idealistic soul when

confronted with the world's conventionality, and the later one which expressed Melville's sometimes sardonic, sometimes embittered reflections on his own career. There is no successful fusion of the two" (193). In accounting for the imperfections, they note that "behind Melville there was no educated literary milieu, no available models, no shoptalk with other literary masters, no rigorously critical friend, no one to assure him of ultimate glory—nothing, in short, to help him hold to the pervading idea that impelled the first half of the book. Yet he had accomplished so much in this book that one becomes anguished as Melville's genius goes tragically to waste" (ibid.). This argument appears to devalue the influence of Hawthorne, with whom Melville carried on a lively correspondence beginning in 1850, and the literary milieu dominated by Emerson. Evidence in Melville's letters and in the text of *Pierre* examined in this chapter points instead to Melville's rebellion against the model provided by Hawthorne's sentimental novel and Emerson's idea of the successful self-reliant literary man.

9. "Introduction," *Pierre* xx.

10. See Murray lxxviii–lxxix, Watson 395.

11. See Hugh W. Hetherington, *Melville's Reviewers* (Chapel Hill, NC: U of North Carolina P, 1961) 238.

12. In *The Piazza Tales*, eds. Harrison Hayford, Alma A. MacDougall, G. Thomas Tanselle, et al. (Evanston: Northwestern UP and Newberry Library, 1987) 372–373.

13. Christopher W. Sten examines sources of Melville's satire in Emerson's lecture, "The Transcendentalist" (1842), rpt. in *Nature; Addresses and Lectures* (1849). See "Bartleby the Transcendentalist: Melville's Dead Letter to Emerson," *Modern Language Quarterly* 35 (1974): 30–44.

14. I am indebted to Charles R. Metzgar for first pointing out to me the relation between "Benito Cereno" and Emerson's address on "The Fugitive Slave Law."

15. See Philip D. Beidler, *"Billy Budd*: Melville's Valedictory to Emerson," *Emerson Society Quarterly* 24 (1978): 215–228, for a different view of Emerson's relation to Melville's last novel. Beidler proposes that *Billy Budd*, like other Melville novels, is "an explicit critique of Transcendental ideas of order" (215). He perceives that transcendental notions of harmony of the true, the good, and the beautiful do not work aboard the *Bellipotent*, which is a "Transcendentalist world gone awry," since "paradigmatic form" proves "at odds with contingent reality" (219). The influence of Emerson, however, is actually much broader and potentially more dramatic than the abstract standards that Beidler mentions. As this study shows, Melville was attracted at least as early as 1849 to such Emersonian ideas as natural aristocracy, instinct versus logic, cracked nature, and polarity or compensation. This chapter demonstrates how these concepts on the nature of man govern the design of *Billy Budd*, as they did in *Moby-Dick*.

16. The individual lecture topics for Emerson's Boston series of 1849 are listed in *The Boston Daily Republican*, January 17, 1849: 2.

17. *The American Adam* 147. Lewis comments that Melville's achievement in

this novel was double: "He brought myth into contemporary life, and he elevated that life into myth—at once transcending and reaffirming the sense of life indicated by the party of Hope."

18. *White-Jacket* 110–111. Critics have observed the similarity of Vere's name to *veritas*, truth (as in "verity"), and *vir*, man in the moral sense (as in "virtue"). Though these meanings suggest the complexity of Vere's character, he is none the less a sailor, and the sailor's sense of the word should compete with these meanings, if not predominate.

19. "All barbarians are rakes," Melville writes at the end of his portrait of John Paul Jones in *Israel Potter*. Unlike Vere, who is completely dedicated to naval conventions and the Articles of War, Jones is described as "a very rude gentleman" who takes orders from no one. "Doctor Franklin," he says, "whatever Paul Jones does for the cause of America, it must be done through unlimited orders: a separate supreme command; no leader and no counselor but himself" (99). On the inside of his right arm is tattooing "such as is seen only on thorough-bread savages" (108).

Chapter 9

1. Quoted in Howard Gardner, *Art, Mind, and Brain: A Cognitive Approach to Creativity* (New York: Basic Books, 1982) 22.

2. "Hawthorne and His Mosses," *The Portable Melville* 414–415. The quotation concludes a paragraph of tribute to Hawthorne's genius, but it is in the larger context of Melville's argument for self-reliance in the new American literature, rather than one based on imitation of European models. Thus Melville is putting into his own words in 1850 the Emersonian argument for literature based on originality dating from *Nature* in 1836 and "The American Scholar" in 1837.

WORKS CITED

Allen, Gay Wilson. *Waldo Emerson: A Biography*. New York: Viking, 1981.

Anderson, Charles R. *Melville in the South Seas*. New York: Morningside Heights, 1939.

"Bad News for the Transcendental Poets." *The New York Literary World*. Ed. Evert Duyckinck. 20 February 1847: 53.

Baird, James. *Ishmael: A Study of the Symbolic Mode of Primitivism*. New York: Harper, 1956.

Baker, Carlos. *The Echoing Green*. Princeton: Princeton UP, 1984.

Barbour, James and Harrison Hayford. "The Composition of *Moby Dick*." *Melville Society Extracts*. September 1980: 2–3.

Baym, Nina. "Melville's Quarrel with Fiction." *PMLA* 94 (1979): 909–923.

Beidler, Philip D. "*Billy Budd*: Melville's Valedictory to Emerson." *Emerson Society Quarterly* 24 (1978): 215–228/

Bible. King James Version.

Bloom, Harold. *The Anxiety of Influence*. New York: Oxford UP, 1973.

Braswell, William. "Melville as a Critic of Emerson." *American Literature* 9 (1937): 318.

Bredahl, Jr., A. Carl. *Melville's Angles of Vision*. Gainesville, FL: U of Florida P, 1972.

Cabot, James Eliot. *A Memoir of Ralph Waldo Emerson*. Vol 2. Boston: Houghton, Mifflin, 1895.

Cameron, Kenneth W. *Ralph Waldo Emerson's Reading*. Raleigh, NC: Thistle Press, 1941.

Campbell, Joseph. *The Hero with a Thousand Faces.* 2nd ed. Princeton: Princeton UP, 1968.

Canby, Henry Seidel. *Classic Americans.* New York: Harcourt, Brace, 1931.

Carlyle, Thomas. *Sartor Resartus.* In *The Works of Thomas Carlyle.* Vol. 1. New York: Scribner's, 1896.

Chai, Leon. *The Romantic Foundations of the American Renaissance.* Ithaca, NY: Cornell UP, 1987.

Coleridge, Samuel Taylor. *The Complete Works of Samuel Taylor Coleridge.* Ed. W. G. T. Shedd. Vol. 3. New York: Harper, 1854.

Conrad, Peter. *The History of English Literature.* Philadelphia: U of Pennsylvania P, 1985.

Davis, Merrell R. *Melville's Mardi: A Chartless Voyage.* New Haven: Yale UP, 1952.

Elder, Marjorie J. *Nathaniel Hawthorne: Transcendental Symbolist.* Athens, OH: Ohio UP, 1969.

Emerson, Ralph Waldo. *The Complete Works of Ralph Waldo Emerson.* 12 vols. New York: Houghton Mifflin, 1903.

———. *The Journals of Ralph Waldo Emerson.* Eds. Edward Waldo Emerson and Waldo Emerson Forbes. 10 vols. Boston: Houghton, Mifflin, 1909–1914. Ed. A. W. Plumstead, et al. Vol. 11. Cambridge, MA: Harvard UP, 1975.

———. "Mind and Manners in the Nineteenth Century." Treatise. Emerson Papers. Houghton Library, Harvard U, Cambridge MA.

———. "Natural Aristocracy." Lecture. Emerson Papers. Houghton Library, Harvard U, Cambridge, MA.

———. *The Natural History of Intellect.* Lecture series, 1848–1850. Emerson Papers. Houghton Library of Harvard U, Cambridge, MA.

Feidelson, Charles. *Symbolism and American Literature.* Chicago: U of Chicago P, 1953.

Finkelstein, Dorothee Metlitsky. *Melville's Orienda.* New Haven: Yale UP, 1952.

"Flogging in the Navy." *The Boston Daily Republican.* 3 March 1849: 2.

Frothingham, Octavius B. *Transcendentalism in New England.* New York: Harper and Brothers, 1959.

Fuller, Margaret. "Emerson's *Essays.*" *New York Daily Tribune.* 7 December 1844. Rpt. *The Recognition of Ralph Waldo Emerson.* Ed. Milton R. Konvitz. Ann Arbor: U of Michigan P, 1972. 20–25.

Gardner, Howard. *Art, Mind, and Brain: A Cognitive Approach to Creativity.* New York: Basic Books, 1982.

Gilman, William H. *Melville's Early Life and Redburn.* New York: New York UP, 1951.

Goddard, Harold Clarke. *Studies in New England Transcendentalism*. New York: Hilary House, 1960.

Hawthorne, Nathaniel. *The Complete Works of Nathaniel Hawthorne*. Ed. George Parsons Lathrop. 13 Vols. Boston: Houghton, Mifflin, 1882.

Herbert, T. Walker, Jr. *Moby-Dick and Calvinism*. New Brunswick, NJ: Rutgers UP, 1977.

Hermerén, Gören. *Influence in Art and Literature*. Princeton: Princeton UP, 1975.

Hetherington, Hugh W. *Melville's Reviewers*. Chapel Hill, NC: U of North Carolina P, 1961.

Higgens, Brian and Hershel Parker. "The Flawed Grandeur of Melville's *Pierre*." *Perspectives on Melville*. Ed. Faith Pullen. Kent, OH: Kent State UP, 1978. 162–196.

Holmes, Oliver Wendell. *Ralph Waldo Emerson*. Boston: Houghton Mifflin, 1884.

Hutchinson, William R. *The Transcendental Ministers*. New Haven: Yale UP, 1959.

Kant, Immanuel. *Critique of Pure Reason*. Trans. F. Max Muller. New York: Doubleday, 1966.

Levin, Harry. *The Power of Blackness*. New York: Knopf, 1970.

Lewis, R. W. B. *The American Adam*. Chicago: U of Chicago P, 1955.

Leyda, Jay, ed. *The Melville Log*. 2 vols. New York: Harcourt Brace, 1951.

Lowell, James Russell. "Emerson the Lecturer." *My Study Windows*. 1871. Rpt. in *The Recognition of Ralph Waldo Emerson*. Ed. Milton R. Konvitz. Ann Arbor: U of Michigan P, 1975.

Marovitz, Sanford E. "More Chartless Voyaging: Melville and Adler at Sea." *Studies in the American Renaissance: 1986*. Ed. Joel Myerson. Charlottesville: UP of Virginia, 1986. 373–384.

Matthiessen, F. O. *American Renaissance*. New York: Oxford, 1941.

McElderry, B. R., Jr. "Introduction" to Owen Chase, *Shipwreck of the Whaleship Essex*. New York: Corinth Books, 1963.

———. "The Transcendental Hawthorne." *Midwest Quarterly* 2 (Summer 1961): 318–319.

Melville, Herman. *Billy Budd, Sailor*. Eds. Harrison Hayford and Merton M. Sealts, Jr. Chicago: U of Chicago P, 1962.

———. *The Confidence-Man: His Masquerade*. Ed. H. Bruce Franklin. New York: Bobbs-Merrill, 1967.

———. "Hawthorne and His Mosses." *The Portable Melville*. Ed. Jay Leyda. New York: Viking, 1952. 400–421.

———. *Israel Potter: His Fifty Years of Exile*. Eds. Harrison Hayford, Hershel Parker, and G. Thomas Tanselle. Evanston: Northwestern UP and Newberry Library, 1982.

———. *Journal of a Visit to Europe and the Levant: October 11, 1856–May 6, 1857*. Ed. Howard C. Horsford. Princeton: Princeton UP, 1955.

———. *Letters*. Eds. Merrell R. Davis and William H. Gilman. New Haven: Yale UP, 1960.

———. *Mardi*. Ed. Harrison Hayford, et al. Evanston: Northwestern UP and Newberry Library, 1970.

———. *Moby-Dick*. Eds. Luther S. Mansfield and Howard P. Vincent. New York: Hendricks House, 1952.

———. *Omoo*. New York: Russell and Russell, 1963.

———. *The Piazza Tales*. Eds. Harrison Hayford, Alma A. MacDougall, G. Thomas Tanselle, et al. Northwestern UP and Newberry Library, 1987.

———. *Pierre*. Ed. Henry A. Murray. New York: Hendricks House, 1949.

———. *The Portable Melville*. Ed. Jay Leyda. New York: Viking, 1952.

———. *Redburn*. Eds. Harrison Hayford, Hershel Parker, and G. Thomas Tanselle. Chicago: Northwestern UP, 1969.

———. *Typee*. Eds. Harrison Hayford, Hershel Parker, and G. Thomas Tanselle. Evanston: Northwestern UP, 1968.

———. *White-Jacket*. Eds. Harrison Hayford, Hershel Parker, and G. Thomas Tanselle. Chicago: Northwestern UP, 1970.

Metcalf, Eleanor Melville. *Herman Melville: Cycle and Epicycle*. Cambridge, MA: Harvard UP, 1953.

Metzger, Charles R. *Emerson and Greenough: Transcendental Pioneers of an American Esthetic*. Berkeley: U of California P, 1954.

Miller, Edwin Haviland. *Melville*. New York: Persea Books, 1975.

Miller, Perry, ed. *The American Puritans*. Garden City, NY: Doubleday, 1956.

———. "The Augustinian Strain of Piety." *The New England Mind: The Seventeenth Century*. Boston: Beacon Press, 1961. 3–34.

———. "From Edwards to Emerson." *Errand into the Wilderness*. New York: Harper and Row, 1964. 184–203.

———. "Melville and Transcendentalism." *Virginia Quarterly Review* 20 (1953): 564–575.

———, ed. *The Transcendentalists*. Cambridge, MA: Harvard UP, 1950.

Parker, Hershel. *The Recognition of Herman Melville*. Ann Arbor: U of Michigan P, 1967.

Paul, Sherman. *Emerson's Angle of Vision*. Cambridge, MA: Harvard UP, 1952.

Perry, Bliss. *The Praise of Folly*. Boston: Houghton Mifflin, 1923.

Poe, Edgar Allan. *The Works of Edgar Allan Poe*. Vol. 3. New York: Redfield, 1859.

Pommer, Henry F. *Milton and Melville*. Pittsburgh: U of Pittsburgh P, 1950.

Pound, Ezra. "A Retrospect." *Literary Essays of Ezra Pound*. Ed. T. S. Eliot. New York: New Directions, 1935.

Porte, Joel. *Representative Man: Ralph Waldo Emerson in His Time*. New York: Oxford UP, 1979.

Reviews of Emerson's Lecture Series "Mind and Manners in the Nineteenth Century." *The Times* of London. 6 June 1848: 1. *The Boston Daily Republican*. 17 January 1849: 2. *The Boston Post*. 25 January 1849. *The New York Daily Tribune*. 6 February 1849. *The Boston Daily Evening Transcript*. 8 February 1849: 2.

Review of Emerson's Collected Poems. *The New York Literary World*. Ed. Evert Duyckinck. 3 April 1847: 197–199.

Review of Emerson's *Essays*. *The New York Literary World*. Ed. Evert Duyckinck. 6 November 1847: 326.

Review of *Mardi*. *The New York Literary World*. Ed. Evert Duyckinck. 7 and 14 April 1849: 309–310, 333–336. Rpt. *The Recognition of Herman Melville*. Ed. Hershel Parker. Ann Arbor: U of Michigan P, 1967. 8–13.

Reynolds, David S. *Beneath the American Renaissance: The Subversive Imagination in the Age of Emerson and Melville*. New York: Alfred A. Knopf, 1988.

Reynolds, Jeramiah N. "Mocha Dick: or the White Whale of the Pacific." *Knickerbocker Magazine*. May 1839: 377–393.

Rosenberry, Edward H. *Melville and the Comic Spirit*. Cambridge, MA: Harvard UP, 1955.

Runes, Dagobert D., ed. *Dictionary of Philosophy*. Ames, IA: Littlefield, Adams, 1959.

Rusk, Ralph L. *The Life of Ralph Waldo Emerson*. New York: Charles Scribner's Sons, 1949.

Sealts, Merton M., Jr. *Melville's Reading: A Check-List of Books Owned and Borrowed*. Madison, WI: U of Wisconsin P, 1966.

———. *Pursuing Melville: 1940–1980*. Madison, WS: U of Wisconsin P, 1982.

Spiller, Robert E., et al. *Literary History of the United States*. Vol. 1. New York: Macmillan, 1953.

Stein, Morris I. *Stimulating Creativity*. New York: Academic Press, 1974.

Sten, Christopher W. "Bartleby the Transcendentalist: Melville's Dead Letter to Emerson." *Modern Language Quarterly* 35 (1974): 30–44.

Thoreau, Henry David. *Walden*. Princeton: Princeton UP, 1973.

———. *The Writings of Henry David Thoreau*. Ed. H. E. Scudder. Vol. 10. Boston: Houghton, Mifflin, 1893.

Vincent, Howard. *The Tailoring of Nekville's White-Jacket*. Evanston: Northwestern UP, 1970.

————. *The Trying Out of Moby-Dick*. Carbondale: Southern Illinois UP, 1949.

Vogel, Stanley M. *German Influences on the American Transcendentalists*. New Haven: Yale UP, 1955.

Watson, Charles N., Jr. "The Estrangement of Hawthorne and Melville." *New England Quarterly* 46 (1973): 380–402.

Whitman, Walt. *Leaves of Grass*. Ed. Emory Holloway. New York: Doubleday, Page, 1924.

Wittrock, M. C., et al. *The Human Brain*. Englewood Cliffs: Prentice Hall, 1977.

Yoder, A. L. "Emerson—Golden Impossibility, Representative Man." *Emerson Society Quarterly* 21 (1975): 241–259.

INDEX